# Bombers

# Bombers

## AN ORAL HISTORY OF
## THE NEW YORK YANKEES

RICHARD LALLY

Crown Publishers
New York

Published by Crown Publishers, New York, New York.
Member of the Crown Publishing Group, a division
of Random House, Inc.

www.randomhouse.com

CROWN is a trademark and the Crown colophon is a
registered trademark of Random House, Inc.

Printed in the United States of America

Designed by Cynthia Dunne

Library of Congress Cataloging-in-Publication Data

Lally, Richard.
Bombers: an oral history of the New York Yankees /
by Richard Lally
1. New York Yankees (Baseball team)—History.
2. Oral History.  I. Title.
GV875.N4 L37 2002
796.357'64'097471—dc21          2001047282

ISBN 0-609-60895-9

10  9  8  7  6  5  4  3  2  1

First Edition

*To my family*

*And to two men who always kept the faith,*
*Julian Bach and Mark Reiter*

## ACKNOWLEDGMENTS

I wish to thank my editor, Pete Fornatale, for bringing his passion, dedication, and intelligence to this project. Mark Reiter, my agent at IMG Literary, has been a loyal ally and friend over the last ten years: During those odd times when I was seized by writer's anxiety, he was always just a phone call away. I must thank the entire New York Yankees organization, particularly the players, and their public relations director, Richard Cerrone. This book would not have been possible without their cooperation. I also want to express my gratitude to the New York Mets. Mets public relations director Jay Horowitz and his assistant Shannon Dalton gave me all the access I needed to complete the segment covering the 2000 Subway Series. I don't have a research staff, but whenever I needed to check a fact or smooth over some unmanageable copy, I was able to turn to one of my Gang of Usual Suspects: Billy Altman, Bill Shannon, John Collett, Jordan Sprechman, Bill Daughtry, and Jim Gerard. Rob Neyer, the fine columnist for espn.com, shared some valuable data on the 1939 Yankees.

I also want to thank those friends and relatives who have supported me with their affection and encouragement throughout my career. I love each and every one of them: my brothers, Joseph and Sean, who know when I need a pat on the back or a good swift kick in the behind; my father, Richard, whose often offbeat perspectives help to keep me sane; my late mother, Anne, who adored Gil Hodges and the Brooklyn Dodgers and taught me to cherish baseball; my future sister-in-law, Jamie; my aunt Kathy; my uncle Tom; the always intoxicating Maria DiSimone, my violet-eyed partner in crime; Eve Lederman, who keeps my face rich with laugh lines; the late Brother Leo Richard and his Clan of the Cave, including Dr. Patrick Murphy, Father Edward Doran, Brother James Norton, Brother Regis, the late Brother Ronald Marcellin, and the late Dr. Robert Englud; my blood brother Al Lombardo, who is as surprised as I am that we survived our teens, and his wife Cathy; Richard Erlanger, the Carlos Castaneda of Fenway Park, and his wife, Jessie, the indisputable belle of Burns Street; Joyce and Emma Altman; the Budny family: Alecks, Michaela, Paulina, Mathilda, and my main man Rasmus, also known as the incredible "Mr. Mookie"; the late Victor Kiam, a beloved mentor who taught me so much about life and business, his wife Ellen, and their entire family; Alan Flusser, who transformed my life and career forever by introducing me to Buddhism; Karl Durr, the Forest Hill Gardens Fox, and his lovely wife, Margrid; W. Michael Gillespie; Ray DeStephens and Brother Dan O'Riordan; Chris Dougherty; James Spedaleri; President Daisaku Ikeda and every member of my SGI family, including Ed and Vivian Neuwirth, Arthur Fitting, Todd Randolph, and David Edwards; and Vesna, Jean, Joey G., and the rest of my rollicking, inspiring gang at Q Thai Bistro in Forest Hills, the best damned restaurant in New York City.

him when teammate Ralph Terry was trying to get the final out of the 1962 World Series, we realize that even the most confident of ballplayers must also grapple with self-doubt. Just like the rest of us.

One thing my editor and I wanted to avoid was a rehash. The challenge in writing a book about a much-storied franchise such as the Yankees was to uncover fresh material or find a new slant on an oft-told tale. For example, it is well known that Billy Martin was the Machiavelli who persuaded manager Casey Stengel to remove Enos Slaughter and Joe Collins from the lineup for the seventh game of the 1956 World Series and replace them with Elston Howard and Moose Skowron. Several books contain accounts of the conversation between Martin and Stengel that led to the switch. However, nowhere could I find Slaughter's reaction to his benching. You'll learn Slaughter's thoughts on the subject, as well as the reaction of Martin's teammates to his tinkering, in the chapter titled "More Than Perfect."

In "Called?" one of Babe Ruth's former teammates at long last addresses whether the Babe called his shot against the Chicago Cubs in the 1932 World Series. Later in the book, former major-league shortstop Eddie Joost shares an anecdote describing what it was like to play for Casey Stengel before he was a genius, a tale that underscores Stengel's merry vindictiveness as well as his fierce competitive drive.

I had not expected to write anything about the 1961 Yankees of Mantle and Maris; so many authors have covered that team already. But then Cincinnati Reds reliever Jim Brosnan disclosed how his club employed a secret strategy against New York during the 1961 World Series, yet were still unable to avoid defeat. Not even the Yankees who played against the Reds that October were aware of what was going on in that Crosley Field scoreboard until I relayed Brosnan's story to them.

We also didn't want to use any archival material that has appeared in other books or publications. *Bombers* is composed largely of material culled from interviews and correspondences that I have accumulated since 1980, first during a nearly two-year stint as a columnist for

## AUTHOR'S NOTE

*Bombers* is a collection of experiences and remembrances, a compilation containing eyewitness accounts of significant events from the history of the New York Yankees. You will not find many statistics within these pages; the focus is on the personalities, how the players met the challenges of their profession, and how they interacted with one another. Narrative passages set the stage for the ballplayers' recollections, which form the very spine of the book. By often offering several firsthand perspectives of the same event—Kurosawa's *Rashomon* has long been one of my favorite films—I hope to give you a seat in the dugout for some of the most dramatic and pivotal moments from the history of baseball's most celebrated franchise.

I also wanted to impart a sense of how baseball is played on the major-league level and how it feels to compete in such a heady atmosphere. When pitchers Frank Lary, Lew Burdette, and Mel Parnell explain how they subdued so many formidable Yankee lineups, their monologues represent pitching primers. Reading David Justice's succinct analysis of a productive at-bat against Al Leiter during the 2001 World Series, we learn that successful hitting often depends on a combination of intellect and muscle, and come away with an understanding of why Ted Williams called hitting a baseball the most difficult feat in sports. And when Clete Boyer, perhaps the finest-fielding third baseman of his generation, admits that he didn't want the ball hit to

*Yankees Magazine* and then as a freelance writer working on a variety of baseball assignments. Approximately 75 percent of the interviews were conducted specifically for this book between June 2000 and May 2001. All of the quotes appear as they were given to me by the subjects, digressions included, except in those instances where someone asked me to tidy up their grammar, smooth out a thought, strike their profanity, or change a date or statistic after checking its accuracy. In the "Subway Series" chapter, I have included quotes from Joe Torre, David Cone, Al Leiter, and Bobby Valentine from their postgame press conferences.

More than one hundred players, writers, managers, coaches, and executives shared their recollections. I owe each of them a debt of gratitude. They include: Robert Creamer, Woody English, Frank Crosetti, Elden Auker, Tommy Henrich, Bill Werber, Eddie Joost, Phil Cavarretta, Bob Cerv, Cecil Travis, Bobby Doerr, Lonny Frey, Dario Lodigiani, Phil Rizzuto, Jeff Bagwell, Whitey Ford, Mickey McDermott, Walt Dropo, Rusty Staub, Joe Morgan, Hank Bauer, Tommy Byrne, Johnny Hopp, Irv Noren, Tom Sturdivant, Mickey Vernon, Mickey Mantle, Bobby Thomson, Larry Jansen, Alvin Dark, Sal Yvars, Jerry Lumpe, Bob Turley, Jim Bouton, Marvin Miller, Ron Blomberg, Lew Burdette, Vic Power, Clem Labine, Moose Skowron, Billy Martin, Enos Slaughter, Johnny Kucks, Carl Erskine, Steve Hamilton, Bud Daley, Roy White, Tino Martinez, Frank Lary, Mel Parnell, Jim Coates, Vern Law, Ralph Houk, Clete Boyer, Ralph Terry, Jim Brosnan, Dick Gernert, Chuck Hiller, Billy O'Dell, Willie McCovey, Tom Tresh, Tommy Davis, Phil Linz, Mike Burke, Pete Mikkelsen, Jake Gibbs, Elliott Maddox, Ferguson Jenkins, Willie Randolph, Oscar Gamble, Bill Lee, Marty Appel, George Medich, Sparky Anderson, Chris Chambliss, George Brett, Amos Otis, Bill Shannon, Earl Weaver, Ken Singleton, Rudy May, Fran Healy, Reggie Jackson, Mike Torrez, Charlie Hough, Bob Lemon, Mike Heath, Lou Piniella, Ron Guidry, Goose Gossage, Bucky Dent, Rick Miller, Don Zimmer, Bob Stanley, Carl Yastrzemski, Mike Caldwell, George Brett, Mike Piazza, Jay Payton, John Franco, Joe McEwing, Benny

Agbayani, Robin Ventura, Glendon Rusch, Jose Vizcaino, Luis Sojo, Scott Brosius, David Justice, Bernie Williams, Paul O'Neill, Roger Clemens, Mike Stanton, Mariano Rivera, and Derek Jeter.

This is their book; they are its authors. All I did was turn on the tape.

# Bombers

## CALLED?

*ig belly, big nose, big shoulders, big bat, big swing, big cigars, bigger cars: Everything about Babe Ruth was big. He was living large before anyone coined the phrase. Ruth was the ultimate consumer of food, booze, women, pitchers, and life. Ultimately, of himself. He was completely of his time—the Roaring Twenties, when many Americans frolicked till dawn in speakeasies, gambling parlors, vice dens, and other illicit venues. Ruth was one of their own, a satyr capable of reveling in an all-night debauch in some whorehouse before racing to the ballpark, without so much as a catnap, to hit two home runs against some Bible-belting, temperate, upright, devoted husband of a pitcher who had taken the mound with a full eight hours' sleep.*

*Yet while he was playing, few beyond Ruth's circle knew of his excesses, that he knocked them back in gin mills as often as he knocked them out of ballparks. Babe cavorted during the so-called Golden Age of Sports, when fans expected their athletic icons to mimic the virtuous comportment of Jack Armstrong, the All-American Boy. Much of what journalists wrote about Ruth back then—the man, not the extraordinary player—was myth, a myth that never fully embraced the breadth of his vibrant, delightfully profane personality.*

*Ruth's on-field exploits needed no embellishment. The Babe was, hands down, the most astonishing baseball talent ever to slip into a pair of spikes, and if you want to argue that point, consider this: Before becoming the game's most prodigious slugger, Ruth was considered the finest left-handed pitcher in the major leagues. So unless you find someone who can morph from Randy Johnson into Barry Bonds, who are you going to put up against him?*

*Uberplayer that Babe was, no one had to exaggerate his accomplishments, an irony since the most enduring Ruth legend started on the diamond. It has the Yankee right fielder strutting to the plate against the Chicago Cubs during the third game of the 1932 World Series and calling his shot—actually predicting with the point of a finger that he would smack the next pitch from Charlie Root over Wrigley Field's center-field fence. Homer he did, to that very spot. But did the Bambino actually call it?*

*Most of the reporters covering that series apparently didn't think so. At least, not at first. In his splendid biography of Ruth,* Babe: The Legend Comes to Life, *author Robert Creamer writes that the day following Ruth's homer, only one journalist, Joe Williams of the Scripps-Howard syndicate, mentioned the called shot in his story. A few days after Williams's piece appeared, several writers—most notably Paul Gallico of the New* York Daily News *and Bill Corum of the Hearst syndicate—carried the angle further. Corum's account of the called shot was particularly curious since, as Creamer notes, he didn't refer to it at all when he wrote his game account in the Wrigley Field press box on the day it supposedly occurred:*

**Robert Creamer:** "It's just my conjecture, but when those two or three writers first wrote about the Babe's call, no one thought that much of it at the time. Then it became a good follow-up story. Especially for a guy looking for something to write about, something a little different, a little refreshing. Also, I think all of them had a vague memory of seeing Ruth point at something, but I think they saw him point in the first inning, which was very clearly written about. So maybe they had that in the back of their minds, sort of equating the pointing in the first inning with the gesture in the third."

*After the game—a 7–5 New York victory—the Cubs denied that Babe called anything. Charlie Root, the no-nonsense, gravel-tough pitcher who surrendered Ruth's homer, said, "Ruth didn't point at the fence, because if he had I would have knocked him on his ass with the very next pitch." Root's catcher, Gabby Hartnett, supported his teammate, claiming that Ruth wagged his fingers, not toward center field, but at the Cub's dugout, where the players "gave him the business, stuff like he was choking and he was washed up."*

*Other witnesses, teammate Lou Gehrig and Yankees trainer Doc Painter among them, were convinced that Ruth did gesture toward center before homering. In his 1947 autobiography, written with Fred Lieb and Bob Considine, Ruth himself, who throughout his life was often deliberately vague about what happened in Chicago, took credit for calling his shot. But when Ford Frick, the ghostwriter for many of the newspaper articles that appeared under the Ruth byline, asked him to set the story straight, the Babe went all foxy on him:*

**Robert Creamer:** "Frick wasn't at that Series, but he told me that he asked Babe later if he did, in fact, point to the center-field bleachers. And Ruth replied, 'Well, it's in the papers, right?' When Frick pressed him on it, Ruth said, 'Why don't you read the papers? It's all right there.' Clearly, he was alluding to the columns by writers like Williams and Corum that had him calling the shot. Ruth also said, 'Ah, I did that lots of times. In 1928, for instance.' Which means he never denied it to Frick, but he never confirmed it, either."

*So, did he or didn't he?*

*Grainy black-and-white images captured on celluloid are the only recorded evidence we have of the event. Over the last twenty years, two films of Ruth's most famous at-bat have surfaced, but, viewed in tandem, they contradict rather than clarify. One shows Ruth gesturing toward what may be center field just before hitting the next pitch out of the yard. The second, shot from a different angle, indicates that Gabby Hartnett's recollections of that afternoon were accurate, that Ruth was wagging his finger at the taunting Cub bench rather than engaging in any prognostication. But now another film has been uncovered from the cinema of memory and its antique frames finally reveal what occurred in Chicago that afternoon:*

**Frank Crosetti (New York Yankees infielder and coach, 1932–68; short-stop, 1932 New York Yankees):** "All right, that's a story I can tell you about. As you know, Mark Koenig, the shortstop, had been with the Yankees and was a great friend of the Babe's. After he left the Yankees, he went from the Tigers to the Pacific Coast League. Koenig had a good season there, so the Cubs picked him up when their own shortstop [Bill Jurges] got injured. Mark played terrific ball with Chicago [Koenig batted .353 and slugged .510 in 33 games] during the Cubs' stretch drive. Chicago won the pennant in a close race, and everybody knows they would have had a tough time doing it without Koenig.

"But when the Cubs voted to divide their World Series shares—you did that before you actually played the Series—they voted Mark only half a share. . . ."

**Woody English (major-league shorstop/third baseman, 1927–38; third baseman, 1932 Chicago Cubs):** "We thought a half-share was fair. Koenig played a little more than thirty games for us, barely one-fifth of the [154-game] season. So ordinarily he would have been entitled to a quarter-share. We thought he did such a great job, we doubled it to a half-share. That seemed generous to us. . . ."

**Frank Crosetti:** "Did that burn the Babe! Not just because Mark was his friend, but because it went against his nature. Let me show you what I mean. During that season [1932] we were playing a series in the old White Sox stadium [Comiskey Park]. Now, in those days they didn't have any security guards at the clubhouse door. Anyone could walk right in.

"I was dressing across from Babe and Myril Hoag, the outfielder; I can still see those steel lockers we had back then. Through the door, comes this old man. He had a beard, hat flopping over his ears, a coat that reached down to his ankles. He must have been seventy or more, and he looked down and out. What you would call homeless today. Babe was still in his underwear. The old guy walks up to Ruth and whispers something in his ear. Babe reaches into his locker, removes his pants, takes a wad of bills from his pocket, and peels off a hundred-dollar bill. He gives it to this fellow.

"Remember, this is during the Depression! You have people on bread lines. They're selling apples on the corner. A guy making ten dollars a week is doing well. So you can see that was a lot of money back then. But to Babe it was nothing. He was the kind of guy who would lend someone two, three hundred dollars, then forget he gave it to them. The old man thanked him and shuffled out the door. I can't tell you how many times Babe did that sort of thing. He was the most generous guy in the world and he couldn't stand tightwads.

"So when he thought the Cubs stiffed his friend, he got on them. Babe would really razz them good. Called them cheapskates, penny-pinchers, tightwads. The Cubs, they razzed him back, making fun of his big belly and calling him Fatso. Someone in their dugout offered to hitch a wagon to him. And they said a lot of stuff to each other you can't print in this book.

"In that game you're talking about, Root got a strike on Babe and, boy, did the Cubs let him have it. Then Root got another strike past Babe—I think that made it 2 and 2—and now they really ripped into him. Babe stepped out of the box. He put up his hand but *he did not point to center field*! What Babe did was turn slightly toward the Cubs dugout and hold one finger in front of his face, meaning he had one more strike left. I was watching and he didn't point to center field like everyone says. It just so happened he hit a home run on the next pitch! Boy, that shut the Cubs up. Babe was like a little kid running around the bases. When he got into our dugout, he said, 'If anyone ever asks me what my greatest moment was, this is it!' He was so excited about coming through, even though he didn't call the shot.

"Naturally, the next day, after a couple of writers wrote that he called the shot, everyone wanted to know whether or not he pointed. But I was with Babe, sitting next to him in the dugout, and, no matter how many questions the reporters asked, he never said that [he called the shot] directly. He also didn't exactly deny it. He just went along with whatever they said, let them fill in the details. That's why the story spread. After they left, and I remember this like it happened yesterday, I asked him what that was all about and he told me, 'You and I both know I didn't point, but if those writers want to think that I pointed to that spot, let them. I don't care.' And that's how it all started. The writers wanted to say he pointed to center field even though he never did, and Babe let them think and write whatever they wanted. He was just having fun with them."

**Robert Creamer:** "The point I keep trying to make to people about this is that even if he didn't point to a particular point in center field, there is no question that he challenged the Cubs—Gabby Hartnett said that as Ruth wagged his finger he said, 'It only takes one to hit it'—and then stuck it to them by hitting not just a home run, but a tremendous home run. A breathtaking shot deep into the bleachers. So it all came together in a nice little story."

**Frank Crosetti:** "You know, the funny thing is, Ruth actually called a lot of home runs, but no one wrote about them. Babe would come in the clubhouse singing—he had a nice bass voice—and say, 'I'm going to hit one today,' and then he would. We were used to him doing things like that, things no one else could do. You know, he wasn't just a great home-run hitter, he was a great hitter, period. Probably could have hit over .400 a couple of times, if he didn't swing so hard on every pitch.

"He and I talked about that one day when I asked why he struck out so much, and he told me, 'I try to hit a home run almost every time I go up to the plate, because that's what the people come to see.' And he still hit over .340. After a while, you stopped being surprised. This was a guy who had more color than any ballplayer ever. Who else could have saved baseball? I know a lot of people today probably don't believe he did that, but I was around then.

"After that 1919 scandal, when the White Sox threw the World Series, I remember, fans felt sick about the game, thought it was all crooked. So they turned away from it. Then here comes this young fellah, he's hitting home runs further and more of them than anyone ever hit before and they're following him on the radio and in the newspapers. Then everyone went back to the ballparks to see him. I have no doubt they would have come back eventually, but Babe got them coming back much sooner. He was amazing. What was that you told me Jimmy Dykes said about him—'Ruth's not human, I think he dropped out of a tree'? I know he meant that as a compliment and he was right. There was nobody like Babe, not before or since. And with everything he did, all the attention he got, the money he made, no one in our clubhouse was jealous of him. Most of the players loved him."

**Robert Creamer:** "That's one thing that stood out, apart from his accomplishments on the field, when I researched my biography of Ruth. I talked to one or two people who had reservations about Babe, who saw him do unpleasant things. But they were in the minority. You have to understand that Ruth was sort of indifferent to what people thought about him. He didn't pretend to like people because he wanted them to like him; he just liked who he wanted to. If people got in his way, he pushed them out of his way. I don't mean brutally; he just ignored them. So I can't say it was one hundred percent favorable, but talking to most old players, they would clearly enjoy talking about the old days with their teammates and other players. But they would just beam when they got to Ruth. The memories were so warm and so much fun."

## AN EYE FOR POWER

*B*abe Ruth was a subversive, a Che Guevera lacking fatigues or philosophy who revolutionized baseball by introducing trot-around-the-diamond power to a game that had been previously played one base at a time. Ty Cobb hated him for the change. Bash a single, steal second, scoot to third on a ground ball, then dash home on a sacrifice fly—that was the Georgia Peach's idea of a rally. Take your bow, Ty, then take a rest. All that work for one mingy run.

*Babe? He would step to the plate with teammates leading off first and second, smack a pitch over the wall, then saunter around the bags—stroll just like an old Southern gentleman enjoying his sun-drenched leisure—while tallying three. Cobb read nothing but threat in that big swing, thought its breeze might blow him right out of the game.*

*Where did all the unprecedented power that Cobb so disdained come from? Before Ruth, other large men had taken their cuts, hitters so brawny their bats looked too small, like toothpicks, when they carried them to the plate. But they couldn't hit the ball out as often or as far as the Bambino. Ruth made stadiums look too small. No park could contain him. He hit a ball during an exhibition game in Tampa, Florida, that Ed Barrow, the Yankees general manager, claimed traveled 579 feet. Other witnesses say it topped 600. No one this side of Mickey Mantle has come close to that distance since.*

*And there was no one close to Ruth throughout most of his career. Babe won his first two home-run crowns by hitting over twice as many dingers as the second-place finishers. In 1920, Ruth's slugging percentage was .847, still the American League single-season record. The average major-leaguer slugged .334 that season. At his peak, the Babe outhomered entire major-league teams. From 1919 to 1929, American League batters hit 4,924 home runs. Ruth accounted for 486 of them, nearly 10 percent of the total. Why, the man hit more home runs than whole nations. It's a fact. In 1927 when he hit 60 round-trippers, all of Ethiopia hit only 59. You can look it up if you don't believe me.*

*After a few seasons of Ruth's relentless long-ball barrages, the owners noticed how all that power had kept the turnstiles jitterbugging around the league. So they introduced a lively ball, put a little hop in it, gave the other hitters a chance to keep pace. It didn't help the Babe mash any more homers, though. He hit that ball so hard any rabbit living in it would have died. God with a picture-perfect swing couldn't have outslugged the Sultan of Swat. Babe had a gift. A mystical force had anointed George Herman in the womb, gave him something special that explained all that crash and flash. Then it neglected to make a pair for any of Babe's rivals:*

**Elden Auker (American League pitcher, 1933–42):** "It was those eyes of his, that's what made him such a great slugger! The thing that will probably surprise you about the Babe was that he wasn't exceptionally strong. People look at all the home runs he hit and figure he must have been a powerhouse. He really wasn't, nothing like a Mark McGwire. Oh, he was no cream puff. Babe had that deep, wide chest. He was certainly stronger than the average man, but not all that much stronger than the average player. We golfed together a lot during the off-season, and I could drive the ball off a tee forty or fifty yards further than he could.

"But at the plate, there was no way I could come close to hitting the ball anywhere near as far as Babe. Hitting a moving object is harder than hitting a stationary one. Hand-to-eye coordination comes into play, and Ruth had this fantastic vision. I believe Babe had the best pair of eyes you'll ever find on a ballplayer. People talk about [Ted] Williams's eyes, but Ruth could match him and then some. It was almost inhuman the way he could read and time a pitch, no matter how fast it came in. And believe me, those pitches were coming in fast. People kid themselves today about how much harder pitchers throw than they did years ago. That's silly. The top pitchers when I was playing—fellows like Lefty Gomez, George Earnshaw, and Wes Ferrell—threw in the mid-90's just like the modern pitchers do. Lefty Grove was even faster than that. Ruth hit all of them.

"With his big swing and that heavy bat—it must have weighed 42 ounces—Babe would strike out more than most hitters back then, though not like those hitters who strike out a hundred or more times every season now. But because of his great eyes, he'd also walk more than anyone in baseball. Heck, Babe had Lou Gehrig, the best RBI man around, batting behind him and he still walked 130, 150 times a season. You think pitchers were pitching around him so they could face Lou? Not hardly. They were trying to throw strikes, but Babe's eyes were so good that if the ball was just off the very edge of the strike zone and it wasn't something he could drive, he'd take it for a ball. How do you think he hit .350?

"Babe also had the quickest, most powerful wrists I've ever seen on a batter. Man, he flicked that heavy bat of his through the strike zone as if it weighed no more than a feather. Ted Williams—I played with Ted on the Red Sox in '39—his wrists were almost as strong and quick as Babe's. Jimmie Foxx was another one who came close. Guys like that could wait longer on the ball than most hitters, so if there is late movement, they're not as easily fooled. They have time to adjust and hit that ball hard.

"The first time I faced Ruth was 1933. I'm a rookie with the Tigers, and he was near the end of the line, but he was still dangerous. I was in the bullpen and Bucky [Harris] called me in to relieve Carl Fischer. Who walks up to the plate but Ruth. First time in Yankee Stadium and I'm facing the Babe! Struck him out on four pitches. Then I got Gehrig out to end the inning. That's two Hall of Famers, two of the greatest hitters who ever lived, and I got them both.

"Babe didn't feel too good about that. Art Fletcher, the Yankee third-base coach, was a real old-time bench jockey. He'd do anything to get under your skin. He called over to me on the mound, 'Hey, Busher, look over here.' I ignored him. He called again, but I still wouldn't look, just kept warming up. Then, as we were throwing the ball around the infield, he finally caught my eye and said, 'You got the Bam [Ruth] all upset. He said he's been struck out before, but it's the first time he'd ever been struck out by a goddamned woman.'

"Fletcher said that because I threw underhand, submarine style. Ruth didn't like that delivery. Several times he told me, 'Elden, I just can't pick up your ball. After you release it, I have trouble following it.' I'd pitch Babe in on his fists, keeping the ball close, so that if he pulled it, the ball would go foul. You could catch him with that pitch. But you had to be careful. If you got it out away from him just a bit, he'd whip those wrists of his and hit it a mile. Babe didn't hit too many balls hard against me because he couldn't pick up the ball, so his eyes weren't helping him. It's like I was pitching to his blind spot, taking away his advantage. Believe me, if he was picking up my pitch sooner, he'd have been hitting it a lot harder."

**Tommy Henrich (outfielder/first baseman, New York Yankees, 1937–50):** "I'm glad to hear Elden mentioned that about Ruth's eyes, because it gets back to an argument I had with Ted Williams about hitting. Imagine me arguing with Ted about hitting! But Williams said when he listed the attributes of a great hitter, strong wrists were his top priority. Of course, he was right to a large degree. You can't hit unless you can break your wrists. Why, when I first saw Michael Jordan try to hit a baseball, I knew with one swing he didn't have it. He couldn't break his wrists!

"So I concede that wrists are important, but they aren't number one. I told Williams, 'Ted, I've got wrists that can pull Bobby Feller's fastball, okay, and no one throws the ball any quicker. But I'm still a .280 hitter and you've hit over .400. What you take for granted is what most of us don't have. Your eyes. When the ball comes to the pitcher, no matter what the speed, you can read the rotation—Ted could actually see the stitches on the baseball spinning—and that tells you what's coming. Most of us can't do that, which is why you're a better hitter than anybody.' Eyes like that, they're a gift, and it's nice to know Ruth had it, too. I'd never heard that before. Call Ted and tell him."

**Bill Werber (major-league infielder, 1930–42; reserve infielder, 1930 New York Yankees):** "Ruth was all talent. Everything he did was based on his natural skills, like those eyes—and I don't know if Elden mentioned how unusually large Ruth's eyes were, which may have accounted for something—and his wrists. Babe wasn't a thinking hitter. I don't mean any disrespect with that observation. He would have told you this himself. While I was with the Yankees, I was sitting on the bench with Earle Combs when Babe hit this towering home run. As soon as Ruth trotted into the dugout, Earle asked, 'What'd you hit, Babe?' and Babe said, 'Oh, hell, I don't know, but it sure went out of here in a hurry, didn't it?'

"Then he gave us a little lecture. He said, 'You fellas go up to the plate and you're thinking about what the pitcher might throw you, a fastball, a screwball, a change of pace, or a curve. Then you're trying to guess what part of the plate he'll throw it to. That's too confusing for me. When I get up to the plate, I don't think about nothin'. I just look for the ball and hit the hell out of it.' Babe was not an educated man; I doubt he read more than a book or two in his life. But he was smart enough to keep things simple at the plate."

## THE TRUTH SET HIM FREE

*C* *hattel. Professional baseball players were little more than that before 1976, when an arbitrator struck down the reserve clause that had bound them to one team for life. Until then, you could have thought baseball, ballyhooed as the National Pastime, wasn't a part of America, as though some amendment to the Constitution exempted players from the protection of the laws forbidding indentured servitude. Team didn't pay you enough to live on? Tough, you had to accept whatever management gave you or find another profession. Didn't like how infrequently the manager penciled your name into the lineup? Go work on an assembly line, you'll get all the overtime you want.*

*Any player who was not a prime gate attraction brought meager leverage to his contract negotiations. Hell, even the biggest stars—the Ruths, Deans, DiMaggios, and Fellers—never got paid what they were worth, not when measured against the profits the owners were hoarding for themselves. Once an organization signed you, they owned you. You were stuck by the short hairs to that club until it was done with you. Unless you could find a loophole, unless you had the guts to buck the system. Like one young player:*

**Tommy Henrich:** "I had signed with the Cleveland Indians organization in 1934 when I was just eighteen. Over the next three seasons, I batted .326, .337, and .346 while going from Class D ball to Class C, and finally to A-1 ball with New Orleans. It didn't seem to me that I had anything left to prove in the minors. Players like Jeff Heath—what a great hitter he was with Zanesville—got brought up to Cleveland or invited to the major-league spring-training camp for a look by the Indians after only one or two years in the minors. But I don't get a call.

"After the 1936 season, I sat home wondering when I was going to get a shot at spring training with a big-league team. Then I'm told that New Orleans had sold me to Milwaukee, another minor-league club that also had a working agreement with Cleveland. So even though they called the transaction a sale, I wasn't really sold to anyone. Cleveland just transferred me from one pocket to another. I didn't see it that way at first, but then I read a couple of stories over the winter that changed my outlook.

"First, one sportswriter wrote that the Boston Braves had tried to buy my contract from Milwaukee. Just one week after that, the *Cleveland Plain Dealer* reported that the Indians were going to trade me and someone else to the St. Louis Browns for [first baseman] Jack Burns. I'm saying to myself, 'One ball club is selling me to the Braves, while another one is trading me to the Browns. Just who owns my contract?'

"Commissioners had a lot more power back then. Judge [Kenesaw Mountain] Landis was working under a lifetime contract. He didn't have to please the owners to keep his job. To my mind, this meant the Judge was the only man in baseball with any authority who was on the players' side. So I wrote a letter to him to find out who I belonged to. I got a quick reply from the Judge's assistant that said, 'Our records show that you are the property of the Milwaukee Brewers.'

"That was one question answered. But I wasn't satisfied, because I discovered Landis hadn't seen my letter. He had been vacationing in Florida when it arrived at his office. So I write again. This time I specifically requested that the Judge himself read what I had to say, that I seemed to be the property of two different clubs. Four or five days later, I get a telegram from the Judge inviting me to present any evidence I had supporting my point.

"The best piece of evidence I had was heresay, a conversation that had taken place between me and Cy Slapnicka, the general manager of the Cleveland Indians. We had talked after I had tried to get more money out of Milwaukee. The front office turned me down, but they said I might be able to get my salary increased if I spoke to Cy. Now, that was interesting. Why on earth, I wondered, does the general manager of Cleveland have to approve a raise for a player on Milwaukee?

"I met with Cy in Cleveland. During our conversation, I brought up the trade rumors I'd heard. Cy was perfectly frank. He admitted that several major-league clubs had made offers for me. Which meant teams were making inquiries with the Indians about player Henrich when, according to the commissioner's office, player Henrich wasn't supposed to be their property.

"When I met with Landis, I mentioned Slapnicka's comments—I identified Cy as a 'Cleveland Indians official'—to demonstrate that Cleveland was acting as if they owned me instead of Milwaukee. You see, my allegation was that Milwaukee was just holding me on the shelf for Cleveland, who already had a lot of good outfielders on their team. Which is why, despite any offers they had for me, they couldn't act on them without Slapnicka's say-so.

"Landis didn't like farm systems. He thought it was wrong for a team to pile up players when there were no spots for them on the major-league rosters. Landis also believed that minor-league teams should operate independently. He heard me out, then told me to go to spring training with Milwaukee in Biloxi. While I'm there, the Judge calls a meeting in New Orleans. He invites me, Cy Slapnicka, [Milwaukee president] Al Bendinger, and the representatives of my former team, the New Orleans Pelicans.

"Our first session lasted from morning to well past noon. You have to imagine my state of mind. I'm afraid that if I don't win this thing, I'm going to be blackballed from major-league baseball for life. So my knees are knocking as we sat before the Judge. I still have this clear image of Landis listening while we made our cases. He'd cross his hands in front of him and rest his chin on them. With that long nose and snow-white hair, he looked like a hawk. But the thing I remember most were his eyes, the way he would stare right through you with these piercing eyes. Boy, was he intimidating.

"The Judge asked Al Bendinger to explain his club's relationship with the Indians. Well, Mr. Bendinger starts giving Landis a lot of gab, but not much information. It was all double-talk. I'm looking at Landis and thinking, 'Come on, Judge, you're not buying this, are you?' But I can't tell how he's taking it. Landis had a real poker face. Finally, when Mr. Bendinger was finished, Landis said, 'That was a very fine speech you just made, Mr. Bendinger. Now would you mind answering my question?' I thought to myself, 'Attaboy, Judge!' Landis wasn't about to get snowed, and right about then I started to feel pretty good.

"Then Landis mentioned my conversation with 'a Cleveland Indian official.' He asked me to identify who it was and I said, 'It was Mr. Slapnicka.' Cy right away said very adamantly, 'I deny that.' The Judge asked a few more questions, most of them based on the information contained in my letters. After I finished testifying, we were about through.

"But before we left, the Judge asked if anyone had anything else to add. No one did. Except me. I said, 'Just one thing. When I said Mr. Slapnicka had told me he could have sold or traded me to a couple of big-league clubs, that happened.' Once again, Slapnicka said, 'I deny that,' which is about all he had to say during that entire hearing.

"The Judge dismissed us and promised he'd render a ruling shortly. Right after Milwaukee broke spring-training camp, Landis called us back to Chicago to cover some additional questions. He listened to our answers, then, one hour later, he voided my contract with Milwaukee. I was a free agent.

"I was happy but, oh my knees, was I scared! I had no idea if I'd be able to get another job with a big-league club. Those owners didn't like troublemakers. But as soon as I got home, there were already telegrams and phone calls coming in from eight different major-league teams. The Browns were one of the first, and they offered me more money than anyone else. St. Louis was a second-division team with a losing record, so there was a good chance I could go into the starting lineup with them right away.

"But a Yankee scout had been following me for two weeks, and did I want to play with New York! They had such a great winning tradition with Ruth, Lazzeri, and Gehrig. I wanted to be part of that. The Yankees signed me for a $25,000 bonus, a heck of a lot of money back then. I think Gehrig was only making $40,000 or so when I joined the club, and he was the highest-paid guy on the team.

"That first season with the Yankees, they optioned me to the Newark Bears, where I hit well enough [.440] that they brought me back up to New York. I gradually worked my way into the starting lineup, and by 1938 I was playing regularly. I stayed around for eleven seasons—missed three years during the war—and played on eight pennant winners, so I guess I made the right choice. I'm glad the Judge saw things my way."

## AN IRON HORSE NO MORE

*G*ibraltar in Spikes," that's what sports columnist Jim Murray dubbed him. But to nearly every other baseball writer and fan, Lou Gehrig was the Iron Horse, a slugging thoroughbred who never missed a race, as dependable as he was invincible. Through fourteen full seasons, he put up numbers that were monotonously staggering. From 1926 to 1937, he topped the 150-RBI mark eight times, hit at least 30 home runs, batted over .325 on ten occasions, slugged over .600 every year, and never scored fewer than 125 runs. His 2,130 consecutive games played stood as the major-league record until Baltimore Orioles shortstop Cal Ripken surpassed it on September 6, 1995. Memorable numbers. Yet, when the men who played with and against Gehrig—athletes all, who were not easily impressed by feats of physical strength—recall this Hall of Famer, it is his almost superhuman power as well as his carriage that they mention first:*

**Eddie Joost (major-league infielder, 1936–55; reserve infielder, 1938 Cincinnati Reds):** "He had more power than anyone you'll ever see— McGwire, Sosa, all of them. When I was in the International League playing for Syracuse, we had an off day and a couple of us went to the Stadium to take in a Yankee game. We wanted to see how the big-leaguers do it. Gehrig gets up, muscles rippling under his uniform, he looked like a giant. Lou smacks this line drive that never goes more than ten feet off the ground and hits the scoreboard over 320 feet away. He hit that ball so hard, it knocked the numbers off the scoreboard! Just think about that. You know that the longer a batted baseball stays in the air, the more force and speed it loses. So how hard must he have hit that line drive to scatter those numbers like that? I've never seen anybody else do that. . . ."

**Phil Cavarretta (first baseman/outfielder, Chicago Cubs, 1934–55):** "The first moment you saw him you knew this was a ballplayer, and I first saw him before he turned professional. Lou and his school [Columbia University] played a game in Wrigley Field. I was just a kid myself, but I loved baseball and got to see the game. Lou was all business at the plate, very disciplined, not like a lot of kids who swung at everything. The moment I saw him I said, 'That's my man.' His approach to the ball wasn't what you would call a full stride. Lou just picked up his right foot, stretched out a step, and put it down. That gave him balance. He'd meet the ball right in front of the plate, which is the key to hitting with power. I thought he looked good up there, and I tried to copy him. But he was so much stronger; he had muscles coming out of his ears! He hit a home run in that game, a line drive you could hang clothes on.

"Everyone on the North Side talked about Big Lou's home run, but I was even more impressed with how he handled himself. All those kid ballplayers walked to their positions, you could see them looking around at the big crowd. Hey, they were on a big-league ballfield for the first time; that will awe anybody. But Lou trotted out to first base like a pro. As soon as he reached the bag, he crouched down with his hands on his knees and concentrated on nothing but the hitter. You didn't see him gawking at the stands. He looked like he belonged out there. . . ."

**Bob Cerv (major-league outfielder, 1951–62; outfielder, New York Yankees, 1951–56, 1960–62):** "Gehrig was a major influence on my life. My dad used to drive a refrigerator truck back and forth to New York. Hauled butter and eggs. I used to make the trip with him every summer. In '37 or '38, during one of those journeys, he took me to Yankee Stadium and I saw Lou Gehrig hit three home runs in a doubleheader against the Philadelphia A's. He hit those balls so hard! Line-drive shots that would have cut a fielder in half if he got in front of them. On the way home from that game, I remember thinking, 'Someday, I'm going to be just like Lou Gehrig. I'm going to play with the New York Yankees.' That was my push to become a big-league ballplayer."

**Elden Auker:** "I told you how Ruth got his power from his eyes and those quick wrists, but he really wasn't that powerful? Gehrig, he could outmuscle a ball, just like Hank Greenberg or Jimmie Foxx, only stronger. Fool him on a pitch, and he still might hit a double even if he hardly got any wood on the ball. People know about the home runs he hit, but he also hit a lot of triples. He was fast for a guy his size, but a lot of those triples came about because he hit so hard. He could smack the ball past outfielders the way other players hit them past infielders. Just bullets.

"Gehrig wore me out. Lou was a low-ball hitter; I was a submariner, threw practically underhand. My strength was low. The only thing I could do against Lou was to go even lower than usual. And that didn't work very often. I tried everything against him. Back then, it wasn't like today, where if you throw anywhere near a hitter, the umpire puts you in jail. If a guy hit you pretty good, you would say, 'Well, let's see how well he can hit lying down.' So I used to throw at Lou's feet a lot, you know, just to keep him loose. Back him off the plate. One day I let one go that fractures his big toe.

"Of course, at the time he was working on that record for consecutive games played. Well, when I hit him, it looked like the streak was over. He could barely walk off the field. That was upsetting. Lou was a friend of mine, and the idea was to move him back from the plate, not put him out of the lineup. I didn't feel very good afterwards, thinking about all those games he had played and how it was ending. But, by the next game, Lou had his shoe cut open and he played with his toe in a splint. He could barely walk, but for a week or two he'd play part of the game, then sit to keep the streak going. He was tough, all right. Nothing could keep him down. . . ."

*Or so everyone in baseball thought. Nevertheless, by the end of the 1938 season, the Iron Horse was a less formidable presence on the diamond. His batting average dropped below .300 for the first time since 1925. He hit 29 home runs with 114 RBI, laudable marks until you provide a context for them: 1938 was a great season for sluggers, one in which AL batters tallied 864 home runs to set a new league record. Though run scoring was up from the previous year, Gehrig's stats were down. This astounding slugger, who annually joined the top tier of hitters in homers, batting average, RBI, or runs scored, failed to finish in the first five in a single significant offensive category other than bases on balls. And Gehrig struck out a career-high 75 times, a 50 percent increase over his previous season's total.*

*During the 1938 World Series, a four-game sweep of the Cubs, Gehrig did hit a respectable .286. It was a cotton-candy batting average, composed of four unimposing singles, one of them coming on a ground ball that could have been fielded had Chicago first baseman Ripper Collins not fallen down on the play. Although he was the most productive RBI man of his generation, Gehrig failed to drive in a single run against the Cubs.*

*After the Series, some whispered that Gehrig was starting to show his years, or that all those games played without rest were finally exacting their price. But the culprits diminishing his abilities were neither age nor wear. Unknown to anyone, an insidious, renegade gene was ravaging the nervous system of this ultimate athlete, short-circuiting the electrical impulses that coordinate muscle with reflex:*

**Phil Cavarretta:** "Those four hits Lou got against us in that World Series had no oomph. He didn't look quite right in the field and on the base paths. And whenever he took a lead, he wobbled. I kept looking at him to see what was wrong. During that series, Lou said to me, 'Phil, I really like the way you play. I like the way you hustle. Don't change.' That was my idol, like I told you before, so when he said that it was like putting his stamp of approval on my career. I never forgot those words, but I also can't forget how he looked when he was talking to me. Old. His face was drawn and lined, and this was still a young man. . . ."

**Cecil Travis (shortstop/third baseman, Washington Senators, 1933–47):** "In that last good season of his, towards the end, you could see something was off with Lou. He didn't look sick at all, but his reflexes weren't quite right, especially in the field. Balls that he used to glove easily were getting by because he was reacting slower. At the plate, the ball didn't sound the same coming off his bat, even when he hit it good. Just didn't have that same loud crack like a pistol shot. His timing was off by a fraction. Balls that would shoot out of the park on the line were dying at the warning track. He was hitting more lazy fly balls. And it seems to me he was swinging and missing at more pitches. The thing that shocked me was how it all happened so quickly. Most of that season, when we played him, he looked the same as always. Strong as an ox, nothing wrong with him at all. Then, within weeks, he started to look tired out there. . . ."

**Tommy Henrich:** "Maybe an opposing player, someone who wasn't seeing Lou every day the way we were, would notice a difference. But to us, he looked like the same player at the end of that [1938] season that he had been the year before. Except he slumped a little longer and didn't hit for power against the Cubs. But the Series only lasted four games, so that doesn't tell you much. I thought that any slump he had just meant he was human like the rest of us. You looked at this guy in the clubhouse, the specimen he was, not an ounce of fat on him. We all figured he could just go on forever. . . ."

**Frank Crosetti:** ". . . But in spring training the following year, you noticed something was seriously wrong. Lou moved slower and he wasn't hitting the ball with any authority. He wasn't getting to balls in the field unless they were hit practically right at him. I thought his back might be bothering him. He had trouble with lumbago off and on. We figured, hey, it's spring training, it's taking him a little longer to get into shape. We didn't suspect he was sick or anything. The guy was made of iron, who figured he'd break down?"

**Tommy Henrich:** "From day one down in that training camp, this was a guy who had gotten old in a hurry. He was only thirty-five, but his reflexes were shot. The papers didn't write this—the newspapermen loved Lou, he was always so straight with everyone—but he couldn't do anything. Couldn't even get out of the way of batting-practice pitches that came too far inside. He couldn't run. You don't think of

Lou as fast, but look up all the triples he hit. When I came to New York in 1937, I was a pretty quick outfielder. Well, he was thirty-four then, I was twenty-four, and he could outrace me!

"But now we're playing the Phillies in an exhibition game in Clearwater. Gehrig's on first and Bill Dickey hits the ball off the right center-field wall. Lou's going for two bases. I look out at him, and for Pete's sake, between second and third, he looked like he was running uphill! His legs are churning, but he's not going anywhere."

**Elden Auker:** "You didn't pay much attention to that about a player as great as Gehrig. If he looked a little slow, you just figured it was taking longer for him than usual to get ready for the season. I certainly had no idea anything was ailing him, and we were close friends. We'd pal around during the off-season, used to wrestle with each other for fun. I was with the Red Sox in '39. After running in the outfield before a game, I would go to the clubhouse to change sweatshirts. This one afternoon, I come out to see Lou with his back towards me, standing at the end of the tunnel smoking a cigarette.

"I snuck up and grabbed him around the neck in a half nelson. We used to do that with each other all the time. I was six-two, two hundred pounds. But Lou was so strong, he'd normally just shrug his shoulder muscles and lift me off the ground. Not this time. I no sooner got my grip on him than he crumpled to the ground and yelled, 'Oh, my God, don't do that.' I was shocked and scared. When I helped him up, I said, 'What the hell is wrong with you?'

"You could see he was upset. He said, 'I don't know, Elden, but all my strength is gone. I can't hit the ball out of the infield. I'm so tired, I can barely get out on the field. I don't know what it is.' That's when we found out he was sick. A few weeks later, he was at the Mayo Clinic—the streak had ended by then—where they diagnosed him with what they now call Lou Gehrig's disease. Terrible thing. It eats away your nervous system until you can't do anything for yourself. He was through as a player, and not much later he was dead. Lou was such a great guy, everyone loved him. When that disease took him, it broke my heart."

*On May 2, 1939, Gehrig, the Yankee captain, carried the lineup card for that afternoon's game against the Detroit Tigers to home plate. For the first time in 2,130 games it failed to bear his name. On June 2, 1941, sixteen years and one day after he started his legendary streak, Gehrig was dead at 37 of amyotrophic lateral sclerosis. All of baseball mourned:*

**Eddie Joost:** "Even if you didn't know him well, you felt like someone in your family died. Here was a guy who was better than 99 percent of the players who ever walked on a field, but he was humble. Never talked about himself, treated everyone with respect. Always put his team first. He had such dignity. In 1939 I was with the Reds when we played against the Yanks in the World Series. We opened in New York. Bucky Walters, Paul Derringer, and myself are getting out of the cab when we see some guy struggling to get out of his car in the Stadium parking lot. Must have taken him five minutes or more.

"We can't figure out what his problem is, but we don't think anything of it until we walk over to the players' entrance. We turn around, and it was Lou. I said to him, 'What the hell is going on with you?' He'd stop playing that season, but we didn't know quite how bad his illness was. He just grinned and said, 'Don't worry, I'll make it.'

"He'd slide his feet a bit when he walked, but he wouldn't let us take him by the arm or help him in any way. Acted like nothing was wrong. After we got into the Stadium, we went off to our locker room, he went to the Yankee side under his own power. You know when you play major-league ball, fans make you out to be a hero because you can hit the ball further or throw it faster than the average person. But you're really not; you're just a guy doing your job. Gehrig, the way he held on to his pride when his fingers couldn't even knot his own tie anymore, there was a real hero."

## PUTTING THE REDS TO SLEEP

*H*ow do you halt hell on wheels rolling downhill? Gehrigless, but relentless, the 1939 Yankees decimated the American League from the All-Star break on to win the pennant by *seventeen games. This was, at last, Joe DiMaggio's team with skills as varied and deadly as the gifted center fielder's. Scuffling with these Bombers was like taking on a prime-time Muhammad Ali. You never knew from which angle the knockout blow would arrive. In 1939, 24 American League hitters drove in 80 runs or more; seven of them were Yankees. New York led the majors in runs scored, home runs, on-base percentage, and slugging average. When it comes to measuring offense, what else is there? The Yankees outscored their opponents by 411 runs, a staggering 2.7 runs per game, and the greatest run differential in history.*

*Even when they weren't slugging, they beat you. On those rare occasions when an elite pitcher such as Lefty Grove or Bob Feller muted New York's power, these Yankees would rise up on their toes to dance along the base paths. Bunt, hit-and-run, whatever it took, DiMaggio and company knew how to short-ball with anybody in a tight game. They could even steal a base or two when they had to. But they didn't have to very often.*

*Defensively, the team was sure-handed and rangy. Who could you drive the ball past? Babe Dahlgren, Joe Gordon, Frank Crosetti, and Red Rolfe were the majors' top-of-the-line infield, a quartet of thieves who hijacked base hits before they could reach a box score. Gordon at second was their leader. Flashing the nervy agility of the college gymnast he had once been, Gordon covered so much ground, many sportswriters joked that New York played Dahlgren—no slouch with the leather himself—at first base only because the rules insisted that someone man the bag:*

**Frank Crosetti:** "Moving to his left or right, it didn't make any difference. Joe would scoot practically to the first-base line to take a hit away from someone, then run to the other side of second to rob the next batter. You never saw anyone quicker coming in on slow grounders, but if the ball was hit over his head, he would go back on it like an outfielder to make the play with an over-the-shoulder catch. Joe had a strong, accurate arm and he could get off a good throw from almost any angle. On relays from the outfield, a strong arm helps a lot, but you also have to get rid of the ball in a hurry. Joe would make that play so quickly you sometimes wondered if he even touched the ball. He could do everything. . . ."

**Bobby Doerr (second baseman, Boston Red Sox, 1937–51):** ". . . oh, yes, you never saw a second baseman with greater range, and he was very strong on the double play. You would go into second base thinking you were going to knock him on his rear end, but he could leap so high into the air like an acrobat. He'd jump right over you and you'd never touch him. Very elusive . . ."

**Tommy Henrich:** "Gordon was one of Joe McCarthy's favorite players, because he put the team ahead of everything. If you asked Joe Gordon how many RBI he had or what his batting average was, he could never tell you. Really, that wasn't put on, he never kept track of his own statistics. All that mattered to him was winning. And did you know he was an atheist? No kidding. But that didn't get in the way of our friendship one bit. . . ."

**Frank Crosetti:** "With Joe at second, Babe—who had such great hands, like Gil Hodges, he would catch anything we threw near him—could play closer to the line and rob extra-base hits. I could cheat a little more towards third on certain hitters because I knew Joe could cover all that ground up the middle. That meant Red [Rolfe], probably the best third baseman in baseball back then, could also play closer to the line and stop those doubles. A player like Gordon made the whole infield better."

*Any batter discouraged by the way Gordon and his playmates whittled his on-base percentage found no solace in hitting fly balls. In left, George Selkirk led AL outfielders in fielding percentage, and it wasn't because he played his position cautiously. "Twinkletoes" was his nickname, and he had all the quick the name implied. Selkirk covered so much territory, he could have been a center fielder on many major-league clubs.*

*It wasn't speed Charlie Keller was selling in right. But he could gallop when he had to, and Mr. Keller was downright clairvoyant when it came to positioning himself against opposing batters. The idea for the man at the plate is to hit 'em where they ain't. Thing is, Charlie had this habit of show-*

*ing up wherever ain't was. And forget about taking the extra base on him. Mounted on Seabiscuit, a base runner wouldn't want to challenge his throwing arm.*

*Of course, Selkirk's and Keller's defensive exploits often went unnoticed. All eyes, you see, were fixed on DiMaggio, graceful and audacious in center, spinning the mob's head around game after game, making catches other outfielders wouldn't even attempt. Oh, the Bombers could haul them in all right. All that impeccable defense supported a pitching staff that had led the league in earned run average, shutouts, strikeouts, and saves.*

*Who, National League loyalists had to wonder, could you send into a World Series to thwart such a formidable opponent? How about a club whose pitching staff could match the Yankees strike for strike, whose attack featured so much keep-running-right-at-you-all-day speed it could disassemble even the tightest defenses? While the Cincinnati Reds couldn't play home-run derby with New York, theirs was a lineup of patient, professional hitters. They religiously worked pitchers deep into the count until they got something juicy to cut at. Then they'd drive it into a gap. In the field, the Reds played hardscrabble, dirty-jerseyed defense; they made mental errors about as often as Dorothy Parker flubbed bon mots.*

*Few teams devoted more attention to its glove work. Cincinnati drilled long hours, rehearsing the most mundane defensive maneuvers under the guidance of manager Bill "Deacon" McKechnie. As Reds left-hander Johnny Vander Meer once observed, "[McKechnie] was the most outstanding defensive manager I ever saw. We were not noted as a heavy-hitting team, so all his insights and skills were directed towards defense, from handling his pitchers to positioning his men in the field. He was so skillful at doing those things, we never had to score too many runs to win. McKechnie knew how to hold a one- or two-run lead better than any other manager." The Reds manager had filled his roster with tough, smart players who were not afraid of getting bruised diving after baseballs. Their skipper had taught them that a run saved in the field was just as important as a run scored, and they would do anything short of sacrificing a limb to keep the opposition from crossing home plate. Surely a bunch like that would give the Yankees all the tussle they could want, right?:*

**Lonny Frey (major-league infielder, 1933–48; second baseman, 1939 Cincinnati Reds):** "Four straight, four straight the Yankees beat us that World Series! When a team sweeps you, it's like you weren't even there. What a nightmare! We were confident going in. With our pitching staff, we thought we could beat anybody. But our team was pooped. The Cardinals had been on our necks all year, and they put on that strong run to almost catch us near the end. We didn't clinch until the last day or so of the season [September 29], so we never had a chance to catch our breaths. A race like that leaves you emotionally drained, tired to the bone. The Yankees won their pennant by all those games early, and they were just lying in the bushes waiting for us. If we had a few more days' rest, we could have given them a battle. . . ."

**Billy Werber:** "I don't know that we were so exhausted. Shirley Povich, the great sportswriter from Washington, came up to my room right before that Series started and asked me what I thought. I told him we were going to win and the reasons were Paul Derringer and Bucky Walters, our top two starters. They were the two best pitchers in baseball that year. I figured they'd shut even the Yankees down.

"Derringer did just that, but it didn't matter. The first game of any series sets a tone. We lost that opener at Yankee Stadium 2–1, a game we should have won. It was tied 1–1 in the bottom of the ninth. Derringer got Red Rolfe on a grounder. Then Charlie Keller hit a ball to right center that either Harry Craft in center or Ival Goodman in right should have caught. But they both shied from it, thinking the other would make the play. It rolled towards the bleachers and went for what the papers described the next day as a booming triple. There was nothing booming about it. We walked DiMaggio, then Bill Dickey singled in Keller for the winning run.

"Afterwards in the clubhouse, Derringer was hot. He called Ival Goodman a gutless bastard for giving up on the ball. Ival popped him one good. Bill McKechnie and some of the players separated them before another punch was thrown. I remember McKechnie yelling, 'Shut the doors!'—to the clubhouse—so none of the reporters would see what happened. That never made the papers, because Bill said he'd fine any player who talked about it $500, a lot of money back then. Ival and Paul made up right away, they were good friends. I guess I can talk about it now without getting fined. . . ."

**Lonny Frey:** "It was unusual for any of our outfielders to let a ball drop in like that, because defense was our strength. I thought our fielders were just as good as New York's. The biggest difference between our two teams was power. We played National League baseball, which meant we used speed, defense, and pitching to win ball games.

"Everybody on our club could run except for our catcher, Ernie Lombardi. When he got up, infielders played all the way back, because they knew Lom couldn't beat out any grounders and backing up gave them a better chance to catch his line drives. He could hit that ball hard, and that's the truth. You remember Pee Wee Reese, the shortstop with the Brooklyn Dodgers? Lom once said he was in baseball for four years before he realized Reese wasn't a left-fielder, that's how far back Reese played Ernie! Still, Lom was a .300 hitter, a batting champion. He'd have hit .375 every year if he could have run even a little bit.

"The speed the rest of the club had wasn't necessarily base-stealing speed. But it was the kind that puts runners on first and third all the time, keeps rallies going. And once we got men on, we kept our base runners in motion with hit-and-run plays. When your runners are moving all the time like that, you pull infielders out of their positions, you create holes for your hitters to drive the ball through. With our pitching, Bill McKechnie would often play for one run in the first inning. He figured if we got one, the other team had to get two. With guys like Derringer and Walters on the mound for us, getting two runs was a big chore.

"In a typical game, Bill Werber, our third baseman, might single or walk to lead off an inning. I'd come up next and move him over with a sacrifice or by hitting a ground ball somewhere. Maybe dunk a single. Then one of our big guys, Goodman, Lombardi, or Frank McCormick, would hit a double and we were on our way.

"I'll give you an idea of the kind of pitching we had both years that we won the pennant [1939 and 1940]. In one game late in the season, we were leading the Cardinals by a run in the ninth. They had Stu Martin, Ducky Medwick, and Johnny Mize coming up. Martin was a pesky hitter who didn't strike out much. Medwick and Mize, well, you know who they are. Hall of Famers, power hitters, but power hitters who made contact all the time. I'm going out to second base as they come up, thinking, 'What on earth is going to happen now?' That one-run lead suddenly didn't look like much. Derringer threw nine pitches. Struck out all three, and not one of them touched a single pitch. Nine swinging strikes.

"Building your club around that kind of pitching, and speed and defense, worked in the National League because the teams behind us—the Cardinals and Dodgers—played the same way. Work out a run or two, then hold that lead. But the Yankees played a different kind of ball, almost like they played a completely different game than we did. Nearly every guy in their lineup could hit the ball out of the park. So you could peck away at them and score here and there, put together three runs over the course of the game. Then one of their sluggers would match that with one swing. That's discouraging.

"Another thing about those Yankees was that every one of their hitters knew the strike zone and worked it to their advantage. Even the guys like Crosetti and Dahlgren, who didn't hit for average, made pitchers throw strikes. They walked a lot and didn't strike out much. Because of the Yankees' power, pitchers tried to work them carefully. That's when they'd get in a hole. Now the pitchers had to come in with something the Yankee hitters could drive. And, man, did they have you then. One of those games from the 1939 World Series [Game Three] gives you a good example of what I mean. We got ten hits, all singles, and scored three runs. They got only five hits. But four of them were homers and they had some walks [five], so they scored seven runs. Murder."

*The most vivid memory from that World Series has Reds catcher Ernie Lombardi prone near home plate while Joe DiMaggio scores a run in the tenth inning of the final game. You've probably seen the picture that makes it appear as if Big Lom, looking like a rhino brought low by a bender, is lying unconscious as the Yankee Clipper capers by. The press called it Lombardi's Snooze. According to the players on the field and in the dugout, though, the press got it wrong:*

**Lonny Frey:** "Lombardi didn't snooze at all; he never even lost consciousness. I remember the play. It was 4–4 in the tenth. [Keller and Crosetti were on first and second] . . . when DiMaggio singled to right field. Crosetti scored to put the Yanks ahead by one. From the way [Ival] Goodman, a great outfielder, by the way, came at that ball, it looked as if he lost it in the sun; he actually kicked it and had to run it down before making his throw. As soon as Keller saw Ival was in trouble, he took off for home.

"After Ival got to the ball, I saw him set himself for his throw. Goodman had a great arm, the best in the league. He always got off a good throw, so I knew the play was going to be close. Keller and the ball arrived at home plate at just about the same time. Keller and Lom [Ernie Lombardi] were both big men, so when Keller crashed into him it must have been like a train wreck.

"I don't remember seeing the actual collision; after I saw Ival get to the ball, I probably had my eyes on DiMaggio, who was rounding the bases with the throw. But when I looked at home plate, the ball had flown loose, Keller had scored, and Lom was on his back. DiMaggio saw that Lom was hurt, so he took off and scored. Now, Lom wasn't out, he was trying to grab for the ball, searching around for it. But with the pain and dust in his eyes, he couldn't find it right off even though it was only a little bit away from him. It was just pure confusion up there. . . ."

**Eddie Joost:** "I was sitting on the bench for that play, so I had an excellent view. When they collided, Keller accidentally caught Lom— remember, he's slightly crouched to set himself for the impact—flush on the jaw with his knee. Lom went down like he'd been hit with a baseball bat. Lonny's right. Ernie was stunned, but he didn't lose consciousness. . . ."

**Tommy Henrich:** "If there was a television replay back then, you would see that by the time DiMaggio was coming to the plate, Lombardi was reaching for him with the ball. He might have been woozy, but he had enough of his wits about him to try to get the out. That 'big snooze' stuff is unfair to Lom.

"There was something else about that play, something DiMaggio did, that people didn't notice because they spend so much time focused on what Lombardi didn't do. As DiMaggio came to the plate and Ernie reached for him with the ball, Joe lifted his leg up over Ernie's hand, then brought it down on home plate. If Joe doesn't do that, he might have gone right into the ball for the out. Just imagine how much presence of mind he had to maintain to make that move while he's flying down from third. Man, oh man, that's quick thinking in a crucial situation. That's what made DiMaggio the best."

**Billy Werber:** "The biggest mistake on that play was made by Bucky Walters. He stayed on the mound when he should have come to the plate to back up Lombardi. DiMaggio never would have scored if Bucky had done his job. He apologized to Lombardi in the clubhouse afterwards. Bet you didn't know that, either. I was at third base for that play and I think Bucky, like me, got caught thinking Lom was going to get up and make a throw to get DiMaggio as he came into third. That's not an excuse for Bucky, but I think he was anticipating a little there. The shame of that play was that Lom got a reputation from it as a poor defensive player. Nothing could be further from the truth. Why, Lombardi would pick wild pitches from Johnny Vander Meer out of the air with his bare hand, he had these huge paws. Yes, if a pitch got away from him, he was slow getting to it and he might have looked awkward and lumbering, big as he was.

"But not too many balls got by Ernie. He could go down to block pitches in the dirt as well as anybody. And you couldn't find a better arm—I ought to know, he threw the ball down to me enough times. Lom threw a light ball, easy to handle, and so accurate he'd drop it right into your glove. You had no problem laying the tag on an incoming runner.

"You look at the pitching staffs we had, near the top in ERA. Who was behind the plate calling the pitches? I can tell you our pitchers rarely shook off Lom. He wasn't what you would call smart, but he knew the hitters, knew his pitchers, and had a knack for making the right call. Don't let that one incident in a World Series deceive you. Ernie was as good as Bill Dickey, Gabby Hartnett, Mickey Cochrane, any of those Hall of Fame catchers in every facet of catching.

"He didn't cost us the Series, but the way the play was written about, you wouldn't know that. We lost because the Yankees out-played us. The guy who really killed us in those games was Charlie Keller. Everything we threw him, if he didn't hit it over the fence [Keller had three home runs among his seven hits], he hit it against the fence. Something ironic about that, because I first heard about Charlie when he was with the University of Maryland. A friend wrote me when I was with the Red Sox about this ballplayer at the school named Keller who was such a good hitter he could be a major-leaguer immediately. I told Bill Evans from our organization that he should go scout this young man.

"Three weeks later, I saw Billy again and asked if he'd had a chance to see Keller. Billy said, 'Yes, and he's a prospect all right, but the Yankees signed him just before I got there.' New York got Charlie for $10,000, which he later told me he used to pay off his father's farm. So just think, if we had been just a little quicker, the Red Sox would have had Keller and he wouldn't have been in that Yankee lineup to inflict all that punishment on us. You can't say what would have happened then.

"Of course, DiMaggio was always impressive, you know what they say, he did everything right and they were telling the truth about that. But he was impressive only as a ballplayer. As a person, he was one horse's ass. When I was in the American League, Joe would come trotting by at third base and I would say hi. Never even looked at me. And that wasn't unusual. I once asked Charlie Keller what sort of a fellow Joe was, and Charlie said, 'I can't say, Bill, the man never said a word to me.' Not a word, and they played eight years together. But those two were a good team in the lineup. They sure batted the ball around against us.

"And the Yankees, especially Monte Pearson, outpitched us, which I wouldn't have believed going into the games. To tell you the truth, one of the reasons their pitchers were so successful against our hitters was that a lot of the guys in our dugout were intimidated by the idea of playing in the World Series. None of our regulars had any experience performing in something as big as that. The spotlight can make a player anxious. Hitters start swinging at pitches they would normally take. Pitchers overthrow. The Yankees weren't bothered by that, because they were in the Series almost every year. It was like they owned the event."

## 56

*D*iMaggio or Williams? Throughout most of the 1940s, that was the debate among baseball fans preoccupied with choosing the best player in the game. Never was the argument more heated than during the 1941 season, when Boston Red Sox left fielder Ted Williams led the league in slugging (.735), on-base percentage (.551), runs scored (135), and home runs (37), while batting .406.

*Normally, such striking numbers would make a player the unanimous MVP. But Williams finished second in a tight vote for the honor that year to DiMaggio, who led the league in only a single category, RBI (125). The voters were undoubtedly swayed by the center fielder's all-around excellence—Williams just wasn't in the Yankee's class as a fielder or base runner. Neither was anyone else:*

**Elden Auker:** "I think the one thing most people don't realize about Joe was how fast he was. I remember the time he impressed Billy Rogell, our shortstop when I was with Detroit. Billy had an amazing sense of timing with the runner going to first. We called him 'One-Step,' because it never mattered who was running, the fastest guy in the league or the slowest, Billy would always gun him out by a step.

"Well, DiMaggio is facing us for the first time, it's his rookie year so we don't really know him. He hits a grounder to Rogell. Not a difficult chance. As usual, Rogell times his throw. DiMaggio beats it out for a base hit. Well, you didn't see that happen too often! When Billy got back to our dugout at the end of the inning, he said, 'Goddamn, that guy can really run.' DiMaggio would run out of the batter's box like a rabbit, but what threw Billy was the way he suddenly accelerated, just turned it on a little bit more as he got near the bag. That was something. . . ."

**Bobby Doerr:** "Had the Yankees let him, Joe would have stolen fifty bases every year. Easy. He was also a great base runner, which is different from being a great base stealer. He was smart out there, always knew when he could get that extra base. And, Elden's right, Joe accelerated like no one else in baseball.

"I should know. One time I had him in a rundown. When I got the ball, he was at a dead standstill, standing straight up. But when I reached out to tag him, he just took off. It didn't even look like he bent his knees! We just barely got him. To see him break out full speed like that from a standing position, well, you knew he was something special. I never saw another player who could do that.

"No one could touch him in center, the way he always got such a tremendous jump on the ball, like he knew where it was going before the hitter made contact. You can't teach that. Great arm, always threw to the correct base. If Joe was throwing to the plate instead of hitting the cutoff man, that runner was usually out at home.

"His brother Dom was a terrific center fielder himself. He played behind me for many years. Dom had great range and a strong, accurate arm. Terrific on pop-ups just behind the infield. Excellent leadoff hitter, always getting on base—and Dom could run. But he wasn't Joe. . . ."

**Dario Lodigiani (major-league infielder, 1938–46; third baseman, 1941 Chicago White Sox):** "You know that song that was popular back then, 'Better than his brother Joe, Dominic DiMaggio?' Well, it wasn't true. Dominic was a great outfelder, better than almost anyone. He got a great jump on the ball. But Joe was a little bigger, and with those longer legs and arms, he could get to more balls.

"I played with Joe in junior high school. He was the shortstop and I was the second baseman. He couldn't play short even though he covered a lot of ground, because his arm was powerful but erratic. He'd let in two runs a game throwing the ball away. Of course, he also drove in six, so it didn't matter. Even in high school he had everything at the plate—that great balance that made it almost impossible to strike him out—you saw in the major leagues.

"In center field, what made him better than anyone was his instincts. He would move almost before the crack of the bat. If the ball was going to be pulled, he'd be leaning to his right. If it was going to be hit to his left, he'd be breaking that way as the pitch came to the plate. Amazing. And he didn't play you the same way on each at-bat. I've seen him run practically all the way to the infield to make a catch on a hitter. Then, same hitter, next at-bat, race all the way back to the wall to take away another base hit on a ball hit over his head. You never saw anything like him."

*At the plate, DiMaggio's supporters readily countered Williams's gaudy offensive statistics with the Yankee's own singular, glittering accomplishment, his 56-game hitting streak, a record that many today consider unassailable. One teammate who saw every hit in the streak believes its impact cannot be measured by statistics alone:*

**Tommy Henrich:** "Maybe if you just go by pure numbers, you would pick Williams as the MVP that year. He's the last major-leaguer to bat over .400, isn't he? But anyone who chooses Ted over Joe doesn't understand what Most Valuable means. I still don't think—even with all the attention it's gotten—the world realizes the real importance of DiMaggio's 56-game hitting streak. He was a one-man gang who brought our whole doggone ball club together.

"We were not playing well early in the season and Joe was having a rough time. It wasn't just that his batting average was off, he wasn't hitting the ball with real power. . . ."

*Joe started the streak with a single against Eddie Smith of the White Sox on May 15:*

**Tommy Henrich:** "I don't recall that he even hit it that solidly; I think the ball came off the handle. . . ."

**Dario Lodigiani:** ". . . it was hit just hard enough and perfectly placed to get by me at third and Luke Appling at short. But the left fielder did have to charge all the way in to field it, so it didn't have that much behind it. Joe didn't look good his three at-bats before that. He wasn't making good contact. . . ."

**Phil Rizzuto (shortstop, New York Yankees, 1941–56):** ". . . which was unusual for Joe, because guys like Henrich, Rolfe, and me, we got our share of rinky-dink hits, but Joe hardly ever got any. He got good wood almost every time up. Joe didn't talk much about himself, but he once told me he could hit the ball so hard it would handcuff the third baseman even if he was playing deep, get to the fielder on a line so fast, he couldn't get his hands down to field it. And it was the truth. He did that more than any hitter I ever saw. . . ."

**Dario Lodigiani:** "Many a time, and I'm not exaggerating, he would hit the ball to me at third so hard and fast I shut my eyes and threw myself in its direction just to block it. . . ."

**Phil Rizzuto:** "After the streak started, he hit nothing but bullets. Even the outs were ripped. I was glad I didn't have to play the infield in front of him, because he hit shots that took off your glove and your hand along with it. . . ."

**Tommy Henrich:** "You could see everything coming together for him at the plate. He got two hits here, one hit there, and, before you knew it, he was mashing the ball. Once Joe started hitting, oh my knees, the rest of us got into the act. When a hitter like Joe gets red-hot, it has a positive effect on your whole lineup. I've heard those people who say it shouldn't matter who hits behind or in front of you; you can either hit or you can't, and nothing will change that. They never played major-league baseball. I know for a fact—I saw what they were throwing me before the streak started—and I tell you I got better pitches to swing at right after Joe got hot.

"Once the pitcher had the two of us getting on base, he had to throw strikes to Charlie Keller. Pitch around Charlie, you're loading them up for Dickey and Joe Gordon. Brother, that's a tough situation to put any pitcher in. With me hitting, the guys in the one and two spots [usually Rizzuto and Rolfe] started seeing better pitches as well. It's the same approach, you don't want to walk them when we're getting production from our power spots. Up and down the lineup and it all started with our big guy batting fourth.

"From then on, we just rolled in. It's hard to pick someone as MVP over a player who hit .400 and slugged the way Williams did, but if the MVP is the player who did the most to help his club win, Joe's the guy, hands down. Why, we won the pennant over Williams and his team—and they were a great club—by 17 games even though we had Johnny Sturm at first base."

*In 1941, the first basemen on the other seven American League teams averaged 15 home runs, 84 runs scored, 87 RBI, and 69 walks while batting .287 in 539 at-bats. John Sturm batted .239 with 3 home runs, 54 runs scored, 36 RBI, and 37 walks in 524 at-bats. Most lineups would find it difficult to overcome such a drag on their offense:*

**Tommy Henrich:** "Johnny was a good guy and a fine fielder, but when you say he was absolutely the worst-hitting first baseman in Yankee history, well, you're right about that. The only reason Johnny was playing first is because Joe McCarthy's experiment didn't work. Nineteen forty-one was the year Gerry Priddy joined us with Phil Rizzuto from Kansas City. They had been a great double-play combination in the minors, so Joe McCarthy was going to play Priddy at second and move Joe Gordon to first base.

"Gordon was such a great athlete you figured he could play any-where. But Priddy was taking it in the neck, you know, choking a bit in exhibition games; you could see he wasn't sure of himself yet. McCarthy had to move Gordon back to second and stick Sturm at first. That was a lot of offense to give up at a power position, yet we still won easily. All because of Joe and the streak."

*During the streak, DiMaggio hit .408 in 228 at-bats with 15 home runs, 55 RBI, and 56 runs scored. His slugging average for that period was .735. The Yankees' record during his run? 41 wins, 13 losses, and 2 ties for a .759 winning percentage, a record that pulled the team away from the rest of the American League. Even Williams was dazzled:*

**Bobby Doerr:** "There probably wasn't a bigger Joe DiMaggio fan than Ted Williams. Especially during that streak. They were rivals, and Ted always wanted that batting crown. But he wanted Joe to keep it going. The thing was, Ted loved hitting and he loved hitters. He'd talk to any-one who wanted to improve as a batter, even guys from the other team. He knew how hard it was to hit major-league pitching day in and day out, so he appreciated what Joe was doing more than anybody.

"We had a scoreboard operator in Fenway. From left field, Ted could find out from him whether Joe had added another game to his streak, and whenever he did, he would yell out to Dom DiMaggio, our center fielder, "Your brother's got another one!" and he'd be just as happy as Dom.

"Joe broke that record [Wee Willie Keeler's major-league-record 44-game hitting streak] against our ball club, but his brother almost stopped him. In his first or second at-bat of that game, Joe hits a hard line drive [off right-hander Dick Newsome] to deep center field. That's a sure double. Dom goes racing back—you never saw anyone move so fast—stretches out, and just barely catches the ball. Another half-inch and it's in there. A great catch, off his own brother of all people, and you're thinking maybe it's not Joe's night. Except a couple of innings later, Joe hits one where no one can catch it. Home run, and there's the record."

*There were several other, earlier games that nearly terminated the streak. On June 17, in game 30, official scorer Dan Daniel ruled a DiMaggio bad-bounce grounder off White Sox shortstop Luke Appling's shoulder a base hit, although some thought it was an error. Even DiMaggio later admitted he had his doubts about that call. The next day, Appling failed to retire DiMaggio on another tough chance. Daniel once again gave the Yankee Clipper the nod. But on June 26, against the St. Louis Browns, Joe was experiencing one of his worst outings of the season. Only the quick thinking of a teammate kept the streak alive:*

**Elden Auker:** "I faced DiMaggio during his streak while I was pitching for the St. Louis Browns. He'd hit in 37 straight at that point. Joe was hard to strike out for a guy with so much power. The reason for that was his stance. He stood flat-footed with his feet spread wide apart in the batter's box. Another guy with quick wrists. He could generate so much power with them, he didn't have to get his entire body into the swing, which means you rarely saw him lunging at a pitch.

"And while he looked almost slender in a uniform or street clothes, Joe was strong as could be. Very much like Foxx, who we used to call the Beast because he had so much brute strength. You know what player today reminds me of Joe? Mike Piazza. You almost never see Piazza take a big stride, there's no wasted motion, and his wrists whip the bat through the strike zone so fast, it just whistles. That's why he hits the ball hard almost every time up. Just like Joe.

"He could be tough on any pitcher, but that afternoon in Yankee Stadium, I was having good luck against him. Struck him out the first two times at bat, which was headline news in itself [DiMaggio struck out only 13 times that season], then popped him up on his third trip. All the time I'm pitching, I'm just trying to get him out. The streak meant absolutely nothing to me, but a base hit did. When we went into the eighth inning, I was losing 4–2 and couldn't afford to give up any more runs. . . ."

**Tommy Henrich:** ". . . Joe was scheduled to hit fourth that inning. We're at home. Which means if we don't get a runner on and we keep our lead, he's not coming up. The streak is over. By then, the newspapers were playing the thing up and we all knew Joe was closing in on Keeler's for the major-league record. So the streak was on our minds, too.

"I can't say Joe acted concerned about it. I've heard how Roger Maris became so tense when he was chasing Babe Ruth's home-run record, he lost patches of hair. Home runs became harder to come by as the time ran out. You can't criticize Roger for that one bit; most ballplayers would have reacted just that way.

"But not Joe. I've got to tell you that DiMaggio was the toughest man on a ballfield I ever saw in my life. Hey, I saw a breakdown of his 61-game hitting streak, when he was with the San Francisco Seals in the Pacific Coast League. What amazed me about it was how many times he kept that streak going with hits in his last turn at bat. So even as a kid, he was tough. That was his nature. He didn't let anything get in his way. All that attention he was getting from the newspapers and the fans, everything that was being written, that can distract someone, get you off your game. You start pressing if you go hitless your first couple of times up. Maybe you'll swing at bad pitches. Yet all through the streak, Joe didn't operate any differently, near as I could see, than any other time he played ball.

"However, I did something out of the ordinary when he was chasing the record. It was during that game against Auker. Johnny Sturm led off the eighth with a pop-up. Red Rolfe goes up to the plate, and I'm heading for the on-deck circle when I get a brainstorm. I think to myself, 'If Red gets on with one out, it still doesn't guarantee that Joe will get up. I could hit into a double play.' Which was possible. Even if I make solid contact, I might hit a line drive to second and Red gets doubled off first. Then Joe's left sitting in the on-deck circle. So I turn back to [Yankee manager Joe] McCarthy and ask, 'Joe, if Red gets on first, is it all right if I bunt? . . .'"

*Now, here's a move to stick a wedge under the eyebrows. Henrich, the consummate team player, a man who cared nothing about his own stats as long as the Yankees won, was offering to make the DiMaggio record his priority with the game's outcome still in doubt. What was he thinking?:*

**Tommy Henrich:** "That's a fair assessment, so let me answer the question candidly. This *was* an unusual request for me. With the Yankees, the third man in the lineup doesn't bunt with one out and a runner on first. And winning the ball game was always number one in my book. But you have to remember we had a lead and the Browns weren't a good club. Johnny Murphy, the best reliever in baseball, was ready if we had trouble in the ninth. And this was something I wanted to try out of respect for everything Joe had accomplished. It was as simple as that. You had to be there, be part of that team, to understand why I thought it was the right thing to do.

"McCarthy knew exactly what I had in mind. He pondered what I said for maybe five or six seconds, then he said, very soberly, "That will be all right." Rolfe got a base on balls and here I come. First pitch, I bunted down first, they throw me out, Rolfe goes to second. Now Auker has to face DiMaggio. . . ."

**Elden Auker:** ". . . I'm not giving what Tommy did too much thought at the time, didn't even connect it to the streak. But it was odd for him to bunt in that situation. It's something that he told you he was afraid of hitting into a double play, because Tommy just plain wore me out. He was the toughest hitter on the Yankees for me. . . ."

**Tommy Henrich:** ". . . yes, I usually creamed him. I have no idea why, but for some reason I picked up the ball coming out of his hand better than most other pitchers. I could always read what he was going to throw. Fastball, breaking pitch, I just knew. I can't prove this, but I think it may have been because I played a lot of softball before I started in professional ball. Auker threw underhand, submarine style. I was used to that from softball pitchers throwing very much the same way. So Elden never gave me much trouble. . . ."

**Elden Auker:** ". . . Joe, on the other hand, didn't like my style of pitching. He told me he couldn't pick the ball up and almost every pitch I threw came in low. Joe could hit pretty much anything, but he preferred the ball high like most right-handed hitters. So when DiMaggio came up to the plate with Rolfe on second, I didn't think about putting him on the open base. Again, the streak wasn't in my mind for even a second. I'm not sure who was in the on-deck circle behind him, Keller or Dickey, maybe Joe Gordon, but it didn't matter. Joe rarely hit me well, and I'd handled him all day. There were two men out, so I was coming right at him.

"My first pitch was a fastball that tailed away a bit. Give Joe credit. He jumped on it. Hit a sharp grounder down to our third baseman, Harlond Clift. It skipped up, skimmed off Harlond's shoulder, and went into left field for a double. Harlond was a great-fielding third baseman, he would have been a Gold Glove winner if they had such a thing back then. If he couldn't come up with that ball I don't know who could. Clean hit, all the way.

"That's how the streak stayed alive. But you remember what I said earlier about breaking Gehrig's toe? Well, looking back on that day against DiMaggio, you can see how close I came to being the man who ended the two most famous streaks in baseball history."

*The streak ended against Cleveland on July 17, 1941. DiMaggio then hit safely in his next 16 games for a 72-of-73-game reel that eclipsed the major-league record that Chicago White Stockings third baseman Bill Dahlen had established in 1894. That earlier mark is now largely forgotten. One suspects the DiMaggio standard will prove more enduring:*

**Jeff Bagwell (first baseman, Houston Astros, 1991–present; 1994 National League MVP):** "Fifty-six, that's just unbelievable, because you have to perform every day to keep it going. Four hundred is also tough, but doable. Tony Gwynn's come close a couple of times. A player trying to hit .400 can go 0 for 5 one day, then 2 for 4 two days in a row and he's still at .400. So you have some margin for error. The streak doesn't give you that. You could go 5 for 5 every game for forty straight games—not that anyone will ever do that—then go hitless for one game and you're back at zero. All those hits you made no longer matter as far as the streak goes. The main thing that I believe will keep Joe's record from being broken is the way relief specialists are used today. Back in Joe's time—and this is taking nothing away from what he accomplished—you usually faced the same pitcher three or four times, starters stayed in longer and you rarely faced more than two or three pitchers a game. Today, a batter might face four different pitchers in a game, each with a completely different pitching style. . . ."

**Joe Morgan (major-league second baseman, 1965–84; two-time National League MVP; member of the Baseball Hall of Fame):** "When Joe played, most relievers were pitchers who weren't quite good enough to start. Today many relievers are the best pitchers on the team. When Pete [Rose] was stopped after 44 games, who struck him out? Gene Garber, a relief pitcher for Atlanta. Relief pitching today is so specialized; to keep any hitting streaks going for very long is extremely tough. The more you face a pitcher, the better your chance of hitting him, because you get a better idea of how his various pitches move, where his release point is, things a scouting report really can't tell you. But the way baseball is played now, you might only see a starter for two at-bats, then the relief specialists come in and you get one shot at each of them. That's tough.

"And from game to game you don't know how many opportunities you'll get to break the record. Suppose your team is in a low-scoring game. You walk twice, the next time up the situation calls for a sacrifice bunt. Now you might only get one chance to keep the streak going, and who knows if the pitcher will give you anything good to hit. . . ."

**Rusty Staub (major-league outfielder/designated hitter, 1963–85; 2,716 career hits):** "Then there's all the pressure you face when you go after a well-publicized record, pressure that many players find tough to handle. Look at Roger Maris when he was going after Babe Ruth's single-season home-run record and lost clumps of hair. And Roger didn't have to hit a home run every day to stay on track with that record. He also didn't face one-third as many media people as players have to contend with today. When he finally broke the record, I understand Yankee Stadium wasn't even half filled. A player going after the DiMaggio streak today would be followed by the media continually, and as he got closer, the stadiums would be packed with all the focus on him. It's hard to perform day in, day out with that kind of constant distraction and under that kind of microscope.

"There is a wild card here that I have to mention. Because of expansion, which we will probably see more of, there are players in the majors today who wouldn't normally be here, particularly pitchers. The modern ballparks are designed to favor hitters, and we all know today's ball has a lot of hop to it no matter what they say. Also with teams scoring more runs, hitters are going to get more plate appearances per game because you are going through the lineup more often. That extra at-bat here and there can mean the difference between the end of a streak and keeping it intact. And you have the DH in the American League, which increases run scoring and creates even more hitting opportunities. So few offensive records can be considered safe. Still, I doubt anyone will break DiMaggio's record anytime soon because of the pressure, and I agree with what Jeff and Joe both said about the quality and variety of today's relievers. . . ."

**Joe Morgan:** "Look, I was Pete Rose's teammate when he went after the DiMaggio record in 1978. He was the perfect player to break it, a batting champion who made excellent contact, a switch-hitter so it didn't matter what arm the pitcher threw with. Pete hit the ball to all fields with authority, so even though he wasn't a power hitter, you couldn't play him shallow and he could bunt. Pete had an excellent eye, so he didn't chase many bad pitches. He got his share of walks, but not so many that he would lose a lot of at-bats. The Reds had a strong lineup that year and Pete batted leadoff, so he got the maximum plate appearance in every game. He also had the perfect temperament for the chase. Pete thrived in pressure situations. He was so focused and relaxed, he could have held press conferences in between at-bats without being distracted. Yet he missed Joe's mark by a dozen games. As far as I'm concerned, you can forget about anyone breaking DiMaggio's record."

## BEFORE HE WAS A GENIUS

*U*h-oh, time to write about Stengel. Just the thought of excavating fresh material on baseball's most essayed personality is enough to provoke the onset of museum fatigue. You know that heavy-liddedness that afflicts you after spending the afternoon staring at too much white space and too many Jackson Pollocks? The task is just too daunting. What don't we know about Casey? The wins, the losses, the fractured syntax and frat-boy pranks, the long nights spent outtalking and outdrinking writers at the hotel bar, all those stories have been told many times over.

Anyone who follows baseball surely knows his record with the Yankees. Seven World Series Championships—five of them consecutive—and ten American League pennants in twelve seasons. No baseball manager ever had a more successful term than the one Stengel enjoyed with New York from 1949 to 1960. That hasn't stopped critics, some of them his own players, from claiming that Casey was merely in the right place at the perfect time, that his clubs won because they "had the horses," and not due to his managing brilliance.

Their memories are selective. They forget that during Stengel's first few years in New York, the Yankees were never preseason pennant-race favorites. They ignore how he took over the Bombers during a transition period—the DiMaggio era was closing, Mickey Mantle's time had not quite arrived—when the club, albeit undeniably talented, was also aging and infirm. It was Stengel's masterful platooning, his clever bullpen manipulations, and his intuitive use of the entire Yankee roster that kept New York winning even as it was rebuilding, the most difficult act in baseball.

Admittedly, before Casey managed the Yankees, his vast strategical knowledge and innovative gambits failed to produce many victories. In nine years as skipper of the Brooklyn Dodgers and Boston Braves, he finished over .500 only once and never reached the first division a single time. Still, poring over old rosters, one can see that all of these were dreadful teams, clubs that probably earned as many—or more—wins under Stengel as they could have with any other manager. Even when the results were wanting, Casey extracted maximum effort from all his charges, even *those baffled by his singular communication style. Searching for a Stengel anecdote that hasn't been recycled umpteen times, I decided to talk to one of them:*

**Eddie Joost:** "Casey was our manager when I was with the Boston Braves in 1943. I was the worst player in baseball that season—I hit .185 even though most of the good pitchers were away fighting the war—and I like to say Stengel was the worst manager in baseball; he did get fired right after the season.

"Actually, he was a pretty good manager, considering we didn't have a single hitter in our lineup, outside of Tommy Holmes, who could frighten even a bush-league pitcher. Just look at our statistics. I told you what I hit and Casey gave me over 400 at-bats, so what does that tell you? We finished last in the league in runs scored by a lot. If we put together two runs in an inning, it was a huge rally. But we finished sixth and were in the running for fifth most of the season. That was an accomplishment for a club like ours. Casey had us hustling, playing good defense, and he knew how to work with a pitching staff. Which was important, since our pitchers were the only thing we had going for us. He was a good baseball man.

"But I did have one problem with him. He spoke with that Stengelese double-talk all the time, and that drove me crazy. I never understood a word he said. You know his routine. He'd go over the opposing lineup and say, 'Now, this guy I saw in the Pacific Coast League and he can chop the ball and run like a rabbit if the grass isn't too long and the field is hard, which is how we liked it when I played for McGraw . . .' And he'd go on like this for ten minutes to make some point about how to pitch to this player and how we should position ourselves on defense, but, honestly, I had no idea what he was talking about.

"Finally, I got tired of trying to translate him. We had big lockers back then, so one day when he's going on and on as usual, I turned my chair around and started reading *The Sporting News*. Kept my back to him the whole time. Oh, did he give me hell! All I could say was, 'Case, I'm sorry, but I've been listening to you for more than half a season and I don't understand one thing you've said. I just can't listen anymore.' He wasn't happy with my answer, but that's the end of it. Or so I thought.

"Two days later I'm playing third base, I forget against who. Tony Cuccinello is coaching third. About the fifth inning we're behind by three, there's a man on first and two men out, when I come to the plate. Tony flashes me the bunt sign. Well, we all know that's a crazy call in that situation. I figure I'm seeing things. But I look down at Tony one more time and, darned if he's not flashing it to me again. So I try to bunt for a base hit and get thrown out.

"Before I go back to my position I go up to Tony for an explanation. 'Cootch,' I say, 'what the hell is going on? How could you give me the bunt sign up there?' Tony says, 'I didn't give you the bunt sign. That was the hit-and-run. We had a little meeting yesterday. You weren't invited. Stengel changed all the signs and he told me not to tell you.' That was Casey's way of teaching me a lesson in manners, showing me who was in charge, and you can bet I got the message.

"I got him back, but not that season. When he was with the Yankees, and I was with the Philadelphia A's, I always got up for those games. First, it was the Yankees. If you didn't get a charge playing the best, why, you shouldn't be in baseball. And I'd become a pretty good player by then, and I suppose I wanted to show Casey. In 1949, his first season with New York, I know he thought I showed him too much.

"The A's played the Yankees tough that season. In fact, we almost cost them the pennant. This one Sunday doubleheader, I hit a home run to tie the score. Then Sam Chapman hit a home run in the tenth to win it. And it doesn't stop there, because I helped beat them in the second game, too. Later the Yankee players told me that, on the train taking them from Philadelphia to Washington, Stengel was hopping mad. He comes into the dining car and says, 'That club in Philadelphia is making you look like fools. They are taking the food right out of your mouths. So I'm telling you all now I don't ever want to see any of you getting chummy with them. You don't even talk to them.'

"I don't know this, of course. Next time we play them, I walk up to the plate, batting leadoff, and tap Berra on the shinguards and say,

'Hey, Yog, what's going on?' Usually we'd have a little chat before getting down to business. Only this time Yogi doesn't say a word. I try again. He won't even look up at me.

"I get on and then move over to second. Phil Rizzuto is standing behind me. I say, 'Hey, Scooter, what's wrong with Yog?' No response. I ask again and under his breath, real nervous, Phil says, 'Don't talk to me. The Old Man says we can never speak to you guys again. He'll fine us if we do. He's mad at you because he says you can't beat Boston or Cleveland but you always beat the hell out of us.'

"Can you imagine that? Well, Casey stopped me from talking to his players for a while, but he didn't stop me from annoying him. Later on, I hit a home run for the A's to beat the Yankees in another ball game. You probably don't know that ballpark [Shibe Park] in Philadelphia. The visitors' dugout in our stadium had this low ceiling, you could just barely walk upright in it. When I hit that home run, Casey was standing by the steps leading to the clubhouse and he yelled, 'That son of a bitch just kills us!' And he was so upset he jumped into the air, hit his head on the ceiling and knocked himself cold. Oh, was he mad when he came to.

"But Casey was a good guy and he didn't really hold any grudges. Especially if he thought you could help him win. In 1952, he called me, the same guy he wouldn't let his club talk to, and he said, 'Eddie, doggone it, I admit that I think you're one of the better players in this league. I tell my guys when we play you don't hit it to short or you're out.' Then he said he was picking me to be Rizzuto's alternate at the All-Star Game.

"The year before, he even tried to bring me to New York. Jimmy Dykes was our manager in 1951 and he told me the Yankees were trying to buy my contract. I said, 'When am I leaving?' My bags were as good as packed. But Dykes wouldn't let me go, because the A's weren't getting anything back but money. Jimmy had this team of young players and he wanted a veteran at short—I was thirty-five at the time—to steady them.

"That was my bad luck. I would have loved coming to New York, even if Casey made me a utility player, which is probably what he had in mind. Nineteen fifty-one, '52, and '53, that's three World Series I would have been in. By then, Stengel could have spoken backwards in the clubhouse if he wanted to, I would have listened to every word."

## THE PRICE OF A NEW FORD

*C*ruising through baseball cyberspace, you might encounter *www.cmgww.com, the Web site for Curtiss Management Group, a company that represents the licensing rights for famous ballplayers, many of them, as Casey Stengel would point out, dead at the present time. One of the living legends on its roster is Whitey Ford. Reading the Ford bio featured on that site, you might be struck by the odd line "In 1946, after a bidding war surfaced between the Boston Red Sox and the New York Giants, the New York Yankees gladly snatched up the rights to Ford...."*

*A three-team bidding war? Only last winter the Boston Red Sox had outbid six teams for the services of RBI man par excellence Manny Ramirez by tendering a contract that would pay the outfielder $160 million over eight years. And nonpareil shortstop Alex Rodriguez, perhaps the most talented player in baseball, joined the Texas Rangers after accepting a ten-year deal worth $252 million. Before signing it, A-Rod gave everyone a hoot by claiming he might have accepted a lower bid from his former team, the Seattle Mariners, except he had to take care of his family. His family being, I guess, Guam.*

*Texas Rangers owner Tom Hicks justified the transaction—his team had agreed to shell out over $60 million more than any of A-Rod's other suitors—by explaining that Rodriguez wasn't just an athlete; he was a brand-name product whose association with the Rangers, its cable network, and other entities directly or indirectly tied to the club, would generate a windfall of revenues far beyond ticket sales and broadcasting fees. A-Rod, in effect, had become Armani in a jockstrap.*

*All those electrifying dollar signs, all the millionaire talk of ballplayers as brands, were enough to overheat the synapses, conjuring visions of Henry Miller screaming in our nightmares, "... Yes, money makes money, but what makes money make money!" It also called to mind that bidding war of Mr. Ford's. Just how much loot had those clubs tossed at him back in '47? Had anyone treated the left-hander as if he were the next Coca-Cola?:*

**Whitey Ford:** "Oh yeah, that was some bidding war. The Red Sox offered me $5,000, the Giants offered me $6,000, and the Yankees topped them with $7,000. Ever since then I've kidded that if the Giants had just offered me a little more money, I would have signed with them. But to tell you the truth, I would have signed with the Yankees even if they'd been the low bidder. I grew up a Yankee fan, and that was the team I wanted to go with."

*Seven grand, it just didn't seem like much, especially when you consider New York had forked over $25,000 to sign Tommy Henrich some twelve years earlier. Factoring in inflation, wouldn't you think a commodity— there's that word—like Ford would have brought in more? Couldn't the famously cocksure and New York street-smart lefty wrangle a few more dollars out of the Yankees brass, especially with two other teams driving up the ante?:*

**Whitey Ford:** "Back then people with good jobs were making sixty, seventy dollars a week. As far was I was concerned, that *was* a lot of money the Yankees offered, especially since I never thought I'd make it to the big leagues. It's true that after I got to the majors, I had that reputation for being cocky. But people didn't really say that about me until after I established myself. Coming out of high school I was only five-nine and barely weighed one-fifty. I didn't throw very hard, so even I didn't consider myself much of a prospect.

"Actually, my first three years at [Manhattan Aviation] high school, I didn't pitch at all. I was a first baseman. Pretty good hitter, too, and I could field. But I wasn't a power hitter, and that's what the scouts wanted at first base. When I tried out for the Yankees at Yankee Stadium, their top scout, Paul Krichell, suggested I try pitching. The only pitching I had done up to that time was pretty much in stickball, you know where you throw a tennis ball against the [strike zone on] the wall? That's how I picked up the curve.

"But senior year, my coach, John Martin, asked me to pitch and I didn't lose a game all season right through to the Journal-American finals. We won that. I pitched a shutout in the finals, 1–0, I think. That's when the scouts really started to notice me. I still wasn't exceptionally fast, but I could get the curveball over for strikes and that was a big plus.

"After I signed with New York, I had two pretty good seasons in the minors. But I still wasn't sure about making it to the majors, even after I moved up in the organization each year. Before the 1949 season, I told the Yankee front office that I was going to play in Mexico. They hated that idea. They were afraid I'd get hurt pitching down there. I didn't care. I told them, 'That club has offered to pay me more than you guys paid me my first two years in the minors, so I'm going.'

"I went to Mexico, caught a case of dysentery so bad I ended up in Lenox Hill Hospital for two weeks. By the time I could pitch again for Binghamton [the Yankees Class A Eastern League representative], I'd missed about a month and a half of the season. But when I got back on the mound, I'd found out that I'd gotten a little bigger and stronger, threw a little harder. Suddenly I was breezing [Ford's record for that season was 16–5 with a 1.61 ERA].

"We just made the playoffs, which we won. After that was when I first really thought I had a chance to do something in the majors. I even phoned Casey [Stengel] to tell him that I was ready to help the Yankees win the pennant against the Red Sox. He said, 'Right now, I need hitters, not pitchers.' You have to remember I'm only in A ball, so you can't blame him for thinking I couldn't help them.

"But I think that call stuck with Casey, because he got me to spring training with the Yankees the following year [1950], even if it was only for a few weeks. He wanted to see what this fresh kid could do. They had Raschi, Reynolds, Byrne, and Lopat, so they didn't have much need for me at first. But I pitched well for Kansas City [the Yankees' Triple-A farm team], then I came back up in June and started winning ball games right away. . . ."

**Walt Dropo (major-league first baseman, 1949–61):** "Whitey and I were both rookies that season, and he finished just behind me in the Rookie of the Year voting. [In 1950, Dropo's first full season, he hit .322 with 34 home runs and 144 RBI.] Right away, I could see this guy was going to be trouble. He was like a master chess player who used his brain to take the bat right out of my hands. You'd start thinking along with him, and then Whitey had you because he never started you off with the same pitch in any one sequence. He could start you with a fastball inside, a curveball outside, then reverse that, or even start you with a change-up. He had, I guess, four pitches, fastball, curve, slider, change, threw them at different speeds to every part of the plate, he could change angles, so it was really as if he had 104 pitches . . ."

**Mickey McDermott (major-league pitcher, 1948–61; pitcher, 1956 New York Yankees):** ". . . and don't forget the funny pitches, the spitter, the mudball, the scuffed ball, Whitey had them all and he could throw them into a teacup without breaking the sides. And, boy, did he have nerves of steel. This guy has the greatest winning percentage of all time because he wasn't afraid to lose! Everybody will tell you I had a great arm, could throw as hard as almost anyone. But, with the game on the line, when a curve or change might get me out of a jam, I'd be afraid to throw anything except my fastball, because if I lost on anything other than my best pitch, I'd be pissed at myself. So I'd throw the fastball, the batter would hit it ninety miles, and I'd lose anyway. Whitey would throw the change for a strike, freeze the hitter, and walk off the mound with another win. He had the confidence to take risks on the mound other pitchers wouldn't."

**Walt Dropo:** "Another big thing about Whitey was that he could get ground balls whenever he had to, and that made him very tough. With men on first and second, I'm batting in an RBI spot, fourth, fifth. My job is to let it fly and drive those runners in with a long ball. But against Whitey, I'm thinking to myself, 'Now, you big Serbian, you have to make sure you don't hit into a double play.' I can't just swing away. Instead I'm going to try to hit the ball up the middle, right through him, which is taking away my power. Ford would get me in a mind-set that took me out of my game. He wasn't overpowering like an Allie Reynolds, a Herb Score, a Sandy Koufax. But Whitey was sneaky fast, meaning when you weren't set for the fastball, he'd slip it by you and it seemed that much faster because you weren't looking for it. It was amazing how he knew precisely the right time to throw that pitch. He played games with everybody, every hitter I talked to. He made them hit his pitch, and it was usually something they didn't like. And, just like Mantle, he had this ability from his first day in the majors on. . . ."

**Whitey Ford:** "Having Yogi behind the plate was a big reason for that. We all know what a tremendous hitter he was, but I don't think Yogi gets enough credit for being a smart catcher. I hardly ever shook him off, not just in my rookie year when I didn't really know the league, but after that, too. Yogi knew all the hitters, what they could hit, what their weak points were. And he knew what a batter looked for in certain situations. Yogi would fool them by calling for crazy combinations. Say I threw a batter two curves for strikes. Now the batter is thinking, 'There's no way he's throwing a third straight curve.' So he looks for the fastball. Yogi would call for another curve. He didn't have a great arm, but it was good enough, and he was quick around home plate, especially on bunts. He helped me a lot. After that June call-up, I went 9 and 1 for the team and we went on to win the World Series.

"Casey had a lot of confidence in me after that. He started me that year in the Series against the Phillies. I was the youngest pitcher ever to make a World Series start [a record since broken]. I have to admit I was nervous before that game started, but once we started playing, I was fine. We were up three games to none, so there wasn't a lot of pressure on me. I'm one out away from a shutout, when the catcher [Andy Seminick] hit this fly ball that Gene [Woodling] dropped in left. The run comes in, and here comes Casey. He signaled to the bullpen for Reynolds. I was disappointed. But I think the sixty or seventy relatives and friends I had at the game were more let down. I walked off the mound before Casey. My family cheered me, but then Casey followed and they booed the hell out of him.

"Sure, I thought I could finish the game, but it turned out to be a good move. Allie got a strikeout [on three pitches to Stan Lopata, pinch-hitting for Robin Roberts] to end the Series. I didn't get the shutout or the complete game, but I got the win. Except for my two years in the army, I never left the big-league club after that. I guess I was a prospect after all."

*The New York Yankees never had to ask Ford to return the $7,000. Talk about value for money. Pitching exclusively for New York, Whitey Ford won 236 games while losing only 106. His .690 lifetime winning percentage represents the major-league record for pitchers with at least 250 decisions. In sixteen seasons, he played an integral role—often as the ace, the go-to guy—on teams that won eleven American League pennants and six World Series Championships. There are no candy bars or soft drinks bearing his name. You won't find* FORD *plastered across the back of any designer jeans. But his plaque resides in the Baseball Hall of Fame.*

## "THEY DIDN'T HAVE STOPWATCHES FAST ENOUGH TO TIME HIM . . ."

*A*fter the Bombers won a second straight World Series in 1950, *many baseball fans outside of New York were hoping the victory didn't signal the start of yet another dynasty; they must have found the news coming out of Phoenix disquieting. Yankees owner Del Webb had brought his team's finest prospects to Arizona in February 1951 for a special instructional camp. How deep was the minor-league system that had spawned these wunderkinder? During the 1950 season, the Yankees held title to 240 minor-league players. Sixty of them—one out of every four—competed on all-star teams that summer. The best of these farmhands were assembled in Phoenix to complete their baseball educations under the tutelage of Casey Stengel and a phalanx of Yankee veterans:*

**Hank Bauer (major-league outfielder, 1948–61; outfielder, New York Yankees, 1948–59):** "I've heard that story that the Yankees had me, Yogi, Billy Martin, Jackie Jensen, and a couple of other younger veterans in that camp as instructors to get around the rules, that we were really there as players to get extra coaching. You weren't allowed to bring players on your major-league roster into an early camp back then. But, no kidding, we really were instructors. I was supposed to work with the outfielders on their fundamentals, but mostly I was there to teach the rookies how to turn on the bases. One of them—I think it was Sturdivant, who was really fast—turned and fell over his goddamn base, so they needed the instruction. . . ."

**Tom Sturdivant (major-league pitcher, 1955–64; pitcher, New York Yankees, 1955–59):** "Actually, what I remember is that Yogi tried to teach us how to make the turn at first base, and that he was the one who fell down while doing it. . . ."

**Bob Cerv:** "There had never been anything like this before that I'd heard of. An instructional camp for the team's best young players before spring training officially started? That was something new, but that's why the Yankees kept finishing on top. That entire organization was devoted to getting every advantage it could over the other clubs.

"We usually held training camp in St. Petersburg, Florida. But [Yankees co-owner] Del Webb had a big real estate development over near Phoenix where the New York Giants trained, so he traded with [Giants owner] Horace Stoneham for that one year. I guess it was so he could be close to the team. He also wanted to show us off to his business buddies, there were quite a few of them around.

"During one team meeting, Mr. Webb told us all about the fabulous real estate opportunities in Arizona. He was encouraging us to invest our money out there. There were a lot of bonus babies in the room. I think Andy Carey had gotten something like $70,000 to sign. I'd only gotten $5,000, so I wasn't buying anything. But some of those players followed Mr. Webb's advice and did very well. We all had a great time, learned a lot. Moose [Skowron] was there along with Carey, Tom Morgan, Gil McDougald, Tom Sturdivant, Tommy Carroll, and me."

*During the first days of camp, Webb, his drinking buddies, Stengel, his coaches, and the assembled press marveled over how these Yankee fledglings positively seethed with talent. Nearly every prospect looked like a burgeon-ing star. Five stood out. Skowron and Cerv displayed uncommon intelli-gence and power at the plate; unlike most rookies, they rarely swung at pitches outside the strike zone. Skowron's ability to drive the ball to the opposite field was particularly impressive for such a young hitter. Carey and McDougald cavorted around the infield like twin Nijinskys; each could range far to their left or right and they were blessed with powerful, accurate throwing arms. Morgan, though not yet twenty-one, carried to the mound a veteran's grab bag of pitches. Fastball, curveball, slider, change, he threw them all for strikes at varying speeds.*

*But no matter how many eyes these promising athletes popped out, any headlines they won in those agued climes would soon fade into footnotes with the arrival of a prodigy. Watching him take his freshman swings against major-league pitching, these rookies must have felt the same blend of awe and envy Salieri experienced when he first heard the adolescent Mozart tinkering at the piano:*

**Bob Cerv:** "Mantle wasn't there at first. Mickey didn't have the fare to get from Oklahoma to Phoenix, and Weiss wouldn't send it to him. I don't think he wanted Mickey rushed. But Casey sure wanted him there, and within a couple of days, he reported. Of course, right away you could see Mickey's power was awesome, from both sides of the plate. Moose and I could hit the ball a long way, so could Jackie Jensen. But no one could match Mickey. He'd hit a ball four hundred feet and you knew from the sound that he didn't even get good wood on it. . . ."

**Tommy Byrne (major-league pitcher, 1943, 1946–57; pitcher, New York Yankees, 1943, 1946–51, 1954–57):** "I would shag fly balls out in left field in that Phoenix ballpark, which was a fair shot from home plate, and there was a fence out there maybe twenty-five, thirty feet high. Mickey would hit the ball over that right-handed and even left-handed, balls that just kept on going, you know, still be rising as they went over the fence. That stood out, all that power, but what I remember even more was the way the opposing teams would sit in the dugout while he was taking batting practice with their mouths gaped open watching the show he was putting on. They were awed by him—he was just a kid—and I was awed by their reaction. . . ."

**Bob Kuzava (major-league pitcher, 1946–57; pitcher, New York Yankees, 1951–54):** "I was still with the Senators when he came up, but word about Mickey got around the other spring-training camps awfully quick. When Ted Williams came to our park or we visited Fenway, everything stopped as soon as he got into the batting cage. We all wanted to see Ted hit, he was in a league of his own. The same was true for Mantle even when he was just out of Class C ball. You didn't have to know who he was. The moment you heard that sound, the ball coming off his bat, it was like a rifle shot. No matter what you were doing, you paused and looked. Especially when he batted right-handed. From that side of the plate, you could forget about throwing him a high fastball. It was just suicide."

**Frank Crosetti:** "Mickey struck out a lot batting left-handed, it wasn't his natural side. But right-handed, even that first year, you couldn't get the ball by him. I honestly didn't see how any left-hander could get him out . . ."

**Johnny Hopp (major-league first baseman/outfielder, 1939–52; reserve first baseman/pinch hitter, New York Yankees, 1950–52):** ". . . which is unusual, because you have to understand when a player switch-hits, naturally he's going to get many more at-bats from the left side, there being so many right-handed pitchers. So it's hard to maintain your stroke batting right-handed. You could go a week without batting against a lefty in a game situation. But Mickey remained dangerous from both sides of the plate, with power enough to hit the ball out of any stadium. Which was also unusual, because most of the switch-hitters I'd seen were Punch-and-Judy types, you know, singles hitters. . . ."

**Frank Crosetti:** "I'm not going to put Mantle against Ruth or DiMaggio or any of the other people I saw as to who was better. I don't compare players. But I would have to say that Mickey had more raw talent than any player I'd ever seen, and he also had good baseball sense. Right from the beginning. Lot of times coaching at third, and I'd be undecided whether to send him home on a play. Before I could decide, he'd go right by me. And they never threw him out, not one time when he ran on his own. Great base-running instincts. Faster than Mays, Rickey Henderson, Lou Brock, all those guys, and he knew what to do with it, too."

**Bob Cerv:** "That's the thing that awed me the most about him. Slow roller to the infield, whoever fielded that ball had to stick it in his pocket, he wasn't going to throw out Mickey. And, batting left-handed, he was a great drag bunter. He'd just drag the ball down the first-base line, and with his speed, you couldn't get him out. He was something to see. I've heard stories about us having footraces against him during that camp, but I don't recall racing him, don't think it happened. The Yankees didn't hold footraces. . . ."

**Tom Sturdivant:** ". . . I know why Bob doesn't remember any footraces. It's because there really weren't any races. What we had were a bunch of athletes standing at the starting line watching Mickey Mantle's ass streaking off in the distance. Mickey pretty much ran by himself, or he might as well have. Oh mercy, was he quick! It was a joke for anyone to run against him, the guy could outrun Kentucky Derby racehorses. Why, he made us look like we were standing still!

"Mickey beat us by so much, the coaches were positive he was leaving early. They didn't have stopwatches fast enough to time him. So they had us race again. Same result. Okay, we're going to go one more time. Man, they would have had us out there all day. I was running next to Mick and I finally told them, 'Hell, no, he's not jumping the gun. Mickey's leaving when we are on the first step, it's just that he's half a block away on the second step.' I think that's when they hung the nickname 'The Commerce Comet' on him, except he was faster than a comet. Fastest thing I ever saw. . . ."

**Johnny Hopp:** ". . . Casey, I think, had the best line about his speed. He said, 'This kid runs so fast in the outfield, he doesn't bend a blade of grass.' You know what he meant, like Mickey was just flying over the ground. . . ."

**Walt Dropo:** "From day one, he was the toughest player I ever played against to defend because you never knew what he would do next. Mickey was not a normal hitter like a DiMaggio, Bauer, or Woodling. As good or great as they were, you had some idea what they might try to do during an at-bat given the situation. But Mickey! With two strikes on him in the late innings of a close ball game, he would drop down a drag bunt to get on base. Nobody does that. Mickey could get away with it because he was so fast, nine times out of ten, he'd get a base hit on that play. How do you defend against a hitter like that? Play in so he can bash a line drive and cut you in two? I don't think so.

"Another thing that made him tough to defend against was the way he hit the ball with overspin. Most people swing with a slight upper-cut. But Mickey often hit the ball up and over, meaning his wrists were flying over the top of the ball as he made contact, so he rotated over and against the ball, creating overspin. When that ball hits the ground it doesn't take a true bounce. You don't know what it will do, take a big hop, a short skip. Very hard to judge when you're playing the infield.

"So you can't play in on him, because Mickey would smash it right by you. You can't play too far back to compensate for how hard he hits the ball, because he can bunt or beat out a slow roller at will. If he hits a ground ball right to you, it might skip over your shoulder before you can get a glove on it. And he can hit the ball 450 feet at any time. All your pitcher can do with a guy like that is throw it up there and pray.

"If Mickey had one drawback, it's that he always went for power. Every swing he took had the same dimension. They were all hard like he was swinging for the fences all the time. Mickey never choked up like Ted [Williams] with two strikes to get a base hit. If he had, and worked in a few more bunts, to my mind he would have hit .400 or better two or three times.

"I really don't think people today, or fans who didn't see him play healthy, know what Mickey was like when we first got a look at him. Think of finding a kid today, fresh from the minor leagues, who could run faster than Rickey Henderson in his prime but has power like Mark McGwire. He wasn't anywhere near as big as McGwire, maybe five-ten and 190 pounds, but all muscle like an Oklahoma racehorse. The more clothes he took off, the bigger he got. Hey, I was six-five, 250 pounds, but he had more power, from the right side, than I did. He hit the ball harder more consistently than anyone I've ever seen."

**Tom Sturdivant:** "Oh, he was stronger than McGwire. We all know how Mickey hit the ball 565 feet that day in Washington [against Chuck Stobbs in 1953]. Big Mac hasn't hit this souped-up ball that far, has he? And that wasn't Mickey's hardest shot. He hit a ball off Pedro Ramos [in 1956] that would have gone further. It would have been the only fair ball to leave Yankee Stadium, except it hit the Stadium façade. That ball was over a hundred feet high and would have traveled well over 600 feet . . ."

**Frank Crosetti:** ". . . it got out so quick, a lot of people didn't even see it, they couldn't follow it with their eyes. They just heard the crack of the ball and bat and another crack when it hit that façade. . . ."

**Tom Sturdivant:** "About the only weakness Mickey had was that his fielding was raw when he came to that camp. We were both infielders, they weren't thinking of me as a pitcher yet. Mickey had a strong arm but he was so wild at shortstop, I think the Yankees would have gone broke buying accident insurance for the fans behind first base if he'd stayed there . . ."

**Tommy Henrich:** "... that's how the stories started that the Yankees moved Mickey to the outfield because he was a terrible shortstop and they didn't think he could play in the infield. I can't say that is completely true. Yes, he was an unpolished infielder at that stage of his career, but he was only what? Eighteen? He'd hardly played the infield professionally. But you just had to take one look at that speed, those reflexes, and that arm, plus how hard he worked—something a lot of people don't know because they think he did everything naturally—and you have to figure that if Crosetti and Rizzuto worked with him, he could have learned to be a good shortstop or third baseman. Just think about that. A switch-hitter who could hit fifty home runs and win the triple crown playing shortstop! Wouldn't that have been something?

"Casey asked me to help turn Mickey into an outfielder because we had a logjam in the infield. Phil Rizzuto had just won the [1950] MVP Award, we had two good third basemen in Bobby Brown and Billy Johnson. Jerry Coleman and Billy Martin were still good young players who played second and short. Then we had Gil McDougald and, oh my knees, he could play anywhere. All of these players were solid fielders who had been playing the infield a good deal longer than Mickey. They knew what they were doing out there.

"But in the outfield, I had just retired, and the last year I played I was really a first baseman. DiMaggio, we all knew, was coming to the end. So we had openings out there, and Casey figured center field was going to eventually be Mickey's spot because he could cover so much ground. I took him to the outfield and taught him all the basics. Right away I could see that he had no trouble catching the ball, went back well once he learned how to get a jump, and boy, could he fly! The biggest things I had to teach him concerned his throwing, his mechanics, and where to throw in different situations.

"First, Mickey had to learn to let that arm out when he threw, instead of short-arming it like an infielder. Then, he had this funny habit. When an outfielder lines up under a fly ball with a runner on, he takes a little hippity hop to get momentum behind his throw. Mickey did the hop, but he didn't start it until he caught the ball. Now, if a runner is on third and has any speed, you're going to concede a run doing that because you're wasting too much time. I taught Mickey to start the hop as the ball is coming down, so he could transfer the ball as soon as he caught it and his body is already in motion. Now you have saved time. Plus, you're getting your body behind the throw. I'd throw fly balls to him, maybe forty feet up in the air, all day, and son of a buck, he learned.

"After we're doing this for a while, we're playing an exhibition game against the Indians. Bobby Avila, one of the fastest runners in the league, is on third. Someone, it might have been [Al] Rosen, hits a medium fly ball, maybe 300 feet to Mickey in right field. The ball's coming down and I'm watching Mickey. Sure enough, while it's still in the air, he starts his hop, grabs the ball, and fires home. A line drive to the catcher, just to the left of home plate where he's in a perfect position to get the runner. Avila's out by six feet. Never had a chance. That placement, where Mickey threw the ball, made the play. I told him when he came into the dugout, 'That was the most perfect throw I've ever seen in my life. You've got it. There's nothing else I can teach you.' And I wasn't lying."

**Mickey Vernon (major-league first baseman, 1939–60; first baseman, 1951 Washington Senators):** "He got off to a good start in his rookie year, but you could see he wasn't disciplined at the plate. He didn't know the strike zone, and word gets around quick when you don't. Pitchers started to take advantage of that big swing of his and his inexperience. I remember Walt Masterson would strike out Mickey three times out of every four with curveballs in the dirt, fastballs outside, even fastballs practically in his eyes . . ."

**Johnny Hopp:** ". . . pitches he never should have been swinging at. But it wasn't that he didn't know the strike zone. Mickey was just so anxious to do well, he was overeager at the plate. He had all this pressure on him, everybody writing that he was the next in line from Ruth, Gehrig, and DiMaggio. Then he started to get this bad publicity. . . ."

*Newspaper articles questioned how the 4-F-rated Mantle, a victim of the bone disease osteomyelitis, could hit such booming home runs when he was supposedly too brittle to serve in the armed forces. Columnists intimated that Mantle was unpatriotic and accused the Yankee front office of pulling strings to gain his deferment. Mantle began finding piles of hate mail waiting for him in his locker. Fans in enemy ballparks greeted each of his at-bats with cries of "Draft dodger" and "Commie." And he heard every one of them:*

**Johnny Hopp:** "It got to be too much for him, and who could blame him? Just a teenager and having to put up with that. He suffered internally and his batting average kept dropping. Finally, he struck out five times against the Red Sox in Fenway Park. The crowd got on him a little bit strong. It hurt him so much, he came back to the dugout and broke down into tears. He said to me on the q.t., 'All I want to do is play ball.' And he wanted that so badly it was killing him.

"A little while later, the Yankees sent him back down to the minors [to the Kansas City Blues], more to get away from the pressure than anything else. Best thing for him. He beat up on those minor-league pitchers for six weeks, got his confidence back. When he returned to our club in August, you could see he was a different player, more relaxed and sure of himself. Mickey still struck out some, he swung so hard, but now those pitchers had to throw more strikes, had to work to get him out. Mickey developed a great batting eye. Once he started making those pitchers come to him, he made them pay. And he kept on making them pay for nearly twenty years."

*There are many stories recounting how self-doubt plagued Mantle throughout his Yankee tenure. A clubhouse prankster, the best teammate a ballplayer could ever want, and a party-hearty boy so generous he was quick to anger if anyone else tried picking up a check in his presence, Mantle frequently drank himself dizzy trying to evade the specters of his father and grandfather. Their deaths at a young age, he believed, forecast his own premature demise. No matter how many honors he won, he was often unsatisfied with his performance between the lines. Teammate Bobby*

Richardson, during an interview for this book, said, "Despite everything he did, I don't think Mickey ever realized how good he really was, although everyone who played with him knew that he was the best baseball player they were ever likely to see." Enos Slaughter remembered Mantle as "the least confident superstar I've ever seen. He took every bad game as if it were the end of the world, as if he'd never get another base hit." And Ralph Houk, who managed Mantle for seven seasons, recalled, "You never saw anyone who wanted to win as badly as Mickey. When his team won, even if he went 0 for 4, he was the happiest guy in the clubhouse. But when we lost, no matter what he did, he was down and he usually blamed himself for not doing enough."

Maybe he never learned what enough was. In a 1995 interview aired only weeks before his death from liver cancer—a public confession so heart-wrenching and intimate, you wanted to avert your eyes from the screen—the profoundly self-critical Mantle summed up his career by saying, "I feel as if I've let a lot of people down."

He didn't. Not on the field, anyway. Mickey Mantle played with the New York Yankees from 1951 to 1968. His career totals include a .298 batting average, 536 home runs, 1,509 RBI, and 1,677 runs scored. A three-time American League MVP, Mantle made the All-Star team sixteen times. He played on seven World Series champions and twelve American League pennant winners. The World Series record for career home runs (18) belongs to him.

Despite retiring irked by his inability to maintain a .300 career batting average, Mantle's lifetime OPS, his combined on-base percentage and slugging average, is higher than those of either Willie Mays or Henry Aaron, the two contemporaries with whom he is most often compared. The members of the Baseball Writers Association of America were impressed enough to elect Mickey to the Hall of Fame on the first ballot in 1973. His inclusion immediately enriched baseball's pantheon. From Aaron to Zuverink, more than 25,000 men have been skilled enough to grace a major-league diamond. Only a handful of them, perhaps five or six at most, can claim they were as accomplished as the Commerce Comet. Ballplayers continue to grow bigger, faster, stronger, yet not one has been able to match Mantle's combination of tape-measure power and Olympian speed. Tom

*Sturdivant said it best: Mickey made everyone else look as if they were standing still.*

## 1951: FRESH OUT OF MIRACLES

*T*he Giants is dead." By August 1951, that's what Dodgers fans like my mother thought—although, stalwart defender of the King's English she prided herself on being, she would never have resorted to such disheveled grammar. Who could blame her and the rest of the Ebbets Field throng for being so smug when the much-hated New York Giants led by manager Leo Durocher sat sandbagged in second place, $13\frac{1}{2}$ games behind Brooklyn? There was going to be a subway series that season. The smart money agreed on that. But there was no way the trains would be stopping in Harlem.*

*Well, you probably know what happened next. The Dodgers, unbeatable most of the summer, suddenly struggled to defeat second-division clubs, while the Giants? Why, they just couldn't lose. On August 12, they started a 16-game winning streak. No cause for alarm, my mother told her friends, it was a dying gasp. No team could sustain a run like that.*

*But run the Giants did, in the field, on the base paths, and up the standings. Durocher's team won 39 of its final 47 games to finish the regular season tied with the Dodgers for first place. A three-game playoff would send the survivor into the World Series. New York took the first game; Brooklyn won the second and was leading 4–1 going into the bottom of the ninth in Game Three.*

*Don Newcombe was on the mound for the Dodgers. The tiring right-hander opened the inning serving up singles to Alvin Dark and Don Mueller. Then he induced Monte Irvin to pop out. My mother sat in the living room of her parents' Flatbush apartment, the votive candles lit and piled high on the cathedral radio carrying the game, her fingers rubbing the onyx from her rosary as she prayed for Big Newk to deliver just two more outs.*

*God wasn't listening. Giant first baseman Whitey Lockman sliced a double to score one run. With runners on second and third, third baseman Bobby Thomson, New York's most reliable RBI man, came to the plate.*

*His arrival prompted Brooklyn manager Charlie Dressen to summon
Ralph Branca into the game.*

*Branca would throw just two pitches. Few remember the first, because
the second became the Shot Heard Round the World, the three-run homer
that extended the season for Durocher's team and crowded my mother's
mailbox with condolence cards gleefully sent by friends who dared to root
for Thomson and his mates in her company. So dramatic was the Giants'
victory, it convinced many that Durocher was managing a team of destiny,
a club so fortune-kissed that it could overcome any opponent, even one of
superior ability. But then the Yankees showed up:*

**Bobby Thomson (major-league third baseman/outfielder, 1946–60; third
baseman/outfielder, 1951 New York Giants):** "The playoffs left us no
time to think about the Series. We won the third game in the late
afternoon. I had a little party that evening with my family on Staten
Island. Around eleven P.M., I had to stand on a chair to remind everyone that we had a game with the Yankees the next day and I had to get
some rest. So it all happened in a blur.

"We felt good about our club, ready to take on anybody. I know that
after all those tense ball games we had played, I was so relaxed at the
start of the Series, I was as good a hitter as I could be. I only got one hit
in that first game, but I hit the ball hard all day. Dave Koslo pitched
great for us to get the win. We beat Allie Reynolds, and he was the
Yankees' best pitcher. It looked like we were on our way.

"But in the second game, Eddie Lopat killed me and everyone else
with all his slow stuff. We just couldn't hit him, and it didn't make
sense. The guys that could throw hard were the ones who handcuffed
you, but Eddie couldn't break glass and he always gave you a good
look at the ball. But you still couldn't time him. He had this big
motion like every pitch was going to come in 95 miles an hour, then
the ball never got up to the plate.

"I moved up in the batter's box, moved back. Whatever I did, he
adjusted. And you never knew what he was going to throw next.
There was no pattern to his pitches. If you got a good swing at him,
he'd attack you another way. That's a pitcher."

**Larry Jansen (National League pitcher, 1947–56; pitcher, 1951 New York Giants):** "The one thing about going from the playoffs immediately to the World Series was that, as a pitcher, I didn't have time to study any information the scouts provided on the Yankees. I pitched a pretty good game against Lopat, but to show you what I mean, Mickey Mantle led off for New York and I had no idea he could bunt. I got two strikes on him and figured it was a good time to throw him a curve. Which left him wide open to drag a bunt for a base hit. I was so surprised and he was so fast, Mickey nearly got a double out of it."

**Mickey Mantle (outfielder, New York Yankees, 1951–68):** "That was the game where I suffered my first major injury in the big leagues, and it happened because of something Casey said to me. Joe DiMaggio had this sore Achilles tendon that had been bothering him all season. Right before the series, Casey said, 'The Big Dago's heel is hurting him bad.' He wanted me to take every fly ball I could reach. I had to think like a center fielder even though I was playing in right.

"In the fifth inning, [Willie] Mays hit this fly ball to short right field. I figured there was no way Joe could get to it, so I took off. Just as I got near the ball, Joe called me off. He was already under it, ready to make the catch. Soon as I heard him yell for it, I put on the brakes. The spikes on my right shoe caught the cover of a drain in the outfield. My knee collapsed under me and I went down. The pain was so bad I nearly blacked out. I remember hearing Joe say, 'Don't move, they're bringing a stretcher.' Next day, in the hospital, we found out I had torn ligaments. Funny, Willie hitting that ball, with all the comparisons people made between us over our careers."

**Bobby Thomson:** "When Mickey went down, we didn't think anything of it. He didn't have a great rookie season as I recall, so, really, we didn't know who he was. As far as we were concerned, he was just another one of the good Yankee prospects. None of us realized this was Mickey Mantle they were carrying off, because he wasn't Mickey Mantle yet. We hoped he'd be okay, but we still had a ball game to win. . . ."

**Larry Jansen:** "...Lopat beat me, 3–1, but we took Raschi in Game Three and I felt pretty good about Game Four with Sal Maglie going for us. Since all seven games were being played in New York, there were no off days for traveling. We were supposed to play that series over seven straight days. But then it rained, and that made a big difference. Sal was all primed and ready to take his usual turn. I believe he lost some of his edge with the twenty-four-hour delay.

"Sal also hadn't pitched in a while; this was his first appearance of the Series, and that hurts a pitcher's control. Even though he didn't walk too many, as I remember [Maglie walked two in five innings], his location had to be off, he was getting his pitches up in the strike zone and the Yankees jumped on them. Reynolds, on the other hand, was making his usual start [on three days' rest] and he came out very strong that day. Allie was tough. Very fast. I once faced him and he threw a ball by me for a strike while I swore he was still in his windup."

**Alvin Dark (major-league infielder, 1946–60; major-league manager, 1961–77; shortstop, 1951 New York Giants):** "Everybody has a different way of seeing things. I don't know that the rain was a turning point, because if it hadn't rained the Yankees were going to start Johnny Sain, and I can tell you he was no hacker. No guarantee we could have beaten him ..."

**Larry Jansen:** "...but we knew Sain from all the years he had pitched in the National League [for the Boston Braves], and our lineup was very comfortable against him. Most of our club had never faced Reynolds before the Series...."

**Alvin Dark:** "I homered off Allie in the first game, one of the strangest home runs I've ever hit. A three-run homer that really put the first game of the World Series away for us, but I didn't feel any excitement at all, that's how numbed I still was from the playoff against the Dodgers. We all were. I got three hits off Allie in Game Four, so he didn't look all that different to me. He was tough both times, a great pitcher, and I was just fortunate. But his ball was moving more in that fourth game and he was just throwing it by most of the hitters in the lineup. I know Bobby [Thomson] came back shaking his head a few times . . ."

**Bobby Thomson:** "I'll tell you how good he was that day. He had the best stuff I've ever seen. Ever. I had just faced Newcombe, and he could throw a ball through the wall, maybe throw just as hard as Allie. But Reynolds threw a heavier ball. Tough to handle. I didn't expect him to be so overpowering. Allie not only threw hard, he had a slider that was either right on the plate or only off by maybe three inches. And when it's that close, its very hard to lay off it. I'd been hitting pretty well for two or three months, but hitting against someone like that is tough."

*After the Reynolds win, the Yankees beat the Giants 13–1 in Game Five, a drubbing so methodical, it was like watching a slow-motion train wreck. The following afternoon, Stengel's pitchers continued to dominate their opponents as the Bombers took a 4–1 lead into the top of the ninth. Yankee fans thought a win was assured, but this was Durocher and company. They just couldn't depart without a final, dramatic flourish.*

*Reliever Johnny Sain was on the mound for the Yankees. Eddie Stanky and Alvin Dark, the two pests who had acted as table setters for the Giants all season, started the inning with base hits. When Whitey Lockman blooped a single to load the bases, Stengel had seen enough. He trudged to the mound, his purposeful stride telegraphing his intention to end Sain's workday.*

*In the stands, fans checked their scorecard. Right-handed power hitters Monte Irvin and Bobby Thomson were scheduled up next. What right-hander would Stengel bring in to neutralize them? Allie Reynolds wasn't available after going nine innings only two days earlier. Tom Morgan and Bob Hogue were rested; both had pitched effectively against the Giants in brief prior appearances. Morgan, 9–3 during the regular season and an experienced reliever, seemed the logical choice. Logic never entered Stengel's mind:*

**Bobby Thomson:** "I have to admit that I was somewhat surprised when Casey brought Bob Kuzava in, because he was a lefty. Monte and I both hit left-handers pretty well. But knowing the way Stengel worked, nothing was unexpected. And once you saw what Bob had, you understood Casey's confidence in him. Bob's ball moved a lot, low in the strike zone, and left-handers who can keep the ball down against right-handers are generally going to be successful.

"Monte hit the ball 400 feet to score Stanky with a sacrifice fly. Kuzava and I had a pretty good battle, but he threw me a good, hard-moving fastball that may have tailed away a bit at the last moment. I hit that pitch well. In fact, I thought it might be an extra-base hit when it left my bat. But I just couldn't pull it enough. With the wind blowing in from left, it was another long out."

**Bob Kuzava:** "Bases loaded in the World Series, you have some butterflies warming up. You can't perform well unless you have that nervousness to push your adrenaline. But once I got into the game, I'm checking the feel of the mound, remembering my signals, going over the situation with Yogi. I'm thinking about what I have to do to get ahead on Monte Irvin, what pitch to throw for strike one. As a reliever, strike one is everything because it puts you in charge. Now the batter's in the hole, you have three pitches to choose from and he has a big guessing game. Sixty thousand fans are screaming, but you are so focused on what you have to do, you really can't hear them and the butterflies are gone.

"I wasn't shocked when Casey brought me in to face those big right-handed hitters. You have to remember, this was the sixth game, not the seventh, and we're in the driver's seat. We were one game to the good and this was Yankee Stadium. My fastball got up there in the low to mid-90s so Casey knew right-handers tended to hit long fly balls to left center off me. That was Death Valley in our park. You could hit the ball over 400 feet and go back to the dugout with nothing. The thing was, you had to be willing to challenge the hitters, to pitch them inside even if that was their strength. Let them try to jack it out of there, because if they can hit the ball that far, you tip your cap to them.

"What I didn't want was to get the ball out over the plate where they could drive it the other way. Monte and Bobby were awfully strong. Either of them could have flicked an outside pitch over our short right-field porch for a home run. So I came right at them and they did pull me, but all they got were 800 feet of outs for two runs.

"It's 4–3 and I see someone coming in to hit for Hank Thompson, who was a left-handed hitter. It's Sal Yvars. Now I'm going to surprise you. Bobby Thomson is the man who hit one of the most famous home runs in baseball history. Monte Irvin led the National League in RBI that season we played against him. Yvars is a backup catcher, but, in a way, I'm more concerned about him than the other two.

"You see, I had pitched against Sal in the minor leagues and he used to whack me around pretty good. A very strong right-handed hitter. As soon as they announced him into the game, Casey came out and asked, 'Do you know this guy?' I told him that I had faced Sal in the minors when he was with Jersey City and that I thought I could handle him. Casey left me in.

"Why did I say that when Sal had hit me well in the minors? Because I felt that was back then, and today my stuff was better than usual. I was confident I could get the job done. My plan was to pitch Sal tight. Strong kid who stood on top of the plate, I didn't want him to extend those big arms of his . . ."

*And what was Mr. Yvars thinking as he came to the plate representing his team's last chance to push the Series to a seventh game? Was this backup catcher salivating at the idea of facing a pitcher he had frequently bested in the minor leagues?:*

**Sal Yvars (major-league catcher, 1947–54; reserve catcher, 1951 New York Giants):** "Me? I was just happy to be there. Kuzava's doing all that thinking about someone who wasn't even supposed to get into that World Series. Leo went through twenty-three guys before he finally calls on me in the last inning of Game Six, even though I hit .317 that year. He was mad at me. About a month before the season closed we had a knock-down-drag-out.

"Here's how it all started. I'm in the clubhouse going to the men's room and I came back to find Leo's goddamned dog had pissed all over my best shoes. Ruined them, and they cost $200. So I tap this cocker spaniel on the ass with my toe—not a kick, really, just a nudge—and the dog starts barking and snapping. Now Leo's kid is crying. Leo calls me into his office and starts bawling me out. But I'm not backing down. Hey, I'm the offended party here. I only had two pair of shoes, and these were my Sunday best.

"Some things were thrown and more things were said. It wasn't pretty. But when it was over, I forgot about it. Leo wasn't good at forgetting. After we lost the second game to the Yankees, two writers, Ken Smith of the *Daily Mirror* and Barney Kramenko of the *Herald Tribune,* go up to Leo and one of them asks, 'What's going on? You pinch-hit with Rigney today with the bases loaded and a chance to take a big lead. He hit .230 during the regular season. Then after he makes the second out of the inning, you send up Ray Noble, another .230 hitter, with the game on the line. He fouls out to end the inning. Meanwhile, you got a .317 hitter on the bench. Isn't he the logical guy to send up?' They were talking about me.

"Leo had the most vulgar mouth in baseball, and he let them have it. Every swearword he knew. After they tell me about it, I go up to Leo in the dugout and say, 'The rumor is you're not using me because of that fight we had. Look, if you can use me to win a game . . .' I didn't get another word out of my mouth. He yells, 'Get this son of a bitch out of here.' I had a bat in my hand. I was so mad, I broke it in half on the dugout roof right in front of him. Believe me, I was hoping he would come at me, because I would have killed the son of a b. on the spot.

"Game Three, we win 6–2, so he doesn't use any pinch hitters. But in Game Four he sends Lucky Lohrke to pinch-hit—Lucky wasn't very lucky that year, he hit about .200—in the fifth, and he uses Rigney again in the eighth. I just sit there while we lose. Bam! I break two bats this time.

"Game Five, same thing. Leo uses three pinch hitters; he doesn't even look in my direction. We lose again. I break two more bats. Louisville Slugger gave us each six bats for the Series, so I'm running out of lumber.

"In that sixth game, I'm in the bullpen warming up Sal Maglie. We're down 4–1 in the ninth when we rally to load the bases. Kuzava comes in. Monte hits a sac fly, Bobby Thomson hits a sac fly. Now the score is 4–3 with Whitey Lockman on second and two out.

"The bullpen phones weren't working, and Leo was signaling for a pinch hitter. He had already used Rigney, Williams, and Noble. Out in the bullpen, Hartung stood up, Leo shakes his head no. Lohrke stood up, no again. It's like we're doing this by sign language. We don't know who he wants. So Leo sends Hank Schenz down to tell us. God, even Hank had appeared in the Series as a pinch runner, and I had no idea why he was even on the club. All he ever did was walk Durocher's dog and watch his kid.

"Hank comes in and says, 'Leo wants Sal.' No one believes him, they all knew about the grudge. I run out there. Casey is on the mound with Kuzava, Berra, and Rizzuto, they're trying to figure out who Leo's bringing in because, by then, they forgot that I was even on the club. When Casey leaves I see Bob is staying in. Oh, boy, that was good news for me, because I used to knock the crap out of him when we were both in the minors.

"As I go up to the plate to face him, the bat boy comes out, all frantic. Guess what he says? 'Mr. Yvars, you don't have a bat.' No shit, I've busted them all in two! So I said, Pick one out for me. I stand next to Lee Ballanfant, the home-plate umpire, while the kid brings out someone's bat.

"I used to pull the hell out of Kuzava in the minors. But I had three broken fingers on my right hand. They weren't bad enough that I couldn't hit, but I didn't think I could pull the ball with much power. Bob doesn't know this, so I figure he would put something extra behind the ball and make it tail away from me. I'm looking for that pitch to drive it up the middle. The way Whitey could run, a base hit ties the ball game . . ."

**Bob Kuzava:** ". . . but I wasn't afraid of Sal pulling the ball in Yankee Stadium. With his strength, it was that opposite-field shot I was worried about. So I decided to pitch him inside. I just got the ball away from him more than I wanted to . . ."

**Sal Yvars:** ". . . it was a fastball that tailed away, just like I figured, maybe four inches outside. I lunged into it, which you do when you want to hit straight away. I hit that son of a bitch solidly, a line drive over Jerry Coleman's head at second. A base hit for sure, and I figure Whitey would score . . ."

**Bob Kuzava:** "I didn't think it was a base hit. I was certain Bauer would catch it for the third out in right field. At first. But with the Stadium packed, that ball was coming out of a crowd of white shirts. Hank seemed to lose sight of it. My heart stopped. I'm thinking tie ball game."

*Right field, late afternoon, Yankee Stadium, the last thing an outfielder wants to deal with is a sinking line drive, flitting in and out of the dusk. . . .*

**Hank Bauer:** ". . . which is exactly what Sal hit. A ball like that, you see it fine coming off the bat, but then it disappears into those shadows. Now you have to pick it up again when it comes out of the shadows, so you had better hope you gauged it right. By the time I saw it, I was in pretty good position, but the ball started to fall away from me. And I'm thinking, 'Holy shit, I'm going to have to dive for this . . .'"

**Sal Yvars:** "If you look at the film, you'll see Bauer rolling over on his ass catching that ball. What you don't see is me kicking first base so hard I was limping for three weeks afterwards. I thought it was dropping in, and I was all set to run into second base. I figure, let them cut off any throw Bauer makes to try to get me out. Meanwhile Whitey scores the tying run. And if I make it to second safely, gravy! Then Maglie comes in with us tied or maybe ahead. Sal had a tired arm, but the way he pitched in big games, don't bet they would have beaten him. Except Sal didn't come in. The ball didn't drop, there was no throw. The Series was over."

**Bobby Thomson:** "Even without Sal getting a hit, we could have won that day and forced Game Seven. There was a turning point in that sixth game that most people didn't notice at the time. In the sixth inning, Johnny Mize was at the plate for the Yankees. And Koslo isn't challenging him, he's nibbling. I'm at third base and screaming at Dave to get the ball over the plate.

"I had played with Mize. He was a dangerous hitter, a Hall of Famer. But John was near the end and couldn't get around on the fastball like he used to. He should have been our out man. What he did still have was amazing eyes, and he really knew the strike zone. Players like that build reputations with umpires. They get a lot of close pitches called in their favor. So I'm yelling at Koslo to get the ball over. This is a guy you don't nibble with, he won't swing. But we walk him, and Hank Bauer comes to the plate . . ."

**Hank Bauer:** ". . . Yogi, DiMaggio, and Mize are on base. Kos has me 2 and 2, throws me a knuckleball. I didn't know he even had a god-damned knuckler! For years, he said he thought that ball was strike three. Well, it's fifty years later and I want to tell you I didn't *think* it was a strike. I *know* it was a strike! I'm out, no doubt about it. Except the umpire calls it ball three. Oh boy, that's a nice present. A call like that changes everything. Now it's 3–2 and Koslo has to get it over or he walks in a run. So I know I'm not going to see that knuckler again and probably won't see any kind of breaking pitch. I look for a fast-ball, and when he throws it, I hit it good. I could feel the bat bend a little when I made contact.

"The wind was blowing in. But in Yankee Stadium when the wind blew in and hit that top bleacher, it blew back out again. Like a jet stream. Monte Irvin in left field didn't know that. He had been play-ing me shallow, and when the ball took off, he couldn't get back in time. It hit the 402 mark for a three-run triple. I did have to hit the ball, but it goes to show you how much difference a little luck can make. If the umpire calls that pitch correctly, I'm out. We don't score those runs. Instead we make the lead hold up and win the Series."

**Bobby Thomson:** "To me, with the way we had to come from so far back to catch the Dodgers, the biggest thing was getting into the World Series. But once you're in, you want to win. A lot of people said, well, winning the Series would have been anticlimactic. No such thing. Beating the Dodgers, that was great and everyone still remembers my home run off Ralph Branca. Giants fans seem happy enough with that. But for the players, the loss to the Yankees made us feel like we didn't finish the job. We left the season undone by not winning it all."

**Larry Jansen:** "It was a record-setting Series for me. Besides losing two games, I gave up Mickey Mantle's first World Series base hit in Game Two, Joe DiMaggio's last Series hit when I held him to a double in Game Six, and the first Series grand slam by a rookie [Gil McDougald in Game Five]. So the Yankees made sure I had a place in baseball history. They did that to a lot of pitchers."

## SIGNING OFF ON THE SERIES

*F*eisty *and unyielding though the 1951 New York Giants undoubtedly were, they apparently needed some help overhauling the Dodgers. Just two days after I finished the preceding segment, reporter Joshua Prager, writing for* The Wall Street Journal, *revealed that Durocher and his players had employed an ingenious sign-stealing system—something more elaborate than the peek-and-whistle method that was so common in baseball—during home games to bolster their offense while they were making up all that ground against Brooklyn. Prager's story, which was corroborated by several former Giants, including Bobby Thomson, Monte Irvin, and Sal Yvars, came as no surprise to anyone who remembered Durocher as the original wise guy wannabe, the kind of preening, machine gun–mouthed sharpie who would buy loud silk ties from a haberdasher simply because the artisan numbered the dapper hood Bugsy Siegel among his clients.*

*It was easy to understand why Durocher would affect the style of gangdom's killer clotheshorse. He and Bugsy evidently attended the same charm school. Leo in a pennant race was a ponce in a knife fight. Rules were for those polite gents who ended their evenings cold on stainless-steel slabs. All those nice guys finishing last. Durocher wasn't up for being one of them. He would grab any edge he could, illicit or otherwise, and snap it like a shiv through your eye if it meant skulking out of the alley with another win.*

*Despite his taste for the faintly criminal, Durocher refused to act as perpetrator for the sign-stealing scam. He wasn't leaving any fingerprints behind. Instead, the manager stationed coach Herman Franks in the Giants clubhouse with a high-powered telescope. Franks would read the opposing catcher's signs before relaying them by means of an electric buzzer to bullpen catcher Sal Yvars. Giants hitters could then key off Yvars to discover what the opposing pitcher was about to throw.*

*It was Le Carré ball, an espionage so successful it helped carry the Giants into the World Series. But the Yankees won two out of three at the Polo Grounds and the Giants had scored only three runs in those two losses. So now we had to go back and ask Mr. Yvars why his Giants couldn't score more often if they knew what Allie Reynolds and his colleagues would be dealing:*

**Sal Yvars:** "The system didn't work against the Yankees for one reason: We weren't using it. Too bad, because we could have used the help, although the way Reynolds pitched in that fourth game, he could have told us himself what was coming and it wouldn't have mattered.

"To understand why we didn't steal any signs against the Yanks, you have to know how our system operated. Leo had an electrician rig a buzzer between our clubhouse and our bullpen. Our clubhouse was all the way out, more than 400 feet from home plate. Franks would stand in there, watching through the scope in Leo's office. Soon as he read the opposing catcher's sign, he'd give a short buzz to our bullpen for a breaking ball or change, no buzz for a fastball, and a long buzz if the hitter was going to get knocked on his ass.

"I'd stand in the bullpen, listening for the buzz and holding a baseball where our hitters could see it. If I flipped, it was a breaking pitch; no flip, a fastball. When Herman gave a long buzz, I'd make like I was stretching; whoever was at the plate would get ready to duck. Eventually, we got it down so good we told Stanky, Dark, and some of the others to deliberately look bad on pitches—you know, lunge at a change-up or a breaking pitch like they were really fooled, when we were far ahead. We were afraid people were going to start talking.

"We kept stealing the signs while we were winning all those games to catch the Dodgers. Then we stole them during the playoffs. But the reason we stopped stealing signs against the Yankees during those games at the Polo Grounds was simple. Leo wouldn't let us.

"That might surprise you. Leo was, at heart, a crook, a real thief. He had no hesitation about using all that equipment to steal signs if it helped us win games. But he was afraid we'd get nabbed if we did it in the Series. Leo had been suspended for a whole season [1947], and he eventually lost his job managing the Dodgers for hanging around with gamblers. Not that the suspension stopped him from gambling anymore. Hell, when Leo was managing the Giants, George Raft called him in the middle of a team meeting with a tip on a horse running at Arlington Park. So help me, Leo gave all of us a chance to get in on it. He actually took the bets down for players in the clubhouse, then had me and Hank Schenz place them with a Chicago bookie. We didn't get back until the third inning that afternoon. He had us placing bets during a goddamned ball game!

"So Leo wasn't afraid of much, but he didn't want any more trouble with the commissioner's office. There were too many reporters around during those games with the Yankees—they were like ants in the clubhouse, on the field, everywhere you turned—and there was a chance one of them might nail us. Could you have imagined what would have happened if they found out we were using buzzers and telescopes to win the World Series? Believe it or not, there were no rules against doing what we did, but you know the commissioner would have had our asses just the same. And the main thing, for the players, with the sign stealing, was just getting to the Series. After we did that, we figured we were on our own."

## THE COUNTING HOUSE

*F*or years, the Yankees front office never contented itself to merely leave opposing teams beaten and battered. Come contract time, it conducted a cold war, which occasionally flared hot, with its own players. General managers from Ed Barrow on must have spent hours practicing how to cry poor mouth whenever some employee entered the office with an outstretched hand. It didn't matter that the Yankees were baseball's most affluent team. They knew that the rich didn't stay rich by showering largesse on every ballplayer who thought his services were worth an extra buck or two.

Until free agency arrived, the hired help didn't have too many weapons to fight back with. The reserve clause bound you to a team for life. If a club's final contract offer didn't suit you, your only recourse was to go home and start eyeballing the Help Wanted ads. Or you could hold out—refuse to suit up until management capitulated to your demands. But then the front office could slaughter you in the papers.

Joe DiMaggio sure discovered that. After a 1937 season in which he batted .346 with a league-leading 46 home runs, 151 runs scored, and a .673 slugging average, the center fielder asked the Yankees to triple his salary from $15,000 to $45,000. His bosses refused, pointing out that New York's team captain and biggest star, Lou Gehrig, was making only $41,000. How, they wondered, could a second-year player expect to earn more than that? Or even close to it? DiMaggio's reply was as terse and stinging as the DiMaggio swing. "Mr. Gehrig," he informed his employers, "is underpaid." The front office didn't agree. DiMaggio was, in effect, forced to go on strike, holding out for more money until late April.

While he and the front office haggled, DiMaggio was publicly portrayed as an ingrate, a grasping, greedy punk of a ballplayer who wanted all this loot, as if there weren't a Depression going on and he should be oh so grateful just to have a job doing something he loved. Many fans—unaware that Joe was very much a working stiff just like themselves, albeit one with a bigger bankroll—bought the image of DiMaggio as avarice personified. They didn't know his actual value to the Yankees was two or three times

*what he was asking, that the Yankees could have paid him six figures with-*
*out missing the extra cash.*

   *When Joe D. finally suited up again, after agreeing to a $10,000 raise,*
*Yankee Stadium filled his head with jeers. He had to win a batting title to*
*win back the crowd. The guardians of the pinstriped purse were uncon-*
*cerned that they had stuck their next big drawing card in the doghouse. It*
*served a purpose, kept everyone in line. Dissing DiMaggio sent his team-*
*mates a message: Mess with us, turn up your nose at our top offer, and we'll*
*bring the whole town down on you. It told the rest of the team that the suits*
*weren't afraid to play hardball with anybody. And they went right on play-*
*ing it with other employees, the stars and the subs, year after year:*

**Jerry Lumpe (major-league infielder, 1956–67; reserve infielder, New York Yankees, 1956–59):** "I first came up to New York in 1956. There was nothing difficult about negotiating with the Yankees back then. Since we had absolutely no bargaining power, you didn't make anything. I had a family early. One year I sent a letter to George Weiss saying, I can't live on what you're offering. In so many words, he replied, 'Well, then you better find yourself another job.' He knew there were fifty people waiting for my spot. Weiss didn't care about players, except for what they could do for him and the team. He was a great owners' man. He kept their money in the till.

   "That first year I started out making $6,000. The next year I got a big raise to $7,200. And there's a story to that. When I was making the $6,000, I went to Mr. Weiss and told him I needed a raise right away, during the season. He wasn't too keen on that, but he finally agreed to up me to $6,600. Except he wouldn't make the raise retroactive, so I only got an extra hundred dollars instead of the $600 I needed! What was an extra $500 to a club like the Yankees? Then, the next year, the team negotiated with me as if I'd actually made $6,600!"

**Hank Bauer:** "Oh, they were a bunch of coldhearted bastards in that Yankee front office. They never just came to you and said, 'Good job, here's a fat raise.' Every contract talk was a struggle. The only way to beat them was to be just as tough as they were. If you were nice, the front office walked all over you. Take Moose [Skowron], who's one of the sweetest guys on the earth. I had to make Moose hold out, they were taking such advantage of him.

"He told me that he hadn't gotten a raise in three years. This is a guy who hit over .300 every season. I said to Moose, 'You better start evaluating yourself. You don't realize how important you are to this club.' By the time I'm finished with him, Moose refuses to sign. He comes to spring training but doesn't suit up. This goes on for a little while until our owner, Dan Topping, gets in touch with him and says, 'Meet me for lunch at my country club.' Moose goes, and Dan is there with Roy Hamey, George Weiss's right-hand man.

"Right off, Topping asks, 'Why haven't you signed?' Moose says, 'Mr. Topping, I was told I can't get more money because I'm not well liked on the Yankees'—this was horseshit, of course, because everybody on our ball club liked Moose, but those are the kind of games they played with you. Moose then said, 'If that is the case, I think you should trade me.' When Topping asked, 'Who told you that?' Moose said, 'I'm not going to tell you.' But I know, because Moose told me, that it was Hamey, who was sitting right there at the table.

"Topping asked, 'How much do you want?' Moose asked for a $12,500 raise. Topping said, 'You've got it.' . . ."

**Bob Turley (American League pitcher, 1951–63; pitcher, New York Yankees, 1955–62):** ". . . that was the funny thing, Dan Topping was a generous guy and you could get more out of him if you could just get past Weiss. In 1958, I was 21 and 7 with 19 complete games. I was lucky enough to win the Cy Young Award and World Series MVP Award.

"I was making $19,000 back then, a good salary for the time, but I'm thinking I'm due a pretty decent raise. Dick Young, the New York sportswriter, called me shortly after the Series and, right out of the blue, asks, 'Bob, how would you like a hundred percent raise, you know, double your salary?' Well, how else could I answer that? I told him I'd be very happy with that. The next day, Dick writes a story headlined 'Turley Demanding a 100% Raise!'

"Oh, did that get Weiss on the phone. He calls me and shouts, 'Bob, what in heaven's sake is going on here? We haven't even started talking yet and you're already making demands like this in the papers?' I explained what had happened and how I hadn't demanded anything yet. He cooled off, we had a little laugh, and that was the end of it.

"I have no idea if that article had anything to do with our subsequent negotiations, but this time, Topping got involved right away. He called a meeting with me and said, 'Bob, I want to thank you for everything you've done for our club. This is not a negotiation. I'm going to make what I think is a fair offer and I hope you'll accept it.' And I said, 'Mr. Topping, if it's what I want then I'll sign the contract.' He offered $35,000, near enough to double my salary, so I accepted on the spot.

"When you argued salary with Weiss and [assistant general manager Lee] MacPhail, they didn't give an inch. They rarely talked to you face-to-face. You negotiated by letter or by phone, and they made sure they never took a collect call from you during those negotiations. They wanted every edge, and if it cost you money to plead your case, they figured that was one more point on their side. And they used the World Series against you. Weiss or MacPhail would say, 'And you know that on top of your regular salary you're going to make all that extra money when you get your World Series share.' But they wouldn't guarantee to make it up to you if you had a great year and the club didn't make it to the Series. I once asked them if they would put that in the contract, but there was no way. . . ."

**Irv Noren (major-league outfielder/first baseman, 1950–60; outfielder/first baseman, New York Yankees, 1952–56):** "You could get around Weiss. At least, I found that to be true. In 1954 I hit .319 to lead the Yankees in hitting. Bill DeWitt, Weiss's assistant general manager who used to be with the St. Louis Browns, offered me a $1,000 raise, from $19,000 to $20,000. I sent the contract back. He upped it all the way to $2,000. I called him and said, 'That's no raise after leading the team in hitting.' DeWitt said, 'Well, that's what we're paying you.' I told him, 'Billy, you're not with the Browns in last place anymore, you're with the

Yankees. Act like it.' Oh, did he hang up on me in a hurry. Three days later, George Weiss called and asked what it would take to satisfy me. I told him I wanted an $8,000 raise and he agreed. Just like that."

**Hank Bauer:** "... that was just DeWitt and Weiss working their good cop–bad cop routine. You'd haggle with DeWitt, Hamey, or MacPhail, they wouldn't budge more than a certain amount, act like their hands were tied by the budget. Then Weiss would tell the player he'd give him a few dollars more and it seemed like you won something. But the two of them knew exactly how far they were going to go. My wife worked for the Yankees and she told me that they had two numbers for every ballplayer. One was as high as they were willing to pay, the other was what they would try to sign you for. There was a big gap between those figures, and they usually got you for a number closer to the bottom one than the one at the top."

**Jim Bouton (major-league pitcher, 1962–70, 1978; pitcher, New York Yankees, 1962–68):** "None of the clubs were paying the players as much as they could have; the Yankees were no different, except they probably had more money to not pay than anyone else except possibly the Dodgers. But we didn't know how underpaid we were, because the owners and general managers had us all hypnotized. They kept pounding into us that if you took away the reserve clause, the mechanism that kept salaries down throughout the game, baseball would collapse. We all believed the mantra at the time that, without that clause, two or three wealthy teams would gobble up all the talent and competitive balance would be wiped out. General managers would also tell us not to discuss our salaries with each other because they wanted to keep us in the dark, and we stupidly followed their instructions...."

**Hank Bauer:** "... if you knew what someone else was making, you could argue what you were worth compared to him. I know because I did that when DiMaggio was on the club. In 1950 I hit .320 and Weiss gives me a contract with a $1,500 raise. I sent it back unsigned. We went back and forth three times like this—his offer never changed, not by a penny—until he called and asked me to meet him in New York to discuss the contract. That was supposed to intimidate you, like being called in front of the firing squad.

"I showed up, my first time in his office. He didn't look at me the whole time. Joe was our big star and he kept bringing up his name, comparing my stats to his. And that was his mistake, because I was able to turn it around on him. I said, 'Mr. Weiss, Joe DiMaggio is the greatest player I've ever seen or ever hope to play with. But he makes $100,000. I make ten. You can't tell me he's ten times the ballplayer I am.' Weiss shut up and gave me a $6,000 raise. . . ."

**Jim Bouton:** "The amazing thing is that most players back then had no idea what they were worth. One time, the Players Association took a poll to find out what the guys thought the minimum players' salary ought to be, so we could present a united front to the owners. I believe the minimum at the time was $6,000 or $7,000 a year. As the player rep polled each player, guys were saying it should go up to eight thousand, nine thousand, ten thousand, a few went as high as twelve thousand. All in that range. When it got to me I said, 'Twenty-five thousand.' They said, 'Oh c'mon for crissakes, knock it off, we have to send this in!'

"I explained that we were all near the top of our profession, even the bench players and mop-up men, and that it was harder to become a major-league ballplayer than the president of a major corporation. I told them we all had Ph.d.'s in pitching and hitting. We were in a monopoly business. The owners were raking in a lot of money and we were not only the labor force, we were the product itself. When you think of it that way, this was not too much to ask for. That's when our pitching coach, Jim Turner, said, 'That's Communist thinking.' In fact, the opposite was true. It was the owners who were behaving like Communists, restricting who we could work for and what we could make. . . ."

**Clete Boyer (major-league third baseman, 1955–71; third baseman, New York Yankees, 1959–66):** ". . . the owners had it to spread around, that's for sure. They just didn't want to. In 1962, our payroll hit the $1 million mark. The club made $12 million that year. Last season, the Yankee payroll was $100 million. Did the Yankees make over $1 billion dollars? Shit no. So do the math, compare our salaries to the team's profits, and you can see they could have paid all of us four or five times what we were getting and still be sitting pretty. . . ."

**Jim Bouton:** "As it turned out, what I said about the minimum salary was way too low, because I had no idea how much money the owners were actually making. Had I known, I would have said $100,000 and someone would have fitted me for a straitjacket. For a long time, I was just like every other player. I really believed the owner's claim that if we abolished the reserve clause, the game would go down the tubes. . . ."

**Marvin Miller (president of the Players Association, 1965–84):** "Jim brought up that very point to me after I finished speaking to the club one afternoon. When I asked him why he felt that way, he said, 'Because if you get rid of the reserve clause, one team will sign all the best players and win all the pennants.' And I said, 'Like the Yankees?' That's when I saw the lightbulb go on. Jim realized that this dominance had been happening anyway, even with the reserve clause, and that baseball and the Yankees were doing just fine."

**Ron Blomberg (first baseman/designated hitter, New York Yankees, 1971–76):** "I think the Yankee front office got looser, more generous, after the team started losing [in 1965]. New York drafted me as the number one pick right out of high school in 1967 when I was seventeen. They treated me like I was golden, gave me a big bonus [$60,000] to pass up college, and brought me to New York to see *Fiddler on the Roof* on Broadway. My parents and I went backstage and met the star, Zero Mostel. They probably figured we'd like that since we were Jewish. And later on I was interviewed on television at Yankee Stadium by Phil Rizzuto *and* Walter Cronkite. My head was spinning, I could tell you.

"Everybody on the team really went out of their way to make me feel comfortable, a teenager coming to the big city from Georgia. No one pressured me. They took us to the Stage Door deli, where they had the best pastrami sandwiches in the world. We went to the garment district and the jewelry districts in Manhattan, and here was a Blumenthal, there was a Goldman. You get in a cab and the driver's name was Silverstein. I figured, how could I go wrong here.

"When I came up to the big leagues in 1971, Lee MacPhail was still there as general manager and he was fairly easy to deal with by then. You didn't read about too many holdouts. Bobby Murcer, Mel Stottlemyre, Roy White, and Thurman Munson were our stars and they usually signed quickly. I became popular with the fans, and the Yankees took care of me. Our front office was so desperate for good players by then, they were actually happy when they had to pay you a high salary. I remember, when they brought Bobby Murcer up to the $100,000 level, about as high as you could go back then [1972], they wanted everyone to know it. And once Mr. Steinbrenner bought the Yankees, their wallets opened even wider. Best thing that could have happened to the team. He wanted a winner and was willing to pay for it. And he hasn't changed, has he?"

## STACKED

*I*n 1919, as general manager and president of the St. Louis Cardinals, Branch Rickey had a brainstorm. Unable to outbid richer clubs for players, he set out to grow his own, thus becoming the creator of baseball's first farm system. Rickey strung together a network of minor-league teams that allowed St. Louis to stockpile several tiers of ballplaying talent throughout its organization. By 1925 he had over 800 players under contract on fifty clubs. When the farm system bore fruit and the Cardinals became a major-league power [they would win five pennants from 1926–34], the other major-league teams began to emulate Rickey's inventiveness. The Dodgers, Cubs, Indians, Giants, and Tigers assembled impressive farm systems in a relatively short time.

*But, given their vast financial resources and the allure of their winning reputation, the Yankees were able to play the farm-system game better than any of their rivals. They didn't just have a few good players scattered throughout their minor-league organization; they had entire teams ready to move up whenever an injury or trade depleted their major-league roster. And they always had some bright young prospect to swap for that established veteran they needed to survive a close pennant race. It was an embarrassment of riches no other team could equal, one that played a major role in maintaining the Yankee dynasty:*

**Bob Cerv:** "In 1951 at Kansas City, the outfield for part of the season was Jackie Jensen, Mickey Mantle, and me. Seven years later, we're all three playing the outfield in the All-Star Game, only for different teams. Mickey led the [American] league in homers that year, Jensen and I finished right behind him. That was a season of special satisfaction to me, because I proved what I could do if someone would just play me every day. Those Yankee clubs were so strong, and they had so many prospects coming up with you in the minors, it was hard for anyone to break in. In 1952 I hit three home runs in the first ten exhibition games. I still couldn't get a spot in the lineup. I don't think I had a hundred at-bats with the big-league club all that season. And the next year I was back in the minors.

"During that 1953 season I was in a lineup with Kansas City, the Yankees' Triple-A farm club, that featured Ellie Howard, Vic Power, Moose Skowron, Bill Virdon, and me. All those guys became all-stars. Power was a terrific player, an excellent line-drive hitter and as good a fielding first baseman as you'll ever see. He couldn't even get a cup of coffee with the big club.

"When you were a part of a minor-league system that strong, you couldn't let up for a second. You never stopped playing your behind off. We had to run out every ball, hustle on every play, make sure we never missed any signs. Because if you got even a little bit complacent, someone would push you aside. Young fans today don't know what it was like back then. We didn't have free agency. You couldn't play out your contract to move on to another club where you could get more playing time. When you were stuck behind a group of stars in an organization, you stayed stuck unless you were traded or sold to a club where the manager put you in the lineup more often.

"If you were good enough to make it to the big-league club in New York, you still didn't relax becaue you knew there were four or five guys in the minors itching to get your spot and they were all good! Just imagine being a catcher in that organization. During the '40s and '50s, you had Yogi behind the plate in New York, a Hall of Famer. Now let's go over some of the catchers the Yankees had in the minors during that time . . ."

*Just glancing through David Neft and Richard Cohen's* The Sports Encylopedia: Baseball *produced an impressive list of catchers that included Sherman Lollar, Elston Howard, Gus Triandos, Clint Courtney, Hank Foiles, Hal Smith, Aaron Robinson, and Lou Berberet:*

**Bob Cerv:** ". . . Everyone you just named got to the majors eventually as starting catchers. Some of them even became All-Stars in the majors and they were all tough outs. Most teams back then had trouble coming up with one good-hitting everyday catcher, and we just found eight of them coming up within a few years of each other. Eight plus Yogi. And we always had good backups to him besides. Why, we could have stocked the whole league with catchers. That's why the Yankees kept winning. They had so much talent at every level that if someone got hurt, you could bring up another top player to replace him without losing a thing. And the guys who were playing for the big-league club every day stayed on their toes because they had all that minor-league talent pushing them."

**Bill Werber:** "Oh, the Yankees were always loaded with talent from the time they got Babe Ruth and started winning all those pennants. In those days, you didn't have a draft of players; a fellow could choose which club he wanted to play for. New York was winning year after year, so that was the organization to be with. I came up to the Yankees as a shortstop in 1930 when I was twenty-two. In the four games I played, I hit .286 and did everything right in the field. You think that meant anything? They didn't bring me up again for two more seasons.

"When Joe McCarthy took me to spring training in 1933, I was competing with Lyn Lary and Frank Crosetti at short. Lary was the more established player, he'd driven in over a hundred runs in a season and was a fine fielder. Crosetti had been the starter on their pennant winner in 1932, then there was me trying to fit in. Lary was the oldest among us, and he was only twenty-seven. You had teams back then that didn't even have one shortstop, and here the Yankees had three.

"And it didn't stop in the infield. Sammy Byrd was an excellent outfielder who could hit .280 with good speed and some power. Have you ever heard of him? Not too many people have. He could have started on a lot of teams, but on New York, he was Babe Ruth's defensive replacement. Babe was getting on by then, so they called Sammy 'Babe Ruth's Legs.' Dixie Walker was on that club. There's a fine player, a future batting champion, and he hit with power [Walker hit 15 home runs in 328 at-bats in 1933 while slugging .500] for the Yankees. Even he couldn't get regular work with them. He was the fourth outfielder.

"I'm sure it was right around this time that the Yankees got that reputation for being arrogant. Well, if you were in an organization with that many talented ballplayers, you had better be cocky or you couldn't survive. Hey, in spring training, 1933, I was certain that I had that starting shortstop job sewed up. I was starting every game, hitting about .350. The Red Sox were looking for a shortstop and they had Jack McAuliffe, their scout, following us. But I didn't think I was going anywhere but New York.

"Joe McCarthy began playing Crosetti so McAuliffe could see what Frankie could do. That's who the Yankees were going to trade to Boston. But Crosetti looked good in those games he started—so good, in fact, New York traded me to Boston instead. Frankie was a good player and we all knew what Lyn could do. But, even as a rookie, in my heart I wasn't impressed by either of them. I figured I was just as good as they were if not better, the only thing they had over me was experience. Maybe that was my mistake, overconfidence. But you had to think that way with all those good players competing against you or you were beaten before you started."

**Jerry Lumpe:** "I think it was even tougher, during the 1950s, being an infielder in the Yankee organization, there was so many of us. I say that looking back. When I was actually playing in the minors, I didn't think of it much. At such a young age, you don't focus on all the talent the Yankees had or how competitive it would be to land a job. You were just grateful to be there.

"I came out of a small town in Missouri with no idea how far I could go. When you finally realized how many players were competing for your spot, you had to think, 'All right, I'll do my best because if I don't make it here, some other club will trade for me.' The Yankees had that history of trading prospects for proven talent during their pennant drives. And everyone wanted New York's minor-leaguers because the organization had a great reputation for developing talent. When the front office traded a prospect, it was usually to a second-division club, which meant your chances of starting improved dramatically. All this meant was that if you could play, you were going to get a major-league job somewhere eventually.

"So there was no reason to get discouraged, and I didn't see too many prospects with their heads hanging down. We were proud to be part of the best organization in baseball. It was like the Yankees had three major-league teams between the big-league club, their bench, and their Triple-A team. But talking to you now, I could see what a challenge it was. When I got there in 1956, the infielders in spring training were Gil McDougald, Billy Martin, Andy Carey, Billy Hunter, and Jerry Coleman. Rizzuto was even still on the roster.

"Woodie Held was there, up from the minors, and he's a great example of how deep we were. What a player he was. Good range at shortstop, one of the best arms in the game, excellent batting eye, and he could hit twenty homers. I know shortstops hitting for power are common today, but in the fifties, Ernie Banks was about the only home-run-hitting shortstop in baseball. Even with all his talent, Woodie couldn't even get a shot with New York, but after they traded him he was a starter for more than ten years."

**Bobby Richardson (second baseman, New York Yankees, 1955–66):** "You never saw so many good young ballplayers. You know, we had Marv Throneberry at Denver. He later got a reputation, from his time with the Mets and the beer commercials, as something of a clown. Remember they called him Marvelous Marv? But there was nothing funny about he way he played baseball when he was in our minor-league system. He hit over forty home runs one season, was an excellent fielder, just another terrific Yankee ballplayer stuck behind a star, in this case Moose Skowron.

"When I was there, our Triple-A regulars could have started for half the major-league clubs. But when we came to the Yankees, many of us were subs. Look at Elston Howard. He sat on the bench behind Yogi Berra for four or five years, then he later went on to become an All-Star and an MVP. He would have made it sooner had he been with another team. In fact, you put him in a ballpark that favored a right-handed hitter—I always thought I'd like to see what he could do in a stadium like Wrigley Field—as a starter from the time he's about twenty-three, and I am convinced he would have been a Hall of Famer. You have to remember, Ellie didn't become our regular catcher until he was over thirty years old.

"So you really had to pay your dues to make it with the Yankees. I would have to tell Jerry [Lumpe] that some of us did find this discouraging. I made the all-star team in the minors every year. In Binghamton, I played every inning of every game and finished second in hitting. At Denver, I was second or third in hitting. But I couldn't get much playing time with the club in New York. My first two times up with the Yankees [1955 and 1956], they sent me back down without Stengel giving me what I thought was a fair shot at showing what I could do. Casey was a tough man to break in under. He didn't mind embarrassing players, especially younger ones."

**Jerry Lumpe:** "He sure wasn't patient with us [young players], I can tell you that. Stengel was constantly on my case, and Siebern's and Kubek's as well. Casey liked his veterans. I'd hit up in the lineup, but if I went bad for a few games, he'd drop me to eighth. Then he'd drop you out of sight. But he'd let veterans work their way out of slumps. I can understand that, because they've proven themselves with past performances. But it's not very good when you're the young player getting passed over. It can damage your confidence.

"In 1956 I started the early part of the season at short for the Yankees, made some errors, and got benched after only ten games. Casey replaced me with Gil McDougald. Okay, I really can't blame him for that, Gil was a great player. But a week or two later, Casey sent me back down to our minor-league club in Richmond and I was pretty much out of his plans for good. Stengel was one of the great users of the press, used it well. He'd criticize a young player in the press to motivate him [Stengel once said of Lumpe to a reporter: "He's the greatest player in the world until you stick him in the lineup."], but that doesn't work with everyone. . . ."

**Bobby Richardson:** "You're a rookie and you read in the newspapers where the manager thinks you couldn't go to your left, or weren't aggressive enough at the plate. This was Stengel's way of having a conversation with you, to make you, he thought, a better player by goading you to prove him wrong. I didn't like that approach, either. He was always complaining that I didn't walk enough batting leadoff, but the Yankees had a lot of power up and down the lineup with Mickey and Yogi, Moose, and Ellie. Then we got Roger. Pitchers don't want to walk you with hitters like that behind you, so I saw a lot of strikes and I had to swing at them.

"He pinch-hit for me once in the first inning. As I came in to the dugout I said, 'Well, why did you start me?' In the clubhouse, he said, 'You go get your little mitt and head out into the bullpen. You're warming up Ryne Duren.' Ryne, as you know, couldn't see very well. He could be very wild and he threw about 100 miles per hour. That was Casey's way of letting me know he didn't like players talking back to him.

"I was somewhat frustrated, not getting a chance to play more. So after Jerry Lumpe and Norm Siebern were traded, I went to George Weiss and said, 'Hey, I want to play more, would you trade me to some ball club that has an opening.' But Mr. Weiss asked me to be patient and assured me I'd get my chance to play. As it turned out, I'm glad he didn't trade me."

**Lew Burdette (major-league pitcher, 1950–67; pitcher, 1950 New York Yankees):** "You think pitchers in the Yankee minor leagues had it any easier? Heck, no. When I beat the Yankees three times in the World Series, everyone wrote I was getting my revenge because they never gave me a shot at the big leagues and ended up trading me for Johnny Sain. That just wasn't so. I wasn't mad at the Yankees for trading me. I was happy because they didn't have a spot for me. But the Braves were a rebuilding ball club—we finished seventh my first year there—so I knew I'd get an opportunity. Mr. Weiss did me a favor.

"I never blamed Casey for not putting me in his rotation when I was there. You know, the best shot I had at making the Yankees came when I threw batting practice to Mickey Mantle and Bill Skowron while they were trying out for the club. The whole time, Mickey and Bill couldn't hit a ball in the air off me. It got so Ralph Houk said, 'I'm not so sure we're looking at the right people here.' And Frank Crosetti yelled, 'Shut up, Ralph, we're looking for hitters, not pitchers.' And it was true. They had Ford, Raschi, Reynolds, Lopat, and Byrne. And Tom Morgan and Bob Grim coming up through the minors. No club could match that. What the hell did they need me for?"

## BLACKBALLED

*I*n 1949, two years after Jackie Robinson broke baseball's color line, the New York Yankees were among the first major-league teams to enlist African American ballplayers. Many columnists charged that the signings were just window dressing. Those critics had a *case. Not one of the initial Yankee signees—Birmingham Black Baron shortstop Artie Wilson, Homestead Gray outfielder Luis Marquez, and Philadelphia Star shortstop Frank Austin—was considered a top-rate prospect, and each failed to last more than a season in the organization's minor-league system. Austin never played an inning of major-league ball; Wilson, nearly thirty when the Yankees signed him, would get 22 at-bats with the 1951 New York Giants while hitting .182; Luis Marquez would total 143 at-bats with three teams over two years and also hit .182. Given the scant evidence offered by their statistics, it is a matter of conjecture whether any of the three could have played their way onto the most powerful roster in all of baseball. But it is unlikely the Yankee brass ever viewed them as potential major-leaguers.*

*Bob Thurman, on the other hand, was one black player who seemed destined for promotion to the Bronx. A left-handed hitter, the 6´1˝, 210-pound outfielder joined the Newark Bears, the Yankees' top farm club, in 1949 and immediately became a local hero. Thurman not only hit home runs frequently, he hit them far. Those who were there claim the average Thurman homer would travel 400 feet; at least one exceeded 500 feet. He could also hit for average (.317 despite a hand injury in his first minor-league season) and was a fast, heady base runner; the* Newark Courier *declared he had "tootsies lined with mercury." Thurman fielded his position expertly. He displayed exceptional range as well as a powerful, accurate throwing arm. Scouts today would call him a five-tool player.*

*Even though Thurman demolished Triple-A pitching and proved to be a potent gate attraction, he was sold to the Chicago Cubs after only one season in the Yankee organization. No one has ever produced any hard evidence to prove that New York dumped Thurman simply to avoid bringing him to the majors, but it certainly appeared to be the case.*

*In 1953 Ruben Gomez, a black Puerto Rican and top-flight pitching prospect, was so frustrated by his inability to rise through the Yankee system, he bought out his contract—an unheard-of move for the times—to sign with the New York Giants. Gomez won 13 games in his first major-league season. The following year, the right-hander notched 17 victories as one of the leading contributors to the Giants' 1954 World Series Championship.*

*The Yankees could have utilized Gomez's talents in '54. Despite featuring baseball's most productive offense, New York finished second to the pitching-heavy Cleveland Indians. Unfortunately, Gomez's success with a crosstown rival didn't embarrass Yankee officials into adopting a hiring policy that embraced greater racial diversity. When pressed on the matter of New York's failure to integrate its major-league squad, general manager George Weiss haughtily replied, "The first Negro to appear in a Yankee uniform will have to be worth waiting for."*

*Godot would have arrived sooner. While other teams, particularly National League clubs, eagerly augmented their rosters with African American talent, the Bombers remained as segregated as a Southern country club. Weiss repeatedly had to tell anyone who would listen that the Yankees would sign a black athlete as soon as they found one who met the organization's high standards not only on, but off, the field.*

*What did that mean, that this mythic African American would have to comport himself in the same dignified manner as Babe Ruth, who used to wow visitors to his home by showing them the trophy he won in a farting contest? Or perhaps the role model for gentility Weiss had in mind was his second baseman Billy Martin, the carousing, punch-happy Oakland roughneck whom writer Ray Robinson once characterized as "a vicious jockey . . . who is beset with all manner of actual and psychosomatic ailments including hypertension, anxiety, insomnia, and acute melancholia." Whatever lofty benchmarks for decorum players such as these had set in pinstripes, the Yankee general manager apparently couldn't find any African Americans who could reach them. As Weiss would assert, "We have been looking for a Negro player [note the singular] for some years. The Yankees will have a Negro player as soon as we are able to find a Negro player among the availables."*

*Hmm. Ernie Banks, Willie Mays, Minnie Minoso, Hank Aaron, Don Newcombe, Bill Bruton, Junior Gilliam, Hank Thompson, Sam Jethroe—they were available among the rich crop of minority players following Jackie Robinson into the majors. Just where were the Yankees seeking that "Negro player," at Klan meetings? Weiss and his scouts had few peers as appraisers of baseball talent. Yet, time and again, this unquestionably brilliant baseball executive allowed his acumen to conveniently desert him whenever that talent didn't happen to be white.*

*Weiss's reluctance to aggressively court players of color invited many members of his organization to exercise their own peculiar biases. In his book* Baseball's Great Experiment: Jackie Robinson and His Legacy, *author Jules Tygiel revealed how one high-ranking club executive, his mouth loosened by a Niagra of martinis, confided to a sportswriter that the Yankees would never bring up a black ballplayer because "we don't want that kind of crowd. It would offend our boxholders from Westchester to have to sit with niggers." In 1953 Yankee traveling secretary Bill McCorry declared, "No nigger will ever have a berth on any train I'm running." Weiss and Yankee owner Dan Topping refused to reprimand him for the noxious remark. These and other incidents gave the clear impression that the Yankees were, in the words of* Pittsburgh Courier *sportswriter Wendall Smith [as quoted by Mr. Tygiel], "a ruthless, vindictive lot" on the subject of race relations.*

*Somehow, two exceptionally gifted African American ballplayers were able to wend their way through the Yankee farm system. Elston Howard, a powerful, dextrous athlete, was so talented he could have starred in the majors as a catcher, first baseman, or outfielder. He was designated early on by the New York front office as "a suitable Negro," meaning Howard was so well-mannered and soft-spoken, management felt his presence in a Yankee uniform would give scant offense to those fans who equated character with color. Howard moved through the Yankee system relatively quickly to become one of the most productive catchers in the franchise's history, a frequent All-Star, and winner of the 1963 American League MVP Award.*

*But another equally skilled African American player who roomed with Howard in the minors never got to wear pinstripes in a major-league game. Militant wasn't a word you heard much in the 1950s, but if you had, it would have been applied to this player. He was a man too proud not to make waves. Because of his outspokenness, Weiss's front office never considered this peerless-fielding first baseman Yankee material, so the team never did anything to encourage his advancement:*

**Vic Power (major-league first baseman, 1954–65):** "The Yankees didn't treat me badly, but they didn't protect me. After I signed with them, they sent me to Syracuse. I'm twenty-three, I'd been playing in Puerto

Rico and Canada, and knew nothing about segregation. And since everyone else on our team was white, no one on our team could tell me about it or understand what I was up against.

"Syracuse itself was okay for me, no trouble. But in spring training we went to Tampa. Colored people had no hotels there, it was white only. The Yankees get me a room in the best house in the colored neighborhood, but the best house was a funeral parlor. So I slept next to a room filled with dead bodies! No one asked me how I felt about the arrangement. They just stuck me with all these corpses.

"I wanted to be a big-league player so bad, I probably wouldn't have complained about it if they had asked. I just tried to adjust. But it was tough. One night, I was window shopping in Tampa. A policeman came over and said there was a city ordinance: No black people could walk downtown after six P.M. I'd never heard of anything like that. But I knew you didn't start trouble with the police, so I went back to the funeral parlor.

"Staying in shape was hard for many black players because we couldn't get good food to eat. The black restaurants served mostly fried foods and barbecue. When I went into a white restaurant, a waitress came up to me and said, 'Sorry, we don't serve Negroes.' I answered, 'That's okay, I don't eat them, I'd like to order some chicken, rice, and beans.'

"She didn't laugh and she wouldn't serve me. So I went to the supermarket to buy cold cuts to make sandwiches, and bananas and orange juice. I brought them back to my little room and ate next to those dead bodies. In Puerto Rico we are very superstitious. We are afraid of dead people coming back. After sleeping in that funeral parlor, I was able to tell my friends that dead people don't walk around at night. But I slept with a bat in my bed just in case.

"Traveling was tough. Yellow cabs wouldn't pick up colored people. I had to walk over a mile every day to and from the park. My teammates didn't segregate me, but they didn't mingle, either. The ones with cars would drive off to the white sections. No one ever offered me a lift.

"Ellie Howard was my roommate, I loved him, a nice guy. More the kind of colored player the Yankees wanted. A little bit a yes-man. But I don't criticize him for that. He had a family to support and did what he had to so the Yankees would promote him. Back then, no one wanted the colored players to make even the tiniest waves. Like, in our clubhouse there was a bathroom that said 'Whites Only.' When I asked where black people went, one of the ballplayers said I talk too much. He thought I was making trouble. But, no, I just wanted to go to the bathroom! The club had a Port-O-Potty, like you see in construction sites, for black players behind the center-field scoreboard. There was a water fountain there for us, too, but the water was always hot.

"The Yankees kept bringing up excuses for why they wouldn't promote me. In 1952, with their farm club in Kansas City, I hit .331 with 109 runs batted in. The next year, in the middle of the season, I was leading the minors in batting, hits, doubles, and RBI, but the Yankees still wouldn't call me up, not even in September [when the major-league rosters expand].

"That's when I started to hear the rumors. People in the front office were saying I was just a minor-league hitter, that I couldn't hit major-league pitching. So I said, 'How can you say that when I haven't had a chance to prove myself?' I'd never hit against major-leaguers. Then there was that quote [from the Yankees owner Dan Topping] saying I was a good hitter but couldn't field.

"I knew what that was about. When Tom Greenwade, the scout who signed me, saw me play, it was in an all-star game in Canada. That day I made an error on a bad hop. Greenwade sent in a report that said I was a poor fielder because of that, and the Yankees kept bringing it up. But when I came to the big leagues, everyone could see that wasn't true. I won seven Gold Gloves.

"Then the Yankees said I was a showboat because of the way I fielded throws with one hand. But I was playing first [base] right-handed. It was easier for left-handers to make the double play, first to second to first. I started catching the ball one-handed so I could get the throw off quicker. I wasn't showboating, but that was what they called it. When writers would ask me about it, I'd say, 'If Mr. Doubleday wanted us to catch with two hands, he would have had us wear two gloves.'

"Some writers told the Yankees they should bring me up as a business move, that I'd attract a lot of Puerto Rican fans to the park. George Weiss told them that Puerto Ricans only buy cheap seats and they didn't spend anything on concessions. So he said I wouldn't bring in any money. I didn't think he knew what he was talking about.

"The big story the Yankee front office spread around about me was that I dated white women. When I heard that I said, 'I didn't know there was anything wrong with white women. If I knew, I wouldn't have gone out with them.' They didn't think that was funny. They were upset with me, but that was hypocritical because one of the Yankee players liked to go out with black women. In fact, this player once offered to 'trade' me, to introduce me to the white girl he was dating if I introduced him to two black girls I knew. I've never publicly said who the player was until now—it was Billy Martin. The Yankees knew it, but they never made anything out of it. They kept it hushed up while they talked about me, which was a double standard.

"I also got a reputation as a troublemaker. Yeah, there were fights. But you have to understand why. One time, in 1953, a pitcher in the other team's bullpen was calling me monkey, gorilla, King Kong, things like that while I played left field. Who wants to hear that? He forgot that to get off our field in Kansas City, you had to go through our dugout. After the ball game, I waited in the runway, baby, and I gave it to him. Kicked his ass. I had to stand up for myself.

"In Tampa, when I complained about segregation, management said the law was the law. I said, 'No, the law is for human beings. If a law says you can't drink when you're thirsty, can't order something to eat when you are hungry, that is not a law because it treats you like an animal, not a human being.' Eventually, the laws changed. They got rid of segregation. At least, that's what we were told.

"That restaurant that didn't serve me, after the civil rights law was signed, I said to myself, 'Now, baby, I'm going back there to eat, right now.' Well, the waitress brought me my meal, a steak, but she didn't bring any utensils to eat it with. So I said, 'I want a fork.' But with my accent it sounded like I was saying, 'I want to fuck.' And I kept saying it. The owner came out, we had some words, and I still didn't get served.

"You found prejudice everywhere, no matter what the law was. In 1953, I'm still with Kansas City in spring training. Our bus stops at some small town between Fort Myers and West Palm Beach. We got out at a gas station for a piss call. But it was a 'whites only' bathroom. The owner took one look at me and said, 'I don't want any black bastards using my bathroom.' What could I do? I had to go bad, but we were in the middle of downtown so I couldn't even duck behind a tree.

"There was a Coca-Cola machine and I figured I'd buy the soda, empty the bottle, and pee in it on the bus. That owner was watching me so I couldn't pour out the soda. Instead, I'm drinking it slow. When we get back on the bus to pull out, the gas station owner comes on and says I have to return the bottle for the deposit. Yeah, like people never drove out of there sipping Cokes. So I said I'd pay him extra for it. He refused. I still wouldn't give it to him.

"He knew what I was planning. We get on the road and pretty soon, the gas station owner is behind us in a car with the sheriff. They pull us over. Both of them come on and the station owner yells to the sheriff, 'It's the black bastard in the back!' He arrests me for disturbing the peace!

"My teammates followed them back and asked if they could pay my bail. The sheriff asks for $500. Everybody pitched in. . . ."

*So here are this gas station owner and sheriff behaving as if they were the two pig-squealing, rotten-toothed, lopside-headed cretins who tried to make Ned Beatty their girlfriend in the film* Deliverance, *arresting Vic Power for the heinous crime of having to relieve himself. How did Yankee owner Dan Topping respond to this injustice? Did he send a troop of pricey attorneys to defend one of his organization's top prospects? Did he publicly commend Power's teammates for standing tall behind one of their own?*

*Did Topping at least offer private words of comfort to his emotionally wounded employee? If you've been closely following the first baseman's account to this point, you already know the answers:*

**Vic Power:** "They did nothing! A few days later, I tried to hire my own lawyer to argue my case. He said, 'Vic, forget about it. No black man has ever won a court case in that town. If you go back there, you're going to have more trouble.' I become a bail jumper, which meant we lost the $500. Now, don't you think the Yankees could have backed me up by reimbursing the players who bailed me out? No way. I had to pay them back out of my salary, and I wasn't making much to begin with. So that bottle of Coke cost me $500, which is why I drink Pepsi today.

"On the field, everything was tougher for black players. Some umpires would never give a black ballplayer a close pitch. That's why I didn't walk much: It wasn't because I didn't know the strike zone or anything. If it was near the strike zone with two strikes, baby, I had to swing. Those umpires made me a good 'bad ball' hitter. Hey, I played twelve years and got over 1,700 hits [for a career batting average of .284] and made the All-Star team four times, baby, so maybe they did me a favor."

*In December 1953, the Yankees traded Power to the Philadelphia Athletics for pitcher Harry Byrd and veteran first baseman Eddie Robinson. New York would be one of the last major-league teams to integrate. Elston Howard would finally break the Yankee color line in 1956, nine years after Jackie Robinson's major-league debut. It would be five more seasons until another African American player, pitcher Al Downing, advanced through the Yankees' system and onto their big-league roster:*

**Vic Power:** "It shouldn't have taken them so long. After I left the Yankees organization, Casey brought Ryne Duren in to face me during a game. Duren threw hard, close to 100 miles an hour, and he was wild. He wore thick glasses and pretended he could hardly see the plate just to scare hitters. White pitchers always threw more at us.

Duren threw a pitch right at my head; I nearly fell down getting out of the way. Casey and the Yankees started laughing.

"I walked over to that dugout with my bat and said, 'Listen, old man. If that guys hits me I'm not going to fight him. I'm going to kick your ass.' That stopped the throwing that day. Pitchers threw at me a lot; I only got hit fifteen times, but that was because I had good reflexes. I had to use a long bat so I could stay off of home plate. They got me good, twice in the head and the face.

"But what hurt me most was not playing at least one season with the Yankees. Ballplayers want to win, to go to that World Series, more than anything. I told people with the Yankees I'd play anywhere they thought I could help the club—left field, second base, third, wherever they said. I had good hands, you could put me almost anywhere; I played every position but pitcher and catcher in the majors.

"Casey liked guys who could play different positions, and the Yankees were always moving people in and out of left field. You would think they could have used me on their bench. I even challenged them by offering to go behind the plate as Yogi's backup. But they never gave me an opportunity to get into the Series with them. That still makes me sad.

"I told all this to my mother. She couldn't believe that if you were hungry in the United States with money, you couldn't get fed, that if you were the best person for a job, you couldn't get promoted. Someone once asked me, if I could reincarnate, what would I come back as. I told him I would want to come back as a ballplayer. That is what I love. But as a white ballplayer. Not because I was ashamed of my color, but because white ballplayers had it so much easier. Especially on the Yankees."

## MORE THAN PERFECT

*M*ention the 1956 World Series and most baseball fans recall little else but Don Larsen's perfect game, one of those events so momentous it cold-cocks memory, jamming the brain cells until they are incapable of storing any competing data or images. I *spoke to thirty-two fans who, either at home or in Yankee Stadium, followed Larsen's masterpiece from first pitch to last. Most of them remembered the game as the closing act of an exciting Fall Classic. It wasn't. Larsen achieved perfection in the fifth game against Brooklyn, a victory that gave the Yankees a 3–2 lead in the Series. As it turned out, New York would engage the Dodgers in two more games, both dandies, before bringing yet another baseball championship back to the Bronx. One Brooklyn pitcher appreciates why Games Six and Seven are so difficult to recollect:*

**Clem Labine (major-league pitcher, 1950–62; pitcher, 1956 Brooklyn Dodgers):** "I probably had the worst timing of any pitcher in baseball history. In 1951 I pitched a shutout to tie the playoffs against the New York Giants. The next day Bobby Thomson hits the Shot Heard Round the World. In 1956 I pitch a ten-inning 1–0 shutout to beat Bob Turley and the Yankees in Game Six. One day after Larsen throws his perfect game. Don's game is all most people remember from that Series. I can understand that, it was such an amazing accomplishment. If I hadn't pitched Game Six, I might not remember it, either."

*As baseball is played today, Labine probably would not have started that afternoon. During the regular season, the right-handed closer had led the National League with 19 saves. Could you imagine Joe Torre starting Mariano Rivera in a World Series game?:*

**Clem Labine:** "... back then, it wasn't unusual. [Dodger manager] Walter Alston only used me for two innings in Game Three, so I was well rested. I had a feeling he might go with me in Game Six. I'd been a successful starter for him in the minor leagues. He certainly didn't give me much time to think about it. [Alston] told me a few minutes after Dale Mitchell struck out [to complete Larsen's perfect game] that I was going the next day.

"If you started a closer in a game today, I imagine the manager would probably expect him to go two or three innings before bringing in the rest of the relievers. Walter wasn't looking for me to keep the game close for our bullpen. The starter, whoever he was, was expected to go all the way; we felt as if we'd let the team down when we didn't go nine. So I was pitching with the idea of finishing what I started.

"The way Turley pitched against me, I could still be out there. I didn't think he'd ever give up a run . . ."

**Bob Turley:** ". . . and I'm thinking the same thing about him. Our first baseman, Joe Collins, kept telling me, 'Just hold them for six innings until the shadows come in, then we'll get you some runs.' Well, we're in the sixth, the seventh, the eighth, and I keep asking Joe, 'Where are those runs you promised, I can sure use them.' . . ."

**Clem Labine:** "Bob easily could have won that game. As the opposing pitcher, you can't stop to admire what the other pitcher is doing. Of course, you're aware he's doing well, but you don't put pressure on yourself by concentrating on it. If you start thinking, 'Boy, this guy's not giving up anything. I better be perfect on every batter,' you're going to get into trouble.

"I just went out and pitched my game. The curve was a good pitch for me. But pitching in Ebbets Field that day, a tiny ballpark, against a lineup as powerful as the Yankees, you want to keep the ball moving down as much as possible to stay away from fly balls. I mixed in more sinkers to keep the ball on the ground.

"Another thing people don't remember about that day is that I got one hit and it nearly won the game. I led off the eighth inning with a drive to left. I thought it might go out, but it hit the top of the railing and skipped into the stands for a ground-rule double. Missed a home run by inches. That double might have hurt us, because I'm sure Turley was so surprised, it woke him up. He got out of the inning without allowing a run. It was a fastball in my power zone. I'm not sure where my power zone was—a lot of pitchers knew where it wasn't—but Turley happened to get the ball in there.

"I remember after I got to second, I was tired. Not so much from the double, but from all the pitching I'd done. So I sat on second base while Junior [Gilliam] walked up to the plate and settled into the batter's box. The umpire came over and asked what I was doing. I said, 'I'm tired and I'm sitting down.' He said, 'You can't do that. It's bush.' So I got up. Those are the kind of little escapades that go on during a World Series that often go unnoticed. Two innings later, Jackie [Robinson] hit that ball out to Slaughter to win that game in the tenth . . ."

*With two men out and runners on first and second, Robinson hit a hard liner to left field. Slaughter took one step in as the ball left Robinson's bat, then had to race back and leap as the drive soared over his head. The base hit scored Junior Gilliam with the winning run:*

**Enos Slaughter (major-league outfielder, 1938–59; left fielder, 1956 New York Yankees):** ". . . Because of that one base hit, I became the first .350 hitter to get benched during a World Series. I go seven for twenty in the first six games, but I paid the price for that ball Robinson hit out to me. That was wrong. Go look at any film from that game. I played what I would consider to be not a deep left field, but one where I have a chance at throwing out Gilliam if Robinson singles. But Robinson hits this line shot off the left-field wall that I couldn't catch even after I jumped for it.

"As soon as that winning run scored, it started. I was coming in from the outfield, a New York writer meets me at third base—actually heads me off before I get to the dugout—just to say I misjudged the ball. I told him he was full of baloney. There wasn't a human being alive who could have caught that ball, it hit three feet up the wall in left center. But now everyone thinks I blew the catch. . . ."

**Bob Turley:** ". . . it's true that ball wasn't catchable, but the reason it wasn't catchable is that Enos took a step in when it was first hit. If he had just stood still, the ball comes right to him, and the game continues. . . ."

**Hank Bauer (right fielder, 1956 New York Yankees):** ". . . yes, Enos read it wrong, but I don't blame him completely. I was a good outfielder in right field and even center. But put me in left field, and I was lost. The sun was in your eyes, the wind played tricks on you out there, and the ball sliced off the bat differently. . . ."

**Clem Labine:** ". . . and that was a difficult ball to judge because of how Jackie hit. Jackie Robinson and Carl Furillo both hit pitches the same way—a little down on the ball rather than hitting it level. So many of the line drives they hit had backspin. When that ball goes towards the outfielder, it looks like it's coming right at you. But then it starts to climb.

"So I understand why Enos took that first step in. I'm sure it looked like a straight line drive to him. A lot of outfielders would have read it that way. Jackie's ball took off on him and there's no way he could recover to catch that."

**Bob Turley:** ". . . yes, but you know that drive Clem hit off of me. Enos should have caught that, too. He was having a lot of trouble judging balls by then. . . ."

*Stengel was usually so supremely confident in his baseball acumen, he rarely indulged self-doubt. But Brooklyn's bare-knuckled response to Larsen's win unsettled him. He dreaded losing two consecutive World Series to the Dodgers. When he contemplated his lineup for the game that would decide it all, he uncharacteristically accepted advice from the one player whose baseball-managing instincts already nearly equaled his own:*

**Moose Skowron (major-league first baseman, 1954–67; first baseman, 1956 New York Yankees):** "After losing Game Six, some of the players were so upset they hid in the trainer's room, where the press couldn't go. Billy Martin was more upset than anyone. He was sitting at his locker, crying. Casey came over and says, 'Is there anything I can do for you?' And Martin finally goes up to him and says, 'We're going to lose this goddamned thing if you don't get that bobo Slaughter out of left field.' . . ."

**Billy Martin (major-league infielder, 1950–61; second baseman, 1956 New York Yankees):** "I liked the way Enos hustled all the time, but he misplayed three balls that game, including a hit [by Junior Gilliam] that he lost in the sun. People don't remember that because he caught the runner at second going for a double. It just looked to me like he was having trouble seeing the ball out there. We just played two games where both sides only scored three runs and I didn't think we could afford to give any away . . ."

**Moose Skowron:** ". . . so Casey says, 'Yeah, and who would you play?' And Billy answers, 'Why don't you get Ellie [Howard] in left field and take [Joe] Collins off first and put Moose back there.'

"Casey had benched me after I went 0 for 4 against Maglie in the first game. The next four games, he sent me up to pinch-hit once. I honestly can't tell you much about Larsen's perfect game. I was so down in the dumps, I didn't care. But come Game Seven, after Billy tells Casey what to do, we look at the lineup card and Ellie's in left, I'm at first. Billy turns to me and says, 'Moose, this is where we separate the men from the boys.'

"I didn't hold up my end right away. We're leading, 2–0, in the fourth. Ellie homers off Newcombe, so now that move looks great. But I struck out in the first, popped up in the third, popped up again in the fifth. Pretty weak. In the seventh, we get the bases loaded against Roger Craig and I step up to the plate. That's when I heard the whistle. It's Casey. I know what's coming. I told [Dodger catcher Roy] Campanella, 'That old man is going to take me out.' Campy, such a great guy, actually tried to cheer me up, he said, 'No, Moose, he's going to leave you in.' . . ."

**Hank Bauer:** "I'm standing there as Moose walks to the dugout, I could see he's upset. All Casey says is, 'Take two shots to right.' Right there, Moose relaxes, you could see all the tension go out of him as he goes back up to the plate. . . ."

**Moose Skowron:** "Craig's first pitch is low and outside, perfect pitch to hit to the opposite field, which is what Casey wanted, right? Except I swung a little early and hit the ball over the left-field wall for a grand slam. I reach home plate and, no, Campy didn't say a word. He was right about Casey leaving me in, but he wasn't happy about the home run. . . ."

**Hank Bauer:** "When Moose gets back to the dugout, Casey pats him on the butt and says, 'That's the way to pull that ball, big fellah.' As if he didn't tell Moose to punch one to right! I heard that, I just about shit in my pants. It was a good thing for us that Billy got so upset with Slaughter. Martin put Ellie and Moose into the lineup, they both homer, we win 10–0 and take the Series. So even back then, you could see the kind of manager Billy would be. A winner."

**Enos Slaughter:** "Even I have to admit it worked out. Billy must have known something because, when you think of it, these were two unorthodox moves. Both Collins and I batted from the left side; Moose and Ellie hit the other way. Newcombe started for Brooklyn, and he was a right-hander. That should have favored Joe and me. If it was a question of defense, well, maybe I wasn't quite as quick as I used to be; I was forty that year. But Elston was a catcher. He wasn't what you would call fast in the outfield.

"All right, you think I can't do the job in left, I went 0–3 in that game against Labine, fine, take me out. But replacing Joe with Moose, that was some call. Joe was a good first baseman. He had [two] hits in Game Six, and the one time he faced Newcombe that series, he drove me in with a solid base hit to center field. Where does Billy know to take him out?"

**Bob Turley:** "It was probably Ebbets Field that influenced Billy's thinking. That was a hitter's park where normally you score a lot of runs, so Billy wanted Moose's power in the lineup. Joe Collins wasn't the home-run threat Moose was, and Ellie had more pop than Enos. . . ."

**Enos Slaughter:** "I think it was easier for Casey to sit me, even though I was hitting so well, because there were people on the club who didn't care for my style of play. I hustled all the time, ran out every play, ran to and from my position every inning. Some players resented that, called me a showboat. They thought I made them look bad. But that's how I had always played. It's what got me to the major leagues.

"In 1935 the Cardinals were going to release me because I didn't run well. [St. Louis coach and future manager] Billy Southworth told me that spring training, 'If we can't improve your running, you're gone.' So every day, before and after everyone left the field, I'd practice running on my toes in the outfield to improve my speed. And I kept running for nineteen years in the major leagues. Even when I was forty, some reporter pointed out that I could still get down to first in 3.6 seconds. That was my bread and butter. So if anyone resented my hustle, it didn't bother me.

"When I found out Casey had left me out of the lineup for Game Seven, that did bother me, not playing. But—and this is the truth, so help me—as soon as we got out to that lead, I forgot about it. We won, and that was all that mattered. Winning was all I wanted to do every time I put on the uniform."

*After Berra hit a two-run homer in the first inning, Game Seven's outcome was never in doubt. Johnny Kucks, an 18-game winner during the regular season, continued a trend of Yankee pitching dominance that had started when Whitey Ford limited the Dodgers to three runs in New York's third-game victory. Over the final 46 innings of the 1956 World Series, Brooklyn, whose 720 runs scored was the second-highest total in the major leagues during the regular season, scored only six times:*

**John Kucks (major-league pitcher, 1955–60; pitcher, 1956 New York Yankees):** "I had my best sinker ever that day; seventy percent of my pitches were sinkers—Yogi hardly had to put down any signs—and the rest sliders. The Dodgers hit only two balls to the outfield. They got three hits, but they were just singles . . ."

**Tom Sturdivant:** ". . . and the Dodgers were lucky they got those! Heck, those last three games we threw against Brooklyn were the best-pitched games you'll ever see anywhere, anytime. To shut down a lineup that powerful. They got seven hits in three games, with six of them singles and one that should have been caught! Don got the perfect game, but the Dodgers didn't hit the ball any harder off of Turley or John, they just happened to drop in. I know this sounds unbelievable, but, an inch here, an inch there, we could have finished that Series with a perfect game and two no-hitters. I'm not kidding."

## HOME COOKING

*Nineteen fifty-six would mark the last time the New York Yankees and Brooklyn Dodgers played a meaningful October game against each other. Brooklyn would move to Los Angeles after the 1957 season. The two franchises had met in seven World Series, with the Bombers winning all but one of them. Their dominance was a continual source of angst for those "waiting for next year" Dodgers fans, who often believed the Yankee victories were as much a matter of luck as superior ability. Few of them realized that architecture—the structure of the teams' rosters as well as their ballparks—had a more profound impact on the outcomes than mere chance:*

**Clem Labine:** "I think we have our fingers on something when we compare the two stadiums. There is no doubt that the Yankees were more adaptable to our ballpark than we were to theirs. Even in 1955, when we finally won the Series, the Yankees beat us three out of four in Yankee Stadium.

"I always said privately that it wasn't hard to pitch to our team, despite all the home runs we hit, if you had good control and threw a ball that moved down. Whitey Ford, Johnny Kucks, Eddie Lopat, and most of the other Yankee pitchers could throw strikes and keep the ball low. They could get breaking pitches over the plate or hit a corner when they were behind in the count. You couldn't throw a cripple [a fastball over the heart of the plate] to our ball club, we'd kill you.

"Furillo could hit at Yankee Stadium. But the last couple of years we played New York [1955 and 1956], Carl would try to hit home runs there and he really wasn't that type of hitter. He was much better hitting the ball to all fields, not trying to jerk it out of the park. When he was swinging for the fences, Carl was a much easier out. Jackie [Robinson] could hit anywhere, but he would hit fly balls that were over the fence in Brooklyn, but long outs in Yankee Stadium's Death Valley.

"Gil Hodges was dangerous, of course, but easy to pitch to because he stepped in the bucket. He tried to pull you, and he couldn't hit outside pitches. Duke [Snider], a terrific left-handed hitter, always hurt the Yankees. He could hit the ball out of any park, and that right-field porch in the Stadium was made for him. But who else did we have? Pee Wee [Reese] would get his hits, but they were mostly singles. We had a lot of right-handed pull hitters in our lineup who could hit homers in Ebbets Field, but weren't as effective in Yankee Stadium."

**Billy Martin:** "Left field and left center in Yankee Stadium, that's where the Dodgers got killed. You looked up and down the Brooklyn lineup and some of those power hitters who had twenty, twenty-five home runs every season would have hit ten playing their home games in our park. They were just an ordinary club once you got them out of Brooklyn.

"Ebbets Field was a bandbox. George Weiss hated playing there because it cost the team money. We hit so many home runs during batting practice, we'd go through all the baseballs. If Mickey had played there his whole career, he would have hit 800 home runs. One year [1953], I hit fifteen home runs. If I had played at Ebbets Field that season, I would have hit twenty-five or thirty. Just look at what I hit there. . . ."

*Martin did not play often enough in Ebbets Field for his offensive statistics to be conclusive, but they are compelling. In 59 World Series at-bats in Brooklyn, Martin, who during his careeer averaged a home run every 54 at-bats while compiling a lifetime slugging average of .369, hit .305 and slugged .542 with three home runs, one for every 19.6 at-bats. Those numbers become even more impressive when you consider that they came against the top pitchers from one of the National League's superior staffs:*

**Tommy Byrne:** "The ball just flew out of Ebbets Field. In left field or left center, you hit the ball 350 feet, it was gone. Same shot to left center in Yankee Stadium, nice easy out. Another thing, the Dodgers lineup was mostly right-handed. Outside of Snider and I guess Sandy Amoros once in a while, I don't remember them having any left-handed batters who could hit the long ball against our right-handed pitchers. . . ."

**Clem Labine:** "The Yankees could send up a right-handed power hitter like Moose Skowron, who was always dangerous in our park, but because he could hit the ball hard the other way, he was a threat in Yankee Stadium, too. Death Valley didn't take away all of his power. Mantle, of course, could hit it out of any park from either side of the plate, so the Stadium didn't mean anything to him. Yogi pulled the ball a lot, but he also hit the ball where it was pitched, off his shoe tops, in his eyes, he could use the whole field in situations. With players like those, the Yankees could score runs anywhere. That made a difference."

*The lineup for the 1941 Dodgers was composed largely of speedy contact hitters, adept at smacking the ball to all fields. Stadium composition made little difference to those batters. In the World Series that season against the Yankees, the Dodgers lost all three games played in Ebbets Field by close scores. Brooklyn's offense was as impotent at home against New York as it was on the road.*

*But the statistics—although derived from a relatively small sampling— lend weight to the contention that the dimensions of the two stadiums played a crucial role in the hostilities the Yankees and Dodgers waged from 1947 to 1956. In the nineteen World Series games played between the two clubs in Yankee Stadium during that time, New York averaged 4.31 runs per game while winning fourteen and losing only four. Of the twenty games held in Ebbets Field, the Yankees won nine for a .450 winning percentage—an acceptable figure given their dominant performance in the Bronx—as they scored 4.75 runs per game, a home/away scoring differential of barely more than 10 percent.*

*Conversely, the Dodgers, averaging 4.65 runs per game, scored almost as often as the Yankees when the Series was played on their home field. But in the Bronx, facing the same pitchers they had hit so well in Flatbush, the Brooklyn offense withered. It could muster only 2.63 runs per game, a 43 percent decline that, five times out of six, proved insurmountable.*

**Carl Erskine (pitcher, Brooklyn and Los Angeles Dodgers, 1948–59):** "Now, that's interesting. With everything that's been written about these two clubs, I've never heard any of those statistics. I'm sure none of our players realized the disparity in run scoring between the two ballparks. Certainly, I never heard any of them complain about hitting in Yankee Stadium, as if they couldn't see the ball as well or anything.

"What Clem said about our right-handed hitters is true, a lot of their best shots were swallowed up in that Death Valley. Campanella was always a big man for us in the lineup. When he started with the Dodgers, he pulled the ball to left field a lot. But when Campy injured his hand, he started pulling the ball to left center. He would hit lofting fly balls that went out in Ebbets Field, but were outs in Yankee Stadium.

"I agree the Yankee lineup was more versatile in this sense: With hitters like Woodling and Mize, who murdered me, or Collins in the lineup they could alternate left-handed and right-handed batters throughout the order better than we could. But I never heard anyone point out that we needed more left-handed hitting. We had a variety of hitters like Sandy Amoros, George Shuba, and Gene Hermanski who platooned in left. After Gilliam joined us, we had a switch-hitter in the infield, although he wasn't a power hitter or RBI man.

"But in order for the front office to fit in another full-time left-handed hitter, what right-handed hitter do you take out of our lineup? You can't take out Jackie. You would have had to displace Campanella, Hodges, Reese, Cox, or Furillo, and they were all so great with their gloves we would have lost something on defense in the exchange. Hard choice to make there.

"I think you have to look at another important piece to this. If pitchers can't execute, a ballpark can't help you. For example, if you have a right-handed pitcher who's throwing mediocre breaking pitches out-side, our right-handed hitters would pop those over Yankee Stadium's right-field porch. New York always had those right-handed power pitchers like Raschi, Turley, and Reynolds who would come inside hard on our right-handed hitters to get a lot of fly balls to left center. They knew how deep that part of the Stadium was and they made it work for them. And a smart left-hander like Whitey Ford, who didn't throw extremely hard, could pitch to that deep part of the Stadium blindfolded."

**Bob Turley:** "One of the things our pitchers had going for us against Brooklyn was the approach the Dodgers took to the plate. Except for Robinson and Reese, they were a team of free swingers. Guys like Snider, Hodges, Furillo, and Campy committed themselves early and swung hard most of the time. Those kind of hitters are vulnerable to good breaking pitches, and most of the pitchers on our staff had excellent curves or sliders.

"People talk about my pumping the fastball as if that was all I threw, but I got a lot of those Dodgers out with breaking stuff, especially sidearm curveballs to Hodges and Campanella. That might also have contributed to this scoring discrepancy. You could throw more breaking stuff to them in Yankee Stadium. . . ."

**Tommy Byrne:** ". . . if you are throwing breaking balls against a power-hitting team in Ebbets Field, anything you hang has a good chance of being hit out. But in Yankee Stadium, you could get away with a hanging curve, especially to a right-handed hitter. He might hit that pitch 400 feet, but there was every chance it would still be nothing but a deep fly ball. . . ."

**Don Zimmer (major-league third baseman, 1954–65; reserve infielder, Brooklyn Dodgers, 1954–57):** "Tommy is dead right about that. Pitchers could get away with more mistakes than they could in Ebbets Field. That was a fairly small ballpark, and you usually had a jet stream going out in left field. In 1955, Game One of the World Series here at Yankee

Stadium, Whitey Ford hung a high slider to me that, when I hit it, I thought, 'Oh, man, I killed that ball.' I hit it out by that 399 sign in left center, except the fence wasn't 399 feet away back then, it was 457. In Ebbets Field, that's a home run easy. Here, Mickey Mantle just ran it down and stuck it in his hip pocket for an easy out. . . ."

**Tommy Byrne:** ". . . And if a pitcher knows he can get away with a hanging pitch once in a while, it stands to reason he's going to throw that curve with much more confidence. "

**Carl Erskine:** "Yankee Stadium also gave the Yankees an intangible advantage. With all that history and so much written about it, the Stadium could intimidate a player—and don't think the Yankees didn't know that. That wasn't so much a factor for us during the '50s, because we got used to playing there. But the first time I faced the Yankees [in the 1949 World Series], many of the players who played New York in the Series [two years] earlier were gone. We were a pretty young club.

"The clubhouses in Yankee Stadium had been renovated that season, and what used to be the Yankee clubhouse was now where the visiting team dressed. I remember that when we got there, the Yankees had still not moved two lockers from the old arrangement. They were Ruth's and Gehrig's. You know Casey was always working some kind of angle. I swear they left those behind to send our green ball club a message, you know, to remind us where we were and what we were up against. Maybe that's one of the reasons we lost that Series in five."

## PAYBACK

*S*elva Lewis Burdette could never deal straight with any hitter. *Everything he served to home plate arrived eely and elusive. A big, wide-shouldered right-hander who searched for his signs through a miner's squint, he may have hailed from Nitro, West Virginia,*

*but his best fastball was more expedient than explosive. It left batters shrug-
ging. They couldn't uncover Burdette's secret, couldn't figure out how he
could overcome them with such underwhelming stuff.*

*Burdette was a Yankee farm-system graduate, although he had pitched
only two innings for the big-league club. New York traded him to
the Boston Braves for Johnny Sain on August 30, 1951. Braves owner
Lou Perini moved the franchise to Milwaukee eighteen months later. By
then, Burdette had established himself as a regular in the Braves starting
rotation. Not a star exactly, but an innings-eating arm his teammates trea-
sured for its reliability. From 1953 to 1961 Burdette would win at least 15
games in every season but one. Few major-league pitchers could match his
consistency.*

*When the Braves entered the World Series in 1957, everyone assumed
Burdette, by now the staff's number two starter, would play some vital role
in its outcome. However, Milwaukee manager Fred Haney believed that
any chance his underdog team had of defeating the New York Yankees spun
on the screwball of Warren Spahn. The Braves' ace was on his way to accu-
mulating more wins than any left-hander in baseball history. That notwith-
standing, an educated fan watching from afar offered a different take:*

**Lew Burdette:** "Right before the 1957 Series, some sportswriters asked
Jackie Robinson who would be the toughest pitcher against the
Yankees and Jackie said, 'There's no doubt in my mind it will be
Burdette.' In our rotation, we had Warren Spahn and Bob Buhl—both
of them won more games than me that season—and both [Gene]
Conley and [Bob] Trowbridge had lower ERAs, but Jackie's naming
me. When he was asked why, he explained, 'Because he never throws
any pitch more than two inches above the knees, just like Whitey Ford.'

"He was right. Key for me in all three of those games I pitched
against New York, and throughout my career really, was control. I
hardly ever walked anyone. Lou Chapman, a writer in Milwaukee,
once charted my walks for me over four or five seasons. We found that
78 percent of my walks scored. Once I saw that, I knew how important it was to get the ball over and keep it down.

"I pitched batters low. The more they fished, the lower I put the ball. If I came upstairs to a hitter, it was inside to brush him back or jam the hell out of him. I was a sinker-slider pitcher. I threw the slider low and away at different speeds. Occasionally I'd throw a sidearm curve, but again keep it low. So even if they hit me, it was hard to put the ball in the air.

"Spahn lost the first game; I started the following afternoon. Let's talk about the second inning of that first game I pitched. Jerry Coleman topped the ball down the third-base line with Enos Slaughter on third. I knew when I fielded it, there was no way for me to get Coleman at first base, but I figured I could tag Slaughter. I picked up the ball, went to my right real quick, and got him. But the umpire was looking towards first . . ."

**Enos Slaughter:** ". . . honestly, he had me but nobody called it, so I just ran home . . ."

**Lew Burdette:** ". . . so that's another earned run I wouldn't have given up. In that same game, we're ahead [4–2] in the sixth. Mantle walks. Berra hits a force-out. Slaughter doubles. [Suitcase] Harry Simpson comes to the plate. With a two-run lead, I can't let Suitcase hit anything for extra bases. Even a long single scores two runs because Enos could still fly, so I want to keep Harry short. If he hits anything a long way, let it be a fly ball that might score a run but gives me a second out. I feed him a sinker low and away. Harry tries to pull it. Taps it back to me off the end of the bat. Double play. They never really threatened again.

"Now, that's a case where the batter got himself out! The Yankees gave me a lot of help like that the whole Series. Their hitters knew I didn't have much of a curve, so they kept trying to pull me. And I kept pitching them outside. My slider was not one of those big breaking pitches, which I consider overrated because it starts breaking too soon. Gives the hitter a chance to read it earlier. My slider generally broke just as the batter swung, which is the best kind to have. It didn't look like much of anything coming to the plate except a nice fastball. But with that late break, you couldn't hit it with the fat part of the bat. Try to pull it, you'd just hit a pop fly or soft grounder. And I had a good sinking fastball that whole Series. . . ."

*Sinker, slider, up and down, in and out, put a little on, take a little off . . . that was it? Did Burdette swipe the balance and pop from the strides of those mighty Yankee hitters tossing only two pitches? Well, he might have been mixing in another little dab, something not quite out of the rule book:*

**Jerry Lumpe:** "I don't know about Burdette being just a sinker-slider pitcher in those games. Lew's ball did come in awfully low, but I'm not sure he had that good a sinker working all the time. Sinkers keep boring down, they don't break as sharply as some of Lew's pitches did. I'm not going to *say* he was throwing a spitter if he won't. But many of those fastballs looked like strikes coming up. Then they'd just drop dead at the plate. . . ."

**Hank Bauer:** "Oh, come on, some of Burdette's pitches were so goddamned moist, you needed an umbrella to hit them. But, hell, give the guy all the credit, because his regular pitches were moving the whole Series. Just putting some moisture on a ball won't get hitters out. You have to have a good arm to begin with and be able to get the pitch over. And a spitball alone isn't enough. You have to work it in with other pitches . . ."

**Lew Burdette:** ". . . It is the hardest pitch in baseball to control, although I'm not going to tell you I ever threw one in a game. But if hitters wanted to *think* I was throwing one, fine. That worked to my advantage, gave them one more thing to worry about. . . ."

**Hank Bauer:** ". . . No one said he was throwing it all the time! Listen, there isn't any pitcher, I don't care if you're Gaylord Perry, whoever, who throws a spitball, can throw that many in a game. Umpires, managers, coaches, hitters, they aren't stupid. If you keep loading up every other pitch or even three or four pitches an inning, someone is going to catch you. So the smart spitball pitcher slips it in once in a while as an out pitch. I bet Lew didn't throw more than ten of them a game.

"And he's right about planting the idea that he's throwing a spitter. Once you show it to the hitter, if it's a good one, you almost don't need to throw it anymore, because now you've planted it in the back of the batter's mind. Even if you don't show another one to him the whole game, he has something else to look for."

**Jerry Lumpe:** "This guy knew how to pitch. Lew not only had excellent control, he also gave you a lot of flailing motion with his delivery. You got all these arms and legs that threw hitters off, whereas a guy with smooth motion, it's easier to time his pitches.

"As far as the spitter goes, when you suspect a pitcher is throwing one, you can complain to the umps to check the ball. Unless he gets caught, you have to deal with it, just like any other pitch. Think of it as an unhittable pitch, and you're dead. Look, a spitball is nothing more than a split-fingered fastball or forkball, except one is wet, the other's dry. The one advantage the pitcher has when he throws it is that the grip is the same as the fastball and it leaves his hand looking like a fastball. So it can be harder to read than other breaking pitches. I agree that spitballers only use the pitch to get big outs, so the idea some people have that Lew threw thirty or forty spitters per game against us is ridiculous. . . ."

*Wet or dry, didn't matter. Burdette pitched as if he knew what those New York hitters were expecting. Watch a film of his performances that Series; what do you see? Yankees swinging over pitches that finished near their shoe tops or lunging outside for balls that nearly unbuckled their belts. Even when a New York hitter connected squarely, the ball usually found a Brave:*

**Lew Burdette:** "Everything was working for me. You pitch that well against a team like the Yankees, you know there's a fair share of luck that comes into it, too. I won Game Five, 1–0, against Whitey Ford. Gil McDougald led off the fourth inning in that game with this deep fly ball. Wes Covington catches it head high in left field, then falls back against the fence. That would have been a double, and the Yankees got two more hits that inning, so there's your one run, maybe more.

"People still talk about that play, but many of them forget that in Game Two of the Series, Wes made an even better catch. With the score tied [1–1] and runners on first and second, Bobby Shantz, a good-hitting little left-handed pitcher, hit a line drive down the left-field line that would have scored two. But Wes raced over towards the stands and backhanded the ball, a much tougher chance because I think Covington had a little more time to get under the ball McDougald hit. Wes wasn't what you would call a good glove man, but he saved me with those catches. If he doesn't make them, who knows? I might have lost both games.

"A key play in that 1–0 game: Mickey tried to steal second in the eighth and got thrown out for the third out. [Milwaukee catcher] Del Crandall didn't have the strongest throwing arm, but he had a quick release. Mickey was a great base stealer—just like Henry Aaron, if he wanted to steal a base, most times it was stolen.

"But I always made the runner at first stop within a certain distance from the bag. Then I'd hold on to the ball, keep him glued to that spot until I saw him relax. I'd look to see his shoulders drop or some kind of a motion that he's letting up. With a man on, I never used a big leg kick. Why give the runner all that time to get going? I would barely pick up my front leg—lifted it maybe three inches—and just slide it forward. A runner can't get hardly any kind of jump when you do that. That's why we got Mickey."

*One–oh, a score to tantalize, with each batter the tying run coming to the plate. Heightening this game's thrall was the New York lineup, so powerful nearly every hitter stepped into scoring position as soon as he left the on-deck circle. In the ninth inning of Game Five, Burdette struck out the first two Yankees he faced before surrendering Gil McDougald's single. To complete his shutout and pull the Braves within one win of a World Series Championship, Burdette wouldn't have to attempt any heavy lifting. He only had to retire the man Ted Williams continually referred to as "the toughest out in baseball from the seventh inning on":*

**Lew Burdette:** "Yogi Berra comes up with a man on first and two out in the ninth. I'd been pumping him all day low and away with sinkers. Now, you keep pitching Yogi the same way, he's going to burn you but good. So I think to myself, 'Damn, I'm going to throw him a flat slider in on the fists.' Left-handed power hitters like Yogi are generally extended-arm hitters, so you give them something that starts outside but moves in on them.

"That slider of mine was near the middle of the plate when Yogi begins his swing. Then the ball runs in on him and I could hear him yell, 'Oh no!' The ball hit on the trademark and he popped it to Eddie Mathews at third. The whole game, that was the one pitch I really gave a great deal of thought to. I changed my way of pitching to him and got him out. That makes you feel good. You know, I have said that was the best pitch I threw the whole Series. It wasn't. It was the best pitch I threw in my whole career."

*Fred Haney had scheduled Warren Spahn to start Game Seven, which suited the Yankees since the left-hander's screwball had failed to confound them in either of his Series starts. New York had driven Spahn from the mound in the sixth inning of the opener. Despite defeating the Yankees in Game Four, Spahn had surrendered eleven hits and was losing 5–4 when Haney removed him for a pinch hitter in the bottom of the tenth:*

**Tom Sturdivant:** "We might not have even been in extra innings, if I could have taken back one pitch. I had a 1–0 lead in the [bottom of the] fourth, when Johnny Logan led off with a walk and Eddie Mathews doubled to make it second and third. A right-handed hitter's coming up with Wes Covington, a left-handed hitter, behind him. Casey didn't want me to pitch to Covington, who had power, with the bases loaded. He came out to the mound and said, 'Babe Ruth couldn't hit a home run today, the way the wind is blowing.'

"So he had me pitch to the right-handed hitter. Who then hit my third pitch just barely over the left-field wall for a three-run homer. When I saw Case in the dugout I said, 'I thought you said Babe Ruth couldn't hit one against that wind.' He growled, 'Well, he ain't Babe

Ruth, he's Henry Aaron.' You think about what he said now and it's really something, Aaron being the guy who broke Ruth's [career] home-run record."

*Vernal "Nippy" Jones, a thirty-two-year-old journeyman outfielder who had spent the previous five seasons toiling in the minor leagues, swung in Spahn's spot. Yankee left-hander Tommy Byrne, working in relief, dealt Jones a bastard curve, a drunken comet that careened past catcher Yogi Berra's glove to the brick wall behind home plate, then Ping-Ponged back to the batter's box. Home-plate umpire Augie Donatelli called it a ball. Jones, already prancing toward first base, offered another perspective. He argued with a skeptical Donatelli that the ball had nipped his right shoe.*

*Despite Jones's pleading, Donatelli remained unconvinced. But Braves third-base coach Connie Ryan supported his player's claim with tangible evidence: a small, dark smudge, an elfin footprint planted on the ball by Jones's shoe. After examining the spot, Donatelli reversed his call:*

**Tommy Byrne:** "I threw Nippy a breaking ball because the wind was blowing out and I wanted a ground ball. He started his swing, then held up and raised his back foot. Once it hit that backstop, it bounced all the way back and was laying right there next to home plate. If the ball had caromed anywhere else, the world never would have known what happened.

"While Nippy and Donatelli were arguing, I tried to get Yogi's attention to pick up the ball and get it back to me. Of course, Yogi didn't know what I was talking about because he was going after the umpire, too. I wasn't certain that the pitch had hit Jones, because hitting his foot did not divert the flight of the ball. That black mark from Jones's shoe polish that Ryan showed to Donatelli was no bigger than the fingernail on my pinky. Soon as Augie sends Jones down to first, all hell breaks loose. Casey and Yogi are screaming. I run in for an explanation, and Donatelli shows me the ball. I said, 'You mean that black spot on the ball is why you sent him to first? That was on the ball *before* I threw it!'

"You should have seen his face! Augie thought he'd really screwed up then. But he couldn't just take my word for it, he'd already sent Jones to first. Of course, what I told him wasn't true. You do anything possible to prevent something like that from happening. If Yogi had gotten the ball back to me [before Donatellli retrieved it], I might have put stuff all over it to cover that mark. Casey didn't argue for too long, then he took me out, brought in Bob Grim to face Red Schoendienst. . . ."

*Nippy Jones's trot to first base started a rally that ended with Milwaukee third baseman Ed Mathews's game-winning home run. Spahn received credit for the victory, but he had left the Yankees unimpressed. Even the outs they made against him were hard hit, and the Bombers were certain they would beat him if he faced them again.*

*Haney was willing to give New York the opportunity in Game Seven; he hadn't lost any confidence in his top starter. The manager had no idea he would be forced to abruptly alter his plans the night before the Series' final game:*

**Lew Burdette:** "Warren came up with the Asiatic flu. Well, hell, I'd been walking around with that little bottle of germs for so long, I didn't know what to do with it, so I sprinkled some on Warren's breakfast. Since Fred had no one else to pitch, I had to start on two days' rest.

"I thought I was up to it. I'd started on short rest before in the minors and won. Never done it in the big leagues, and here we are in Game Seven. But when I was pitching in rotation, in the middle of my three or four days off, I'd come on in relief rather than just throw on the side. In fact, I preferred getting my throwing in that way. Four or five times that season, Haney brought me in to pitch the last inning when we had a big lead or were far behind.

"So I was ready when he gave me the ball. And I still felt good even after Bauer doubled to lead off that game. I had to let Hank get that hit to keep his streak going [*Note:* It was the fourteenth consecutive World Series game in which Bauer had recorded a base hit. In 1958, he would set a World Series record by pushing the streak to seventeen straight.], you tell him that when you talk to him. Then Slaughter taps back to me and I spin around to chase Hank back to second . . ."

**Hank Bauer:** ". . . I'm thinking go to third all the way, but what I couldn't see since I was running and Lew's body blocked me out, was that Burdette had caught the ball on an angle that carried him into a position where he could cut me off from advancing to third . . ."

**Enos Slaughter:** ". . . meanwhile, I'm thinking Hank's in a rundown. I run my tail off towards second . . ."

**Hank Bauer:** ". . . so I'm going back to second. Something like that happens so fast, you don't know your teammate's running to the same bag until it's too late . . ."

**Lew Burdette:** ". . . as soon as Hank gets to second, the rules say the bag is his, so when Enos arrives there, too, [Milwaukee shortstop Johnny] Logan has him out. I think the Yankees had one scoring threat after that until the last inning of the game. We were leading 5–0 by then. I get Berra on a pop-up before McDougald singles. Kubek flies out [to Hank Aaron in right]. Then the Yankees come up with two of the flukiest hits you ever saw. Coleman breaks a bat popping a single to right. Tommy Byrne hits this ground ball to Felix Mantilla at second that goes off his glove.

"Skowron's the next batter. At that point, the last thing I want is a double down the line, because then it's 5–3, with Bauer coming up as the tying run. Now here's my problem. In that situation, you don't want to give a hitter something he can pull for extra bases. I want to pitch Moose away, but that's his strength. He could hit pitches to the opposite field with power as well as anybody. What do you do?

"A pitcher can throw to a hitter's strength and make it work against him if he doesn't make the pitch too good. So I'm going to pitch Moose away, but I'm going *real* low and away. If he takes it for a ball, fine, but maybe in a pressure situation like that I can get him fishing. Well, he swings and I don't know what he was looking for, but he pulls the ball. To hit a ball that far outside that hard, when you're trying to pull it, tells you how much power Moose had. He hits this sharp ground ball . . ."

**Moose Skowron:** ". . . down the third-base line, and if it gets past the bag, we might have three runs. But Eddie Mathews backhanded it and stepped on third to force McDougald for the out. Hell of a play. Oh, that was frustrating, making the last damned out of the Series on a ball hit like that. And, boy, was the front office ever steamed at me. Weiss blamed me for losing the whole World Series. Not just because of that one out. It was for something dumb I did before the Series even started. I picked up an air conditioner and injured my back.

"When I played that opening game against Spahn, I had to wear such a heavy corset, I could hardly move. After I grounded out, I told Casey to take me out. I couldn't play again until Game Seven, and what did I do? Oh-for-three. Terrible. I felt like I let everyone down, but Weiss made me feel worse. You know, I hit over .300 four straight years [from 1954 to 1957] and could hardly get a raise out of him, but after missing those games against Milwaukee, Weiss was so upset he tried to cut me $3,000."

*Skowron's back woes would haunt him intermittently throughout the 1958 season, sapping his power for long hitless stretches. Moose played through the pain, but his batting average (.273), slugging average (.424), and on-base percentage (.320) were not only career lows, they were under the league norm for first basemen. It was a bad season. Skowron ended it looking forward, knowing that October is baseball's month for atonement, the time when you could expiate all your failures with a single clutch swing:*

**Moose Skowron:** "As soon as I knew we were playing the Braves again in the [1958] World Series, you better believe I was motivated. It's like

I was on a mission. Right off, I got a base hit against Spahn [in the first game], then I homered off him. But we lost, so I wasn't happy. I didn't do much in the next three games [1 for 11], and we lost two more times. This wasn't going the way I hoped. One more loss, we go home. And maybe Mr. Weiss decides it's time to trade the first baseman. . . ."

*If Skowron and his teammates needed any further incentive to step up their play, Milwaukee delivered it to them in boldfaced, trash-talking head-lines:*

**Moose Skowron:** "Yeah, the Braves started mouthing off in the papers. Johnny Logan said we were washed up and someone else, Burdette or Spahn, said, 'If they were in the National League, the Yankees wouldn't even be in the Series. They'd finish fifth.' You don't say something like that about our club, not with Bauer, Mantle, Ford, and those guys. They knew how to win, and you had to kill them to beat them. . . ."

*Yankees challenged were Yankees engaged. When Stengel's players took the field for Game Five, they weren't certain they could turn around the Series, but they were determined to leave some welts on the Braves, just so Milwaukee would remember it had been in a scuffle:*

**Hank Bauer:** "Burdette should have kept his mouth shut. Him, Logan, Spahn, and Crandall were all popping off. Your team has pride, that's a motivator. You're not going to let the other club just roll all over you. Being down three games to one in a seven-game series, coming back is tough. But you know that saying 'Take it one game at a time'? That's how you have to think.

"You don't say, 'Hey, we have to win three in a row now.' Sounds too hard. Instead, just win Game Five. Now you're down 3–2. The next day you wake up knowing that if you win the game that after-noon, the Series is tied. Now anything can happen. Either way, you have to win three in a row, but if you don't think about it as three in a row, it's easier. I think we had some help once the Braves thought we were done. They stopped bearing down, forgot how to play. . . ."

**Bob Turley:** "Some of us were a little tight during the comeback. But I remember Mickey Mantle standing up in our bus, which was more quiet than usual, and saying, 'Hey, damn it, we're going to win this thing, so let's get excited now!' and that loosened us up, got our spirits up again. I shut out the Braves 7–0 in Game Five and saved Game Six by getting Frank Torre—Joe's older brother—on a soft liner to McDougald. Moose came through. . . ."

**Moose Skowron:** ". . . I drove in the winning run in Game Six. Just a single, but I was gettting good cuts again. Now, with everything even, the pressure is all on them. Who wants to blow a World Series everyone thought you had already won? Milwaukee sends out Burdette for the final game, figuring he'd nail our coffin just like the year before. He wasn't as sharp this time. We took a 3–2 lead [in the eighth], and with Andy Carey on first, Ellie [Howard] on second, I came up against Lew.

"Now, here's a story for you. In 1951 Mickey Mantle and I are in New York, working out with the Yankees for a week. I had just signed out of Purdue; Mickey was already in the minors. I'm eighteen, he's nineteen. Usually in batting practice like that, the pitcher's just there to lay the ball in for you, trying to give you something to hit. But the pitcher that day wouldn't let us know what he was throwing. He was pitching like it was a major-league game, just stuck the bat right up our asses. It was Burdette.

"Now I come up in that seventh game and Lew throws me a high slider. I hit the ball into the left-field bleachers for a three-run homer. That Milwaukee crowd immediately shuts up, you could hardly hear a peep in the Stadium. As I rounded third base, I turned to Burdette and shouted, 'That makes up for the way you treated me when I was a young punk!' I remembered and I made sure he did, too. My home run made it 6–2 and we didn't need any more. Turley was on the mound [in relief] and the Braves couldn't touch him. He was our big man that Series, along with Hank. . . ."

**Bob Turley:** "I was lucky enough to shut out the Braves in Game Five, save Game Six, and then win Game Seven. They make a big deal about my pitching so well over three straight games, but I didn't think it was that special. You have to remember I pitched Game Two in Milwaukee [a Yankee loss on October 2] and hardly broke a sweat. The Braves had me in the showers after only five hitters. I got one guy out and that was it.

"I was very well rested when I pitched Game Five [October 6] on normal rest and I finished strong. Then we had a travel day off. I only had to get out one batter in Game Six [October 8]. So I wasn't straining when Casey called me in to relieve Larsen [in the third inning] for Game Seven [October 9]. It was practically the same as pitching on two days' rest, which wasn't that uncommon in a World Series. Burdette had done it against us the year before.

"In fact, I was a better pitcher when I was a little fatigued, my control was sharper and my pitches moved more. I probably had my best stuff in that final game. Good as I pitched [Turley allowed one run in $6\frac{2}{3}$ innings], we don't take that Series without Hank Bauer. He hit home runs in two of our wins. . . ."

**Hank Bauer:** "Yeah, I had four of them that Series. I wasn't doing anything special, I don't think. Hitters go through streaks where they see the ball better. But no matter how big it looks, you still have to hit it. Last game, Burdette hangs a slider to me. That's home run number five. Except, I get a little anxious and fouled it off, straight back. Lew came halfway home to get a new ball from the umpire and he said to me, 'You know you're not going to get that one again.' Moose got one of his sliders and hit it just right. . . ."

**Moose Skowron:** ". . . soon as Bob got the last out, I felt vindicated from the year before. After I retired, some lawyer told me I'm the only guy who ever hit home runs in three different seventh games of the World Series [1956, '58, and '60]. I didn't even know it, but I'm proud of that record because you know in the seventh game, that's when everything counts. It's like what Billy Martin said: 'It's where we separate the men from the boys.'"

## A KILLER CONFESSES

*L*ooking at his extraordinary record against the Yankees—5–0 in 1955, 7–1 in 1957, 27–13 lifetime—you get the idea someone forgot to tell Detroit Tiger right-hander Frank Lary that opposing pitchers were supposed to cower in the presence of pinstripes. Lary never tiptoed out there on the diamond. He came right at the Yankees oozing animus and cool. Rarely overpowering, the right-hander could throw any one of four pitches for strikes at any point in the count and he wasn't afraid to challenge hitters inside.

You had a chance if you guessed what was coming, but as soon as Lary got those boys from the Bronx looking for something hard and quick, he'd change 'em up and sit 'em down. A Yankee hitter, wary that Lary might unfurl one of his slower offerings, would tell himself, "Wait. Don't overswing. Let the ball get up here." But most of the time the pitch ambling to the plate would find the batter's arms a bit too far out in front, his hips a tad too far back, his hitting apparatus all askew. The player—bamboozled, embarrassed, thoroughly vanquished—would return to a dugout of teammates shaking their heads in bewildered acquiescence. Once again the ultimate Yankee Killer had murdered their pleasure:

**Frank Lary (major-league pitcher, 1954–65; pitcher, Detroit Tigers, 1954–64):** "You're asking me why was I so successful against the Yankees, good as they were? Well, I'll tell you. My first full season in the American League was 1955. I pitched with Detroit until 1964. New York won nine American League pennants during that time. Great teams every year. But those Yankee ball clubs that I faced didn't have anyone who stole bases. Oh, Mickey could fly, but Stengel didn't want him to hurt those gimpy legs, so Mantle didn't [try to steal] much. That whole team was geared for power, but since the Yankees didn't steal, I could concentrate more on the man at the plate. Forget about that guy on first, he's not going anywhere. That helped me a lot. Whereas teams like the White Sox with [Nellie] Fox, [Luis] Aparicio, Jim Landis, and Jim Rivera running all the time could drive me to distraction.

"Now, I'm a country boy. Any country boy will tell you if you have a mule for a long time, you know what that mule will do. You pitch against a team enough times, you learn what it will do. I had enough pitches—fastball, slider, sinker, change—that if a Yankee hit something off of me, I could switch to something else. Most of them were big swingers. Guys who swing hard are easier to pitch to. You can get them to do a little fishing. I didn't walk a lot of batters in spots where I could get hurt, and I fielded well. All of that helps against a team like the Yankees, because if you made an error against them or start helping them to get on base, man, they'd take advantage of it.

"I threw a hard slider, didn't break real big, maybe five or seven inches, but I could change speeds on it, even easier than I did my fastball. That threw a lot of Yankee sluggers off. Let's take Roger Maris, for example. This boy became a dead pull hitter after he came to New York. Had the right-field foul pole in Yankee Stadium been over just another three feet, forget about McGwire breaking his record, because Roger would have hit 75 or even 80 home runs, he hit so many shots that were just barely foul that way. I'm not kidding. Against Maris, especially in Yankee Stadium, I threw a bit of a sinker, kept the ball away. If I got ahead of him, I'd go to the hard slider inside, and you better believe I mean way inside, enough to break his bat handle.

"Now, with Mickey, my approach was a little different. Mickey was a good old boy from Oklahoma, a country boy like myself. Every pitch that was thrown to him, he swung as hard as he could. Just aired it out. Never choked up, not for a single at-bat. Why, the wind from his swing could blow you off the mound. A much bigger swing than Roger took. Anytime a hitter swings that hard, you don't want to give him any help. Throw as hard as he swings and he's going to hit that pitch out of the state. So you change speeds, mix in some slow pitches. And you don't get behind. Go 2–0, the .300 hitter becomes a .450 hitter, 0–2 he becomes a .200 hitter—even a great player like Mickey Mantle. You have to keep that in mind; you can't let those big swingers intimidate you."

*Another renowned Yankee slayer, Boston Red Sox left-hander Mel Parnell, approved of Lary's strategy and wondered why other pitchers didn't emulate it:*

**Mel Parnell (pitcher, Boston Red Sox, 1947–56):** "Oh, you had to pitch them inside, absolutely! Too many pitchers, especially young ones like Chuck Stobbs and Mickey McDermott when they first joined the Red Sox, were so intimidated by the Yankees, afraid they would pull them, they kept pitching them outside. When you did that against a team like the Yankees, if you're just a little too far outside, they won't swing. They were such a disciplined group of hitters, they'd take that pitch for a ball. If you missed, the ball's towards the middle of the plate where the hitter can swing with his arms extended. That's his power! But by pitching inside, sometimes way inside, I could get the hitter to swing quite often because he still got a good look at the ball, but if he connected, he wasn't hitting the ball on the sweet part of the bat, it was more on the handle side. . . ."

**Frank Lary:** ". . . but you couldn't pitch them the same way every time up. You had to keep them thinking, surprise them once in a while. Once in Yankee Stadium, I threw Mickey Mantle a fastball right down the middle. He takes it for strike one. You have to figure Lary got away with a pitch there, now he better go outside on him. I throw another fastball right over the middle. Strike two. Now everybody in the stands knows I absolutely have to go outside, way outside, to see if he'll go fishing for a waste pitch. So I throw another fastball. Right over the heart of the plate. He took it again for strike three. Three fastballs right down the middle and Mickey took all three!

"I never tried that again, no one is that crazy. But on that day, in that situation, I pitched against logic and won. It was a feeling I had and that comes from knowing the hitter and thinking along with him. We were ahead and I could afford to take the risk. I'd have pitched differently if there were runners on at the time. Go to the sinker more, keep that ball down if there is no one on third, but if a man was on third, I'd have jammed him with sliders.

"So I had good luck with Mickey, Roger, even Yogi. That was the heart of their order. But they had some guys who weren't easy for me. You know, I always said the toughest hitters to get out were the left-handed and right-handed ones, I had no trouble with anyone else. Moose Skowron wasn't someone you wanted to face too often. He wasn't just a big slugger trying to hit the long ball all the time. Smart hitter, went with the pitch, thought along with the pitcher, and could hit the ball the other way as hard as anyone. Guys like that were always hard to get out.

"I guess Elston Howard was the toughest. Strong, dangerous hitter who had a short swing and he waited on the ball so well. That man wasn't appreciated as much as he should have been. He had a lot more power than people realize. Put him in another park, say, Fenway or Tiger Stadium, he'd have hit 35 home runs a year, easy. I did not like to see him getting up. Probably the start that I remember most against them was that July 4 game in 1961. We were in first place, a game in front of the Yanks, with a doubleheader in Yankee Stadium. [Don] Mossi loses the first game to Whitey Ford. Now we're tied.

"The second game, the score is 1–1 in the tenth inning. Maris had hit a homer off me in the eighth. I come up in the tenth—starting pitchers were expected to be finishers back then—with two men out and Steve Boros on third. The pitcher gets two strikes on me. So now I'm thinking: Steve has pretty good speed on third, it's two out, I've got two strikes on me, their infield is playing back. I figure the pitcher doesn't want to waste a pitch here. Why give me a chance to work out a walk and bring up the top of our order? And he can't take a chance of throwing anything in the dirt, because a wild pitch brings in Boros from third.

"You see, I'm thinking like a pitcher now, not a hitter. So I'm looking for something in the strike zone. I closed my eyes, then stuck the bat out for a bunt. Does that surprise you? It surprised everyone else. Soon as I made contact, I took off. Steve scored easily and I beat out the throw at first base. We won, 2–1, to go back into first place by ourselves.

"That didn't last too long. We won over 100 games and finished second. At the end of that season, Whitey Ford won the Cy Young

Award and that sort of rubbed things in for me. No secret there. It was politics. I think those New York reporters pushed for him. You tell me. I won 23 games and completed 22 of them. Some other guy wins 25 and completes 11, how can he win the Cy Young? Whitey only finished a few points better than me in ERA, and I played in a much tougher ballpark for pitchers. Detroit was a hitter's park, Yankee Stadium was made for left-handers. Hey, I'm not knocking Ford. He was a terrific pitcher. But I hit a triple off of him one time. You always want to beat the best, so I always got up for Whitey and the Yankees more than the other clubs. I would bear down just a little bit more. If I pitched that way against everyone, who knows how many games I would have won?"

## STENGEL'S FINAL RIDDLE

*M*az-er-os-ki. *The consonants are jagged, like glass shards forever lodged in the hearts of any Yankee fan old enough to recognize the name's significance. During the 1960 World Series against the Pittsburgh Pirates, the Bombers shattered numerous postseason offensive records, including most runs scored (55), most extra-base hits (27), and highest batting average (.338). New York second baseman Bobby Richardson set an individual Series standard with 12 RBI, while his teammate Mickey Mantle was nearly as prolific with 11 runs batted in. Three New York wins came by scores so one-sided—16–3, 10–0, and 12–0—the Pirates appeared to be on the short end of a mismatch.*

*But those three victories were all New York would celebrate. Despite its unprecedented offensive production, New York lost the Fall Classic in seven when Pirate second baseman Bill Mazeroski hit the ultimate walk-off home run, a 9–9 tie-breaker in the bottom of the ninth inning at Pittsburgh's Forbes Field. It was a climax that left the losing pitcher and his teammates feeling frustrated as well as numb:*

**Ralph Terry (major-league pitcher, 1956–67; pitcher, New York Yankees, 1956–57, 1959–64):** "You never want to lose, but when a hitter beats your best stuff, you tip your hat to him and get over it. The thing is, when I came in to face Mazeroski, I didn't have my best stuff. That game, Casey had me warming up a half-dozen times. I was supposed to be a long man, and I got up the moment Turley ran into trouble in the first. Then I kept getting up nearly every inning. This is the World Series, so each time I'm warming up with everything I had. But Casey kept bringing in someone else, first Stafford, then Shantz, then Coates. I nearly pitched a whole ball game before I came in that afternoon. So, shit, by the time I got in there to face Maz I couldn't blacken your eye with my fastball.

"My first pitch was a slider, high. It probably didn't have much life to it because [catcher John] Blanchard came running to the mound right after I threw it and said, 'Hey, you've got to get the ball down!' Next pitch, I threw Mazeroski a cut fastball that I tried to get low. It came in waist high over the plate. Nothing on it. It was like a batting-practice pitch. Some guys, especially in a situation like that, might have been so overeager to hit a pitch that fat they might swing too hard and pop it up or foul it back. Maz hit it just right, so you have to take your hat off to him.

"He hit it good, way over that ivy-covered wall in left field. Nothing Yogi could do but watch it go out. Soon as I saw it leave the field, I walked off the mound. I felt terrible, like I had let the whole team down, especially Casey."

*Terry wasn't alone in his funk. Moments after Yogi Berra abandoned pursuit of Mazeroski's game-winning drive, a stunned Mickey Mantle sat sobbing in the Yankee clubhouse. Teammates who approached the center fielder found him nearly inconsolable. Mantle would later refer to the 1960 World Series as the most galling defeat of his career. And why not? His club had outscored, outhit, and outpitched the Pirates throughout most of the Series, only to lose everything on the last swing of the season.*

*But there was a reason for Mantle's angst beyond the final score, a puzzle that to this day continues to nag his teammates and their fans. Who cares whether we ever uncover the identity of Jack the Ripper? What does it matter if aliens crashed near some military installation at Roswell? For anyone who claims pinstripes for veins, there is only one mystery worthy of obsession: Why didn't Casey Stengel start Whitey Ford in the first game of the 1960 World Series?:*

**Whitey Ford:** "Casey and his coaches wanted to hold me out until Game Three. I don't know why, because I never asked them. Back then players just did as they were told. That was probably the only time the players and I got annoyed with Casey. . . ."

**Jim Coates (major-league pitcher, 1956–67; pitcher, New York Yankees, 1956–62):** "Annoyed? Lord, we all wanted to kill him. . . ."

**Whitey Ford:** ". . . They all thought I should have pitched the first game. If I had, that meant I could have pitched Games One, Four, and Seven. But the way they had it set up, I pitched only twice and threw two shutouts. We scored twice as many runs as the Pirates [55–27] in that series and still lost on Maz's home run. Oh, did that hurt! Everyone on the team was really upset afterwards. . . ."

**Vern Law (pitcher, Pittsburgh Pirates, 1950–67):** "The Yankees may have been upset, but we couldn't have been happier. Not relieved, necessarily, just pleased that Whitey would only pitch two games against us. Ford had a great reputation as a money player, a guy who comes through with a pennant or championship on the line. You'd have to say Casey's decision might have made a big difference in the outcome of the Series. Whitey did shut us out twice the two times he faced us. No one on our club would have wanted to see him out there for Game Seven. To this day, I have no idea why Casey didn't set up the rotation so that we'd face Whitey three times. But I thank him for it."

**Ralph Houk (reserve catcher, New York Yankees, 1947–54; coach, New York Yankees, 1958–1960; manager, New York Yankees, 1961–63, 1966–73):** "I sat in on the meetings with Casey and the coaches when we discussed the rotation for the World Series. I think there was concern about Whitey starting in Pittsburgh with that hard infield our scouts had talked about. Whitey got a lot of ground balls and the Pirates had all those right-handed hitters. . . ."

*Once Stengel eliminated Ford from consideration, the manager and his coaches wrangled vehemently over who would start Game One. Pitching coach Eddie Lopat campaigned for right-hander Bill Stafford, only 3–1 as a rookie but so utterly self-assured, Lopat was certain the momentous assignment wouldn't faze him:*

**Clete Boyer:** "If they weren't going to use Whitey, Stafford was my pick, too. Tough kid, afraid of nothing, and he was a right-handed Whitey Ford with stuff that had great movement low in the strike zone. Hard thrower, never walked anybody. When he finally pitched in the Series [twice in relief], the Pirates couldn't smell him [6 IP, 5 hits, 1 walk, 2 strikeouts, 1.50 ERA]. I'd have been very confident that he could have handled them in that first game. . . ."

*Like Boyer, Stengel appreciated Stafford's nerve, but he was disinclined to trust rookies in October. Houk and Crosetti persuaded Casey to make what appeared to be the orthodox choice—right-handed Art Ditmar, who, at 15–9, had been New York's top winner during the regular season. Despite Ditmar's excellent record, the selection further confounded his teammates:*

**Ralph Terry:** "Going by what Houk says, that's a strange pick they made, isn't it? If Pittsburgh had such a hard infield, why start a sinkerballer like Art Ditmar? And right-handed, left-handed, who cares? This is Whitey Ford we're talking about, he got everybody out. I know Casey wanted Whitey to start that first game in Yankee Stadium. You couldn't beat Whitey at home. But, here's the thing. Whitey could only start one game of the three in Yankee Stadium. So what difference would it have made if he started Game Four there instead of Game Three?

"Suppose the worst happened and the Pirates won those first three games against us. Who else would you want on the mound at home to stop a sweep besides Whitey? I still can't figure this out. One thing no one mentions is that the dimensions of Forbes were very much like Yankee Stadium, so that was a great park for Whitey. He proved that in Game Six when he shut the Pirates out. . . ."

**Bob Cerv:** "There's a lot more to this story than people know, but I don't want to get involved with it. I might know, but I'm not going to tell you. I wasn't running the team, they were. We were angry the moment we found out Whitey wasn't getting the ball. The team wasn't pitching our best pitcher against their best. And none of us could figure out why Casey started a sinkerball pitcher [Art Ditmar] against a National League team. Those Pirates were all low-ball hitters like most guys in that league. See, today it doesn't make much difference, one league to the other, but back then the high strike was American League. Under the armpits, chest-high was a strike.

"But in the National League, you got strikes at the knees; those were balls in our league. National League pitchers threw low strikes and that's what their hitters were used to swinging at. Ditmar's best pitch played to the Pirates' strength. But the guy to talk to about why Whitey didn't start would have been George Weiss. Mr. Weiss used to talk to Stengel every day before a game. He was involved a little more than people realized. And that's all I'm going to say about it."

**Bobby Richardson:** "I doubt Mr. Weiss had anything to do with it. The Yankee front office didn't understand the move either, and I believe it ultimately cost Casey his job. But as far as anyone persuading Casey to hold back Whitey, uh-uh. Casey would have spoken with his coaches and then made up his own mind.

"You have to understand that Stengel was a gambler who had complete confidence in his hunches. I remember many a time when someone like Andy Carey might have gone two for three, and he's coming up to the plate in some critical spot, a right-handed hitter with a left-handed pitcher on the mound. Suddenly, Casey would say, 'Hold that gun, come back and let Lumpe hit.' Now, with Lumpe you are sending a left-handed hitter against a left-handed pitcher, which doesn't make any baseball sense but it usually turned out well for Casey. Holding Whitey back until Game Three was a typical Stengel move, one of those unorthodox hunches that usually worked. Only this time it didn't.

"Even today, I honestly believe Whitey would have pitched a third shutout or kept them to two or three runs so we would have beat them. Remember, we scored nine runs in that final game. Can anyone imagine our losing with that many runs and Whitey on the mound? You have to give Casey some backhanded credit. Most managers would have been afraid to start the Series with anyone except Whitey, but Casey went with his hunch."

**Bob Turley:** "I'm going to disagree with Bobby to this extent—I don't think this was simply a matter of a hunch backfiring on Casey. We've all heard about how he aged in '59 and '60, but those are mostly stories about him falling asleep on the bench during games as if it was just a question of an elderly man feeling fatigue. Or forgetting people's names. He did that all the time. But there was something else going on. Casey was losing it. He would call out for pinch hitters or relievers who had been long since traded from the club and he made moves that were questionable, not quirky. . . ."

**Jim Coates:** ". . . I dearly loved the man. He helped my career by giving me a chance to pitch a lot in my first full year with the club [1959]. But Bob is right. When Casey would talk to you that season, you could see he had the right idea in his head, but he couldn't quite express it. Like an old outfielder who knows how to make the catch, but his legs can't get him there in time. Casey was a step behind his own thoughts that whole season. . . ."

**Bob Turley:** ". . . that seventh game, for instance, which I started and got knocked out in. Casey brought in Bobby Shantz to relieve me and Bobby did a great job, even though his arm was killing him. Casey knew it, too, but he told Bobby to keep going as long as he could. Meanwhile we have Ryne Duren, all rested and ready to pitch. He'd pitched great against the Pirates in two games already, but Ryne doesn't get a call. Luis Arroyo sat there, too. Luis's screwball would have been tough on all those right-handed Pirate hitters and he kept the ball down. Instead of calling for either of them, he's got Bobby pitching all those innings in pain, Ralph Terry warming up so many times he's draining himself, and then he brings in Jim Coates instead of Arroyo or Duren to give up that three-run homer to Hal Smith [which gave the Pirates a 9–7 lead after eight], and that just killed us. That same Series Casey pinch-hit for [Clete] Boyer with two men on, nobody out in [the second inning of] the first game for no good reason at all. . . ."

**Clete Boyer:** ". . . my first season as a regular and he sends Dale Long to hit for me! Why even start me, if you're going to embarrass me like that? If I'd been a veteran with six or seven years in, I would have killed that old bastard for what he did. But forget how I felt personally, Turley's right, this was bad baseball. If the manager didn't think I could hit the starting pitcher [Vern Law], then he should have started someone else, say, Gil McDougald at third, then brought me in for defense. Instead he burnt up two players, me and Dale Long, in the second inning and got shit for it, not a run. Long flew out and Bobby [Richardson] hit into a double play. . . ."

**Bob Turley:** ". . . No, those weren't hunches backfiring. Stengel had been a great manager, and I don't mean to speak ill of him, but that was a man who should have retired the season before. He just didn't have it anymore. And after we lost the way we did, the front office realized it. He was gone."

*Events suggest that Yankee owners Dan Topping and Del Webb agreed with Turley's assessment. Two days after the Mazeroski home run they fired Stengel and replaced him with Ralph Houk.*

**Ralph Houk:** ". . . but I don't think they fired him just because we lost to Pittsburgh. During the Series, when we were ahead two games to one, there were rumors that the Kansas City A's wanted to hire me as manager. [Yankee assistant general manager] Roy Hamey came to me and said, 'Ralph, don't do anything foolish. Don't be too quick to take that job in Kansas City.' He didn't promise me a job or say that Casey was on the way out. But certainly what Roy said indicates that the decision to retire Casey was made before the Series even started."

## THE 1961 WORLD SERIES: CANCELING RED OCTOBER

*I*mages of raw power, of baseballs rapidly growing smaller as they climbed over distant fences, dominate our remembrances of 1961 in the Bronx. It was the year Yankee teammates Roger Maris and Mickey Mantle waged their Battle for the Bambino, the race to break Babe Ruth's thirty-four-year-old record for most home runs in a season. Ruth had slugged 60 homers in 1927. By July 2, barely the midpoint of the 1961 season, Maris had hit 30 home runs while Mantle followed right behind him with 28. It was around then that the press first started casting attention on the Babe's home-run record. Mantle was the betting favorite to usurp Ruth. The center fielder already had four home-run crowns to his credit and had hit 40 or more homers in three different seasons, including 52 in 1956. Topping 60 or more home runs seemed well within his range.

Many fans, journalists, and players at first reacted skeptically to Maris's assault on the record. The right fielder simply lacked Mantle's slugging bona fides. Maris had never led any league, major or minor, in home runs. He had never hit as many as 40 homers in a season. As one teammate, who deeply appreciated Maris's all-around skills, later recalled, the left-handed hitter did not even arrive in New York sporting a classic Stadium swing:

**Bud Daley (major-league pitcher, 1955–64; pitcher, New York Yankees, 1961–64):** "No one could have predicted what Roger would achieve with the Yankees. It never occurred to me that he would become a home-run champion or come anywhere near Ruth's record. I played with Roger on four clubs—Indianapolis in the minors, Cleveland, Kansas City, and New York in the big leagues. At Indianapolis, he wasn't a home-run hitter at all. The A's traded him to New York just after the 1959 season, and that year he only hit 16 homers for us.

"What Roger was was an excellent line-drive hitter with a quick, compact swing, someone you thought would hit .300 every year but with only 15 to 20 homers. Even when he went to Yankee Stadium, I didn't think he'd hit many more home runs because he wasn't a pull hitter. Roger hit the ball to all fields. Not a spray hitter, he'd hit with authority, a lot of doubles deep in the gap to drive in runs. I'd expect him to get his share of triples, too, because he was very fast. Had he stayed in Kansas City, I bet he would have remained a completely different batter. A possible batting champion, but not the home-run king.

"It was when he came to New York that he taught himself to pull the ball. His first year with the Yankees [1960] I could tell when I pitched to him that he was looking to drive the ball to right field more as the season went on. Roger almost led the league in home runs that year [his 39 were second to Mantle's 40], and I thought that was as high as he could go. But he saw that short right-field porch in Yankee Stadium, and this shows you how smart he was. He kept adapting. That's why the home runs came."

*They came in profusion for Maris, Mantle, and their teammates in 1961. Maris hit his record-setting 61st home run of the season against Baltimore's Tracy Stallard on October 2. Mantle finished second in the race with 54. The Yankees would hit 240 home runs as a team to set a major-league standard that would last for nearly forty years. Seven different Bombers reached double digits in homers to give New York a lineup that could take over a game with one swing in any inning.*

*But like most pennant-winning Yankee teams, this squad didn't have to continually body-slam opponents to win. With baseball's deepest pitching staff and strongest defense, New York was adept at killing teams softly on those rare occasions when the power slept. The only elements the Yankees lacked were proficient table setters at the top of the lineup. Bobby Richardson (.295 OBP) and Tony Kubek (.307 OBP) were far below the league average in on-base percentage (.331), yet the rest of New York's batting order was so muscular, it still scored 841 times.*

*Though the Yankees compiled 109 victories in 1961, they did not go the entire season unchallenged. Detroit shadowed New York right up until Labor Day, when a series of lengthy Yankee winning streaks relegated the Tigers to second place. Detroit finished eight games behind the leaders. It was enough to make even the toughest Bengal cry:*

**Frank Lary:** "Do we have to talk about that? Isn't that awful? Win 101 games and wind up eight games out! People see those standings today, it looks like we weren't in the race, even after we stayed with them right up to the first week of September. The big difference was their power. We had Rocky Colavito [46 home runs] and Norm Cash [41], but we couldn't match them through the rest of the order. I don't think [Al] Kaline hit even 20 home runs that year. The Yankees had [six] players with 20 or more. We did outscore them, but you have to remember, we played in a great hitter's park. Yankee Stadium is a pitcher's park. The Yankees would have scored many more runs playing on our home field. And New York had a sensational defensive team with Richardson and Kubek at second and short, that was the best double-play combination around. Clete Boyer, you couldn't match him at third. And Moose was underrated at first. He had real soft hands and could dig tough chances out of the dirt to save his team throwing errors. Not that they made too many of those.

"By comparison, our infield wasn't exactly a strength. Jake Wood really wasn't a second baseman; he would have excelled as an outfielder with his speed, but you couldn't compare him to Bobby Richardson, who was much smoother and had better hands. Chico Fernandez was competent at short but not in the class of Kubek. He didn't have Tony's range. That Kubek, he never seemed to make an error that cost his team a game. Richardson was the same way.

"And it seemed like we played everyone at third base, mostly Steve Boros. Again, competent, but that Boyer, he was amazing. Why, you couldn't bunt against him most of the time, he played so close to home. A third baseman plays that close, you think you can get a lot of hard-hit balls by him, but Clete's reflexes were so good, he'd catch them all.

And his arm was a cannon, strong and accurate as any third baseman you'll ever see. Defensively, our outfield compared well with theirs. Colavito, Kaline, and Bruton covered a lot of ground and they could throw. But it wasn't enough.

"The Yankees also had more guns in their rotation. We could match them one to three. In fact, I thought we were tougher—you think they wouldn't have liked to have Don Mossi and Jim Bunning in their rotation?—but their four and five men were better than ours and their bullpen was deeper. Our main man, Terry Fox, in some ways, had an even better year than [Yankee closer] Luis Arroyo. But Terry couldn't pitch as often as Arroyo. Luis pitched almost as many innings as a starter; it seemed like the Yankees used him every day. He had a great slow screwball with control. And Luis had guys like Hal Reniff and Jim Coates to help him. Terry didn't have much help."

*As expected, the Yankees, touted by many in the press as the most power-ful baseball team ever assembled, easily defeated the Cincinnati Reds, four games to one, in the 1961 World Series. The two teams played forty-five innings against each other; Cincinnati held the lead in only ten of them, and half of those came in the Reds' second-game victory. New York so thor-oughly outclassed its opponents, the Series was one of the least memorable ever played. Nevertheless, the victory left a lasting impression on a Reds relief pitcher who learned, like Lary and the Tigers, that this Yankee club was something more than just a gaggle of sluggers:*

**Jim Brosnan (major-league pitcher, 1954–63; closer, 1961 Cincinnati Reds):** "They took us in five, but it felt like a sweep. Immediately after New York beat us, I wrote a piece for *Sports Illustrated* titled 'It Was Embarrassing, Wasn't It?' That pretty well summed it up. I appeared in three of the five games and did well only in the first one. My second appearance [Game Four], the Yankees belted me around pretty much at will. Larry Merchant, the sportswriter, came up to me in the club-house afterwards and asked, 'Why did Hutch [Cincinnati manager Fred Hutchinson] leave you in so long? Was he mad at you?' I said, 'No, I just think he had a lot of confidence in me, misplaced as it was.'

"Everybody knew going in how much power the Yankees had. The Maris-Mantle home-run race underlined that, plus they got a lot of ink for having three catchers—Ellie Howard, John Blanchard, and Yogi Berra, although Yogi really wasn't a catcher anymore—who hit more than 20 home runs. But our club had power, too; I thought in a short series we might be able to stay with them in that facet of the game.

"But what impressed me most about that team was something you really don't hear much about because of all the focus on their sluggers. And that was the effectiveness of their pitching staff from top to bottom. They shut us down despite the fact that in Crosley Field, *we knew every pitch that was coming*. You remember Brooks Lawrence? Good pitcher with the Reds during the fifties, but he retired the year before we won the pennant. We had him up in the left center-field scoreboard stealing every sign the Yankee catchers gave. Brooks was on the telephone with Otis Douglas, a conditioning coach I guess you would call him today.

"Hutch picked Otis for this assignment because he had a loud, distinctive voice that carried well. Lawrence would relay the pitch to Otis. If it was a fastball, Otis would yell at the top of his lungs, something like 'Get a good pitch, Vada!' or 'Bring that run in, Frank!' You could hear him a block away from the park. On breaking pitches, he kept quiet. Very simple, right? Not much you could do to screw up that system. It didn't make any difference. We played three games against New York in Crosley and scored five earned runs, even with our hitters knowing every pitch they would throw. Pathetic."

**Ralph Houk (manager, 1961 New York Yankees):** "No way I knew that was going on. I can't believe that their hitters knew what was coming and didn't hit better than they did. They had a strong hitting team, so I'm very much surprised by this. But our pitching was strong, and Jim's right, it was overlooked because of our tremendous offense. . . ."

**Clete Boyer:** "This just proves that stuff about the Giants stealing the pennant in 1951 was all horseshit. Shit, you think we didn't know

Sandy Koufax was going to throw a curve on an 0–2 [in 1963]? We still couldn't hit him. Knowing what pitch is coming doesn't tell you anything about movement or location, speed. You still have to hit the ball. . . ."

**Bud Daley:** "I've never heard what Jim told you about Lawrence stealing signs, but that sure explains a lot of things. I got the win in the final game of that series in Cincinnati. They'd knocked out Ralph Terry with three runs in the third and Houk brought me in to pitch [6⅔ innings] while we came back to take it, 13–5.

"Usually when I worked that many innings, I'd strike out four, five, six hitters. I only had one strikeout that day. And I didn't walk anybody, which was also odd because I walked about a man every other inning that season. In fact, I don't think Cincinnati walked much that entire Series. . . ."

*The Reds, who averaged 4.6 walks per nine innings during the regular season, drew only eight bases on balls in five games against Yankee pitchers. Only three of those walks occurred in the three games played in Crosley Field. One of those was an intentional pass to pinch hitter Jerry Lynch in Game Three:*

**Bud Daley:** ". . . That tells you the Reds came to the plate swinging. I remember thinking I didn't have particularly good stuff that afternoon because they were right on my curveball, which was my strikeout pitch. On a 3–2 count, I'd throw a breaking pitch, they'd jump on it nearly every time. Fortunately, we caught most of them.

"But Wally Post, who I played with at Indianapolis, hit a home run off me with two outs. Wally was a big, strong hitter, especially against lefties, but that home run was suspicious. There was a runner on first, I threw him a fastball and he jumped all over it like he knew it was coming. The way he stepped into the ball tells me something.

"You know, stealing signs would work with me only with a runner on first or no one on. With a runner on second, it wouldn't mean anything. Then I would give the signs to my catcher rather than the other way around. What did I give up, five hits that day? And all five of them came with no one on or a runner on first.

"None of what you're telling me is upsetting, because we won. And what Brooks Lawrence did wasn't unusual. Heck, the Yankees had Bob Turley stealing signs for them for years. So we knew all about stealing signs. But he would just watch from the bench and whistle on certain pitches. Using binoculars and a phone, I'm surpised anyone would do something so elaborate for an entire home stand in a World Series and get away with it.

"Funny thing about that last game I pitched. My first Series appearance [Game Three] was two days earlier. I relieved [starter Bill] Stafford to get Vada Pinson out [in the seventh]. Not a bit nervous. My spot came up third in the lineup that inning; Blanchard pinch-hit a home run for me to tie the game.

"But when I came in for that last game I had two men on, two men out, a left-handed hitter up, and I swear I thought an umpire would call a balk on me, my knees were shaking so bad. Sure, we had them down three games to one and Terry had handed me a 5–3 lead. But you don't want to be the guy who lets the Reds back into the Series when they're down.

"[Reds first baseman Gordy] Coleman was my first batter. Left-handed slugger, don't give him anything he can pull over the fence. Give him a low breaking pitch he can pound into the ground, let our infielders throw him out. He couldn't run a lick. So what does he do? Bunts down the first-base line for a base hit! Here come the butter-flies. I'm thinking, 'Nice beginning.' But we got out of the inning without them scoring, and by the time I got to our dugout, I was fine. Then our hitters just took the game over. We only hit two home runs, but we scored thirteen runs. . . ."

**Jim Brosnan:** "The thing we found out about the Yankees is, they didn't have to hit home runs to beat you. Usually you have an exten-sive book on a team of hitters you're facing for the first time in a big series. New York's lineup was so good, our book amounted to Hutch telling us, 'Go at them with your best stuff and don't give them anything good to hit.' Well, thanks for the advice, Hutch. But what else could he tell us?

"Even the singles hitters like Kubek and Richardson could hurt you. You're right, those two didn't take many pitches for guys batting at the top of the lineup, but they made good contact all the time. There wasn't any easy out in the lineup. With Johnny Blanchard, Bob Cerv, and Hector Lopez around, there wasn't even an easy out on their bench. I bet you they had bat boys who get a pinch hit if they needed one.

"I can't tell you how good the Yankee defense was, because we didn't hit the ball hard enough or see them long enough to test them. Kidding aside, in the first game we played against them, at the Stadium, Gene Freese hits a ball just about down the line for a double. Except Boyer intercepted it with a backhand grab, then threw Freese out from his knees.

"Same game, a later inning, Dick Gernert [pinch-hitting for starting pitcher Jim O'Toole] hits the ball wide to Boyer's left, towards the hole at shortstop with Kubek shading towards second. Sure base hit. Except Boyer dives, lands on his stomach, his body prostrate . . ."

**Clete Boyer:** "Whitey Ford made that play, not me. A good infielder knows his pitcher and works off whatever stuff he has for that particular game. I knew Whitey was going to throw Gernert that hard sinker of his outside and there was no way Dick could pull that ball. I had confidence in Whitey's stuff and I knew he would put the pitch exactly where he wanted it. So I was playing off third base towards shortstop. That's what gave me a chance to make the play. Now, here's the power of negative thinking: As I dove for the ball, I'm thinking there is no fucking way I'm catching this thing. But I extended my body as far as I could and the ball shoots into my glove. . . ."

**Bobby Richardson:** ". . . For any other third baseman, the play probably ends there. Great stop, but a man on first with an infield hit. Somehow Clete comes up with the ball, springs to his knees, and throws Dick out by three steps. It wasn't even close. . . ."

**Dick Gernert (major-league first baseman, 1952–62; reserve first base-man/pinch hitter, 1961 Cincinnati Reds):** "The reason he got me by so much is because I messed up. When that ball left my bat I was so certain that it was a base hit, I took my time getting out of the batter's box instead of busting it. I didn't think there was any way anyone would come up with that ball hit where it was. Years later, when I became the farm director for the New York Mets, I made it a point to tell every player that they had to run full out on every play. I learned a lesson that day. . . ."

**Bobby Richardson:** "Brooks Robinson was a great defensive third baseman and perhaps he would have gotten to that ball. But I don't believe he or any other third baseman could have thrown out Gernert. To be able to get so much behind a throw from your knees, that's a gift. Brooks didn't have an arm anywhere near as strong as Clete's. No third baseman did. . . ."

**Jim Brosnan:** ". . . There wasn't anyone in our league like Boyer, not with those reflexes and that arm! Impressive. Nothing I saw of the rest of that team indicated they had any weaknesses in the field. Even Yogi in left might have been a displaced catcher, but you could see he knew what he was doing out there.

"And everyone on that team, with the exception of Howard, Skowron, and Blanchard, could run. Not just fast runners, but smart. I don't think our outfielders threw out any of them trying to take an extra base. Oh wait, Pinson got Yogi at the plate when he tried to score after Skowron singled off my knee. I'm sure Yogi was thrown out only because he was so concerned about my condition. How could I forget that, the ball nearly crippled me.

"Moose was another surprise for us. We had no idea what a fine hitter he was. Our scouting report said he was a high-fastball hitter. You could get him out with off-speed pitches or breaking pitches down. Forget that. He hit everything we threw, no matter where we threw it or how fast. Hit it hard all over the stadium."

**Bud Daley:** "The reason we ran the bases the way we did was our scouts. Their report on Cincinnati said if you hit a ball in the hole a bit in the outfield, take the extra base because their outfielders never hit the cutoff man. I know of three doubles we had that should have been held to singles because they missed that throw to second base. Good throws and our guys were out. So it just wasn't the team on the field that beat you. The whole organization was devoted to winning. . . ."

**Jim Brosnan:** "Our club, on the other hand, was pretty one-dimensional. Slumps weren't rare for us. The only reason we won the pennant was because the Braves and Dodgers had worse slumps than we did as the pennant race wore down. It was common for us to go through periods when our lineup didn't hit at all. Cincinnati was a free-swinging team, lots of power, but no speed outside of Vada [Pinson], Frank [Robinson], and Don Blasingame. When our big boppers went cold, they went ice cold.

"Defensively, Pinson was outstanding in center. Frank Robinson was a decent right fielder who played hard all the time. But Gene Freese was at third and Gordon Coleman was at first. Not much range there. Wally Post and Jerry Lynch shared left field. Both ideal designated hitters. Let me put it to you this way: We had two second basemen, two left fielders, and two shortstops dividing time and we could have used all six of them playing simultaneously. I'm still not sure they would have covered all the ground they needed to.

"So it was a mismatch. I had two moments of glory. I pitched a scoreless eighth inning in the first game when we were only two runs down. And I struck out Maris on a 3–2 change in Game Five. I had a good change, would throw it anytime in the count. Roger just stood there staring at me like he'd been violated. Wouldn't leave the plate. He hadn't seen my change before, and he was stunned I would throw it at that point in the count. Swung right through it, too, a good pitch low and away.

"Years later, I was writing a series of children's books called *Little League to Big League* and I interviewed Roger for it. He didn't remember my name at first. Most of the Yankees wouldn't remember our names, because they didn't see us for very long. Finally, it dawned on him who I was and he said, 'You . . . you fuck . . . you threw that change-up to me 3 and 2 in a World Series game!' He pretended he was still upset. Then he laughed and gave me a good interview. Still, I thought it interesting he remembered that pitch.

"But I guess there wasn't much else to remember about that Series. His team ran us out of the stadium even though Mantle hardly played. Just before the Series started, the trainer stuck him with a dirty needle, gave him a shot that became infected. He was out of the Series after the first game.

"So the Yankees lose their best player, play three games in a park where we know every pitch their pitchers are going to throw, and they still crushed us. That was a team that could destroy your confidence. Just before the final game of the World Series, there were at least eight suitcases already packed, four of them by our regulars. They knew it would be over that day and we were going home. When Hutch found out I was doing that piece for *SI*, he said, 'Just be kind.'"

## "THOSE YANKEE FANS NEVER MADE ME FEEL LIKE I LET THEM DOWN. . . ."

*That's how Ralph Terry recalls the reception he received from the New York sporting crowd in the aftermath of the Mazeroski home run. The boos and catcalls fans often used to express their disappointment in a player's perfomance, Terry hardly ever heard any of those. Instead, he was met by a family's applause, tender and accepting, the first time he stepped onto the Yankee Stadium diamond in 1961; he rarely did anything on the mound over the next two seasons to stifle those cheers. 16–3 in '61, 23–12 in 1962, Terry ascended into the elite class of major-league hurlers once Yankee pitching coach Johnny Sain convinced him to abandon his off-speed curve, a slop-drop breaking ball so slothful, hitters could read whole passages of Faulkner before it arrived at the plate to be pounded into the distance.*

*In its place, Terry and his mentor substituted a slider that signaled fast-ball to the batter right up to that moment when it sidled from the hitting zone to dart unmolested into the catcher's glove.*

*Terry finished the 1962 season widely heralded as the best pitcher in the American League. A satisfying designation, but he craved something beyond the kudos. Déjà vu with a twist, another Game Seven, one more shot at risking heartbreak in October, that's what this right-hander was looking for:*

**Ralph Terry:** "I knew that I did the best I could with what I had against Mazeroski that day, and professional ballplayers understand that no one pitch or play loses a ball game. But a loss like that hurts, your first reaction is to take a lot of the blame on yourself. You just have to move on or you're finished. The reaction of the New York fans was tremendous. If they had booed me every time I came out, it might have been difficult putting it behind me. Winning all those games in '61 and '62 helped a lot, but of course I was hoping for a second chance to prove myself. But that's something you can't control. You can't allow something like that to eat at you. Very few people get second chances at anything in this life. You have to be pretty lucky to get another shot."

*Luck and the elements combined to give Terry the opportunity he desired in 1962. He entered the World Series against the San Francisco Giants that year slotted behind Whitey Ford in Ralph Houk's pitching rotation. Ford won the Series opener in San Francisco on October 4. Terry lost Game Two, 2–0, the following afternoon. He came back to beat the Giants, 5–3, on October 10 in Yankee Stadium to put New York ahead in the Series, three games to two.*

*Terry's win should have been his final start of the year, except the weather intervened. When the Giants and Yankees returned to the West Coast for Game Six, Hurricane Frieda greeted them with a downpour so heavy it would have sent Noah scurrying to find his travel agent. Both teams sat idle through three days of rain. The San Francisco manager still believes the delay favored the opposition:*

**Alvin Dark (manager, 1962 San Francisco Giants):** "That downpour cost us, because the Yankee pitching staff was a little thin after those games in New York. In Game Three at Yankee Stadium [October 7] , Felipe Alou hit a line drive off [Yankee pitcher] Bill Stafford's [right] leg. Stafford finished that game and beat us [3–2], but he could barely walk off the mound when it was over. He was out for the rest of the Series. The very next day, we lost Juan Marichal when he hurt his hand in a game we won [7–3]. So both teams were short one starter.

"But I thought that our staff was better fixed to handle that loss. With Marichal out, I still had Jack Sanford, Billy Pierce, and Billy O'Dell, who I had been using as an extra left-hander in the bullpen. We also had Bob Bolin in the bullpen, and he had been a successful starter for us.

"When the Series resumed [on October 15], Billy Pierce made his normal start. That should have been Stafford's start. Because of the delay, Whitey Ford was able to pitch in his place and we beat him. Had we continued play on October 12, the way we were scheduled to, Ford still could have started in place of Stafford. He would have been pitching on three days' rest, which was not abnormal for Whitey. But Ralph Terry would not have been able to pitch Game Seven the next day [October 13], not after beating us on October tenth. Who could the Yankees have started?"

**Ralph Houk:** ". . . Now that we've gone over my options, there's no question that without that rain, I had a difficult decision to make. Ford, Terry, and Stafford would have been unavailable. Two of my other starters, Rollie Sheldon and Jim Coates, did not have good years in 1962 and I preferred using Coates in long relief.

"Bud Daley was an excellent spot starter for us, but he was left-handed and the Giants' power, with Mays, Cepeda, and Alou, was mostly right-handed. So I probably would have started [Jim] Bouton. Bouton was a rookie and, yes, he did pitch only .500 [7–7] that year, but he was solid down the stretch for us. You know he wasn't afraid of pitching pressure games; he later proved that in the World Series in

1963 and '64. Knowing his makeup, I would have been comfortable starting him. You have to remember Terry couldn't have pitched, but Jack Sanford pitched against Ralph in Game Five, so he wouldn't have been able to start, either, and he pitched great ball against us . . ."

**Alvin Dark:** ". . . but we would have started Billy O'Dell in that game and he was a nineteen-game winner that year, while Bouton wasn't established yet. You also have to keep in mind that Jim hadn't pitched that whole Series so he hadn't pitched in a game for at least two weeks. What kind of control would he have had? I would have liked our chances with that matchup. Instead, we got all that rain and Ralph Terry in Game Seven. . . ."

*Terry was overpowering that afternoon in Candlestick Park. His fastball and slider carried more octane than usual and his control was unerring: Through the first eight innings, Terry allowed no runs, no walks, and only two base hits. He never threw as many as two consecutive balls to a single Giants batter. Meanwhile, his teammates could do little with San Francisco starter Jack Sanford or reliever Billy O'Dell. One run was all New York could muster against them, and that had scored on a bases-loaded double play. Giants second baseman Chuck Hiller was the middleman on the twin-killing:*

**Chuck Hiller (major-league infielder, 1961–68; second baseman, 1962 San Francisco Giants):** "That was in the fifth inning with Skowron on third [Boyer on second, Terry on first]. We started the play when [Tony Kubek] hit a sharp grounder to [Jose] Pagan at short. Perhaps in a later inning, Jose tries to cut down Skowron at home. Moose wasn't very fast. But bases loaded, nobody out, this early, if we could give up just one run in that inning we'd be happy. So we gave no thought to getting Skowron. Terry had pitched well against us in both of his other starts, but he wasn't overpowering in either game. Don't get me wrong, he had excellent stuff—he didn't win 23 games by accident that year—and great control. You just didn't think of him as the type of pitcher who was going to shut us down completely. We had a great-hitting ball club. I think we led the league in home runs that year, led the majors in runs scored, and that's with Pagan and I hitting barely ten home runs between us. We never dreamed the Yankees could beat us with only one run."

*But Terry maintained his 1–0 lead into the bottom of the ninth. San Francisco pinch hitter Matty Alou led off the bottom of that inning with a bunt single. Now each Giant batter loomed at the plate a potential Mazeroski, able to forever tarnish Terry and his teammates' season with one swing. Terry responded to that threat by striking out Felipe Alou and Chuck Hiller. As Terry dried his fingers on the rosin bag, into the batter's box came that king of one-swing knockouts, the National League home-run leader, Willie Howard Mays. Most pitchers knew the best way to pitch to Willie was not to pitch to him at all. Terry, though, had a plan:*

**Ralph Terry:** "You didn't want to throw Willie too many sliders unless they are down and away, because that pitch moves away from him. If it's up, he can get his arms extended to drive the ball. You have to jam him with fastballs that cut in on him so if he swings you're moving away from the fat part of the bat. Saw off his handle. You also don't want to give him any fastballs up in the strike zone. I don't care if you throw harder than Nolan Ryan, he'll murder you there. I threw him two fastballs that moved to the inside part of the plate, close pitches that the umpire called balls. My next pitch was a fastball outside, but low and away, a good spot against a right-handed power hitter. But this is Willie Mays. He opened up his stance and drove that ball the other way, towards the right-field corner. Great piece of hitting. I'm thinking tie ball game and who knows, if the ball skips past Roger [Maris], the way Willie runs, maybe it's a triple. But Roger cut the ball off [on a bounce] and came up throwing all in one motion. . . ."

**Bobby Richardson:** "Roger had a great arm, but he had strained it during the second half of that season and wasn't throwing as well as usual. I had been compensating for that by hustling towards right field on relays. When I got out there this time, Roger hit me with a picture-perfect relay. Roger's accuracy made the play, because I didn't have to lunge for the ball at all. I was able to quickly wheel and throw home. . . ."

**Clete Boyer:** ". . . Bobby threw a seed to Ellie [Howard] for a strike. A hell of a play, but look at the films from that game. Matty Alou should have scored standing up. I saw the whole thing and as the ball was coming in, I'm thinking, 'Screw it, the game is tied.' But the third-base coach held Alou up, a mistake in our favor. I would have sent Alou and the game would have been tied, because there was no way we would have nailed him. . . ."

*Instead the score remained 1–0 with two men out and runners on second and third. Left-handed hitter Willie McCovey was scheduled to bat next for the Giants. In only 229 at-bats, the outfielder had hit 20 home runs while slugging .590 and compiling a .372 on-base percentage. McCovey was particularly productive against right-handed power pitchers, and he had already solved Terry twice in this series for long balls—a home run in Game Two and a triple in the seventh inning of this very game. So when Ralph Houk jogged to the pitcher's mound while McCovey took his practice cuts, the manager in the Giants dugout was already anticipating his next move:*

**Alvin Dark:** ". . . I figured Ralph had to pull Terry. That's what I would have done. Right away I'm trying to figure out what left-hander the Yankees could bring in so I could counter with a right-handed hitter. New York had Marshall Bridges and Bud Daley in the bullpen. I probably would have gone with Harvey Kuenn, especially against Bridges, who could be a little wild. Harvey was a terrific contact hitter, a veteran not too likely to overswing or offer at a bad pitch. Not a home-run hitter, but he was capable of getting an extra-base hit to drive in both runs. He was the perfect man for that spot . . ."

**Ralph Houk:** ". . . except I never had any intention of taking Ralph out. He still looked strong to me. I knew Kuenn would probably come up if I had brought in a left-hander to face McCovey. Now I would have been stuck with a left-handed reliever facing a dangerous right-handed hitter. We could have intentionally walked Kuenn, but then I would have to bring in a right-hander to face the next man, Orlando Cepeda, who was also right-handed . . ."

*Cepeda was one of the National League's most prolific sluggers. Over the previous five seasons he had averaged 32 home runs with 110 RBI. The Yankee scouts considered him the Giants' deadliest hitter with runners in scoring position.*

**Ralph Houk:** ". . . so I liked the matchup of Terry and McCovey better than any other combination. Ralph was probably the best pitcher in our league that year. I trusted him enough that I just wanted to know his preference. A manager is going to have his own idea about what he wants a pitcher to do in a situation like that, but you have to make sure the pitcher is comfortable doing it or it won't work out. . . ."

**Ralph Terry:** "When Ralph asked me what I wanted to do, I told him to forget about walking McCovey. The day before, Cepeda had gotten three hits [and two RBI]. At the time, McCovey was a young player who hadn't done that much yet. Cepeda was the established RBI man. In that situation, I'm more worried about a base hit scoring two runs than the home run. The only reason you might pitch around McCovey is that you get a force play at every base, but it wasn't worth the risk. I knew if I walked McCovey, the bases were loaded, we're in the Giants' ballpark with all their fans going wild, and there's a National League umpire behind the plate. Not an ideal spot.

"I also remembered how the Giants had gotten into this World Series. They had beaten the Dodgers in a playoff by scoring the go-ahead run on a bases-loaded walk. That had happened only a week before, so it was still fresh in my mind. Some of those balls the umpire called on [Dodger pitcher] Stan Williams were pretty close, he could have called them strikes, so I didn't want to take any chances. With the bases loaded in a one-run game, so many things can go wrong. An infield hit scores the run, a hit batter, a walk, passed ball. I just thought it was better to pitch to McCovey. . . ."

**Ralph Houk:** ". . . as soon as Ralph told me what he wanted to do, I reminded him, 'This kid is probably going to be hungry, he's going to try to win the ball game. Pitch him away the best you can and don't give him anything to hit down the middle,' then I went back to the dugout. . . ."

**Bobby Richardson:** "When I saw what we were going to do, I was somewhat surprised by the decision. The base was open. The runner on second was the winning run, so McCovey's run didn't count. Conventional wisdom says you don't pitch to the left-handed power hitter there. But I believe you put yourself in a big hole when you load the bases and try to pitch too carefully to the next hitter. You have no room to maneuver if you fall behind the batter. You pretty much have to give him something fat to swing at, and if there's a base hit, game over. So I was with both Ralphs on this. I thought, 'Make McCovey hit your pitch. If you walk him, fine, we're still ahead, then we'll deal with the next hitter.' . . ."

**Clete Boyer:** "I was the only infielder who came to the mound for that meeting, because I had this bad feeling. I figured Terry would intentionally walk McCovey to load the bases and pitch to Cepeda. I'd had a good Series to that point. . . ."

**Billy O'Dell (major-league pitcher, 1954–67; pitcher, 1962 San Francisco Giants):** ". . . yes, our scouting report said to pitch Clete outside and that was as wrong as could be. Every time we threw him an outside pitch, he hit it hard. He hit a home run off of me that put the Yankees ahead to stay in the first game . . ."

**Clete Boyer:** ". . . and I always wanted the ball hit to me. As far as I was concerned, I was the Ted Williams of defense. But now, all I could think was that Cepeda was then going to rake a grounder to me that would hit off my ankles or knees then bounce through into left field for a two-run single and the ball game. Or that I would field Cepeda's grounder and throw away the ball. The wind in Candlestick Park must have been blowing forty miles an hour, and even the most accurate throw could get carried into the dugout. Either way, if Cepeda got up I was going to be the goddamned goat. Honest to God, my knees started shaking thinking about it.

"McCovey, on the other hand, there was no fucking way he'd hit a hard grounder to me off Ralph. He was strictly a pull hitter back then. The best he could do on any ball hit my way would be to pop it up. So I was hoping Ralph would pitch to him. I swear, I didn't care if McCovey hit a three-run homer over the fucking scoreboard, I would have traded that rather than be the goat. When Ralph said he wanted McCovey I patted him on the back and said, 'Go get him, big guy!' . . ."

**Chuck Hiller:** ". . . which was just fine with us. The moment we saw Terry was going to pitch to Willie, everyone in our dugout thought the Yankees had just handed us a huge break. . . ."

**Billy O'Dell:** ". . . I didn't know if it was a break or not, because I assumed Ralph wouldn't give McCovey anything good to hit and we'd have to start all over again with Cepeda. McCovey had hit the ball hard off Ralph all Series, so why face him. . . ."

**Ralph Terry:** "I'm sure the Giants thought I was crazy, the way Willie had already hit me, but I felt good. My plan was to go right after him with good stuff around the strike zone, high and tight, low and away . . ."

**Willie McCovey (major-league first baseman/outfielder, 1959–80; outfielder, 1962 San Francisco Giants):** ". . . but I came up figuring I'm not going to see anything close to a strike here. I expected Terry to try to get me to swing at a bad pitch, which is the worst approach a hitter can take. . . ."

**Alvin Dark:** "Isn't that something to find out forty years later? Had I known that, I would have called time and told Willie to look for Terry to make good pitches. As a manager, I didn't believe in pitching around a hitter in that situation. How many Juan Marichals or Whitey Fords are there, pitchers who can put the ball exactly where they want to 99 percent of the time? You might intend to throw a pitch outside the strike zone but still get it in the wrong spot, someplace the hitter can get the fat part of the bat on it. And with a man on third, there's always the chance that a pitch off the plate will get away from the catcher. I always told my pitchers, If you don't want to pitch to someone, walk him intentionally. Don't fool around nibbling at the strike zone. So I would have assumed Terry would be thinking the same thing. . . ."

**Willie McCovey:** ". . . well, it was my mistake, because that first pitch from Ralph was a breaking ball, low and away, but over the plate. I was so surprised that Terry threw a strike, he caught me off balance. I jumped at the pitch and pulled it just a little too much . . ."

**Bobby Richardson:** ". . . Willie hit this looping fly ball down the right-field line. When it left his bat I thought Roger had a chance to catch it. I forgot for a moment that this was Candlestick Park. Those swirling crosswinds carried the ball deep into the seats, but foul . . ."

**Willie McCovey:** ". . . and that was the ball game right there, that pitch. If I hadn't been so surprised and overeager, I might have hit that ball out fair . . ."

**Ralph Terry:** ". . . instead, it was strike one. Now that I've got him looking outside, I wanted to come inside on Willie hard so he can't open up those arms. I put everything I had into that fastball, it might have been the hardest pitch I threw all day . . ."

**Willie McCovey:** ". . . and right before Terry threw that pitch, Richardson moved over a step to his right at second base . . ."

**Bobby Richardson:** ". . . oh, everybody says and writes that, but I didn't change my position a step. McCovey was a left-handed pull hitter and I had moved over to play him in the hole before Terry threw his first pitch. In fact, that was pretty much where I played Willie the whole Series. I didn't have to take another step when Ralph threw him that second pitch . . ."

**Willie McCovey:** ". . . I'm sure Ralph wanted to jam me with that fast-ball, but it stayed over the plate and I was right on it. I don't think I could have hit that ball any harder . . ."

**Chuck Hiller:** ". . . if he gets under that ball, it goes 450 feet and out of the park. But instead the ball stayed down on a line towards the middle of the infield. Our home dugout was angled so that when Willie first hit that ball it looked like a sure base hit, we all thought the game was over and we'd won. It took a moment to realize that Richardson had got his glove on that ball . . ."

**Bobby Richardson:** "It was certainly the hardest-hit ball I've ever caught. Mickey [Mantle], batting right-handed, was one of the few players strong enough to hit a ball like that, with all that overspin. You hit the top of the ball, it starts out high, then comes straight down. It looked like a sure base hit when it left Willie's bat, but it was not really a difficult chance. It came right to me on a line and I caught it chest high. Over the years, people have made it out to be a more difficult play than it was . . ."

**Ralph Terry:** ". . . well, it was a great play, as far as I was concerned. When I came off the mound with that win, I couldn't have been hap-pier, pitching the clinching game of the Series for my teammates. Happy and relieved. I realized at that moment just how much of a burden the Mazeroski home run had been, how I'd been carrying it around with me for two years. When I got McCovey out, the monkey was finally off my back."

## KKKKKKKKKKKKKKK—KOUFAX!

*N*ew York fairly swaggered through the summer of '63, notching 104 victories while scoring 714 runs and winning the American League pennant by 10½ games. 104 . . . 714 . . . 10½ . . . *impressive figures all, but who remembers them? Only one number comes to mind when most recall that team and that season—15. That's how many Bombers went down on strikes as they lost to Los Angeles Dodger left-hander Sandy Koufax in the opening game of the 1963 World Series at Yankee Stadium.*

*What could it have been like that afternoon for those helpless, flailing Yankee batters? Like trying to hit pure thought or mist? Or rage? Yes, that was it. Sandy Koufax's fastball had all the force and velocity of that emotion. A living, punishing thing, it screamed at hitters as it flashed towards home plate to disarm and disrupt.*

*Dismantle.*

**Whitey Ford:** "There weren't too many left-handers who could give Mickey as much trouble as Sandy did. Koufax was very fast in both games he pitched against us, but not as fast as you might think. I had played with at least two guys who threw harder than Sandy—Bob Turley and Ryne Duren, although Duren was a reliever and only had to throw hard for two or three innings at a time. Herb Score was probably faster. But Sandy had a terrific curve to go with that great fastball. It would start high, look like it was going to be a ball, then roll off the table. Batters would give up on it. If you were left-handed, he could start it at your chin and it would break over the plate. I blame myself for losing that first game to him [5–2]. John Roseboro hit a fly ball 297 feet down the right-field line for a three-run homer. That was a bad pitch by me, a hanging curve . . ."

**Jim Bouton:** "I have to disagree with Whitey's assessment of Sandy. I've never seen a pitcher before or since who was faster than Koufax. But the reason I think Whitey said what he did is that Koufax's motion was so deceptive, so beautifully smooth, it didn't look like he was throwing that hard. There was no effort to it. You ever watch one of those jumbo jetliners coming in? They are enormous, but they move just as fast or even faster than those smaller planes. Only you can't tell that by watching them, because the jumbo jets are so majestic and smooth.

"That was Koufax's delivery. It lulled you so his fastball seemed to arrive at the plate much faster than you thought it would. I mean, Mickey from the right side was an awesome hitter, especially if you threw him a fastball. Koufax could throw him three fastballs chest high and Mickey was behind and under every single one of them. That, to me, is the best indication of how hard he was throwing. . . ."

**Bobby Richardson:** "His fastball looked like a rocket taking off. You don't hear anything about his change-up, but it was devastating, because it looked just like his fastball until you swung. Whitey told you about his curveball. In that first game, Sandy had Yankee Stadium's center-field background with all those white shirts to throw out of. That was too much. On that day, he was the best I've ever seen. I was a contact hitter, didn't strike out very much, but I struck out the first time I faced him.

"The second time up, I was trying to be a first-ball hitter. He was throwing strikes, so I thought, 'Don't be fancy, just jump on that first good pitch.' I struck out again. When I struck out the third time, I walked by Mantle, who was coming into the on-deck circle. He said, 'There's no use my even going up there.' Did we score two runs off him that day? Amazing. I can't remember how we did that. . . ."

**Tom Tresh (major-league shortstop/outfielder, 1962–69; left fielder, 1963 New York Yankees):** "We got those two runs in the first game when I hit a home run off Sandy in the eighth when we were already down by five. Honestly, you can't say I had good luck against him, because he also struck me out three times. His stuff was so overpowering, I came away feeling he was the most dominating player I'd ever faced.

"My strategy against Sandy was pretty simple. Early on I realized I couldn't hit his curveball, so I eliminated that. I also couldn't hit his change-up unless I was looking for it. Hard as he threw, if you went up there looking for a change, you were crazy. So I eliminated that. I figured my only chance was to keep looking fastball and hope I could catch up to one.

"What made Sandy special, I think, was the way his fastball rose. Not too many guys had fastballs that could do that. Dick Radatz, the reliever for Boston they called the Monster, had a fastball like that. Denny McLain, the year he won 31 for the Tigers. But you can't name too many others. You know, we used to talk about the high hard one. Then the strike zone got lower. Up until this season [2001] when the umpires are supposed to call the high strike again, there hasn't been a high hard one for nearly twenty years. You could lay off any pitch above your waist.

"But back in 1963 there was a high hard one and Koufax had the best. You had to swing at that fastball of his that started at your armpits, because that was a strike. But it seemed to pick up velocity on the way to the plate—which is scientifically impossible—and end up around your neck. He made hitters swinging at that pitch look ridiculous.

"Now you might say, Why not take that pitch if you know it will shoot out of the strike zone? It's not that easy. No matter how you try, you can't lay off that ball with two strikes on you because not every one of his fastballs rose like that and there was no guarantee he would throw it. If Sandy was 2 and 0 on you, you could look for the fastball. And he might still blow it by you. But at 0 and 2, 1 and 2, which he seemed to be that whole game, you had no clue. With me, he might throw the curve in the dirt, waste a change, or throw the fastball because he figures I'm looking for something off-speed.

"And if he had to throw a curveball for a strike, he could overmatch you with it. That breaking ball of his came straight down. That's difficult to handle, because it doesn't stay in your hitting plane very long. Compare that to the average curve that cuts across the strike zone. You have more time to get the fat part of the bat on that. Of course, Sandy was human. He couldn't have been as sharp as he looked against us every time he took the mound. My God, no one would have hit him."

*As Tresh noted, Koufax wasn't perfect in 1963. He had lost all of five games while winning 25 and leading the major leagues in ERA (1.88), strikeouts (306), and shutouts (11). The National League batted just .189 against him. Jim Bouton claimed Koufax's delivery was so flawless, it lulled hitters at the plate. The left-hander's domination was often so complete, it could lull his teammates as well:*

**Tommy Davis (major-league outfielder/designated hitter/third baseman, 1959–76; left fielder/third baseman, 1963 Los Angeles Dodgers):** "Koufax was a joy to play behind when he was at his peak, because every time he went out was as good as an automatic win. But it was almost as tough to play behind Sandy as it was to hit him. He had games when he was so unhittable, you became lax. In the outfield, you would kneel down, then get set. He strikes a batter out, you do it again. Then he pops somebody up. You do it again. After a while you have to remind yourself to get set because you don't think anyone is ever going to hit a ball to you!

"One game, I was back on my heels when Henry Aaron hit a line drive over my head that I should have caught. I was so embarrassed, I wouldn't go back to the dugout when the inning was over. I just sat out in the bullpen. But that's what could happen playing behind Sandy. After a while you became a fan, just watching him mow guys down, and it was difficult to remember that you still had to do your duty.

"Sandy's curve in that first game of the Series was as good as I'd ever seen it, which is why he dominated the Yankees. It was the kind of curve that could fool the umpire as well as the hitter. From left field, I'd see Sandy throw a curveball that would start out over guys' heads and Roseboro would catch it below the guy's knees. The umpire would call it a ball. I'd say to myself, 'How could that be a ball if it started above the batter's head and ended at his knees? It had to go through the strike zone someplace.' But the umps didn't call too many balls on Sandy in that Series. He put the ball where he wanted it on nearly every pitch."

**Phil Linz (major-league infielder, 1962–68; reserve infielder, New York Yankees, 1962–65):** "I got a pinch-hit single off Koufax in the final game of the 1963 World Series and considered that a great moral victory. As a right-handed fastball hitter, I felt very comfortable against him. But I think he was practicing voodoo out there. Sandy threw right over the top, so smooth there was nothing deceptive about his motion. I got a really good look at the ball as it left his hand. God, it was a like a softball, it looked so big. But as it approached the plate, so help me I'm not crazy, the ball got smaller. A fastball is supposed to lose speed as it approaches the plate. Well, with Sandy, you'd see the ball good, swear you had the fastball timed, then during the last ten feet, whoosh! The ball just took off. I saw that and thought, 'Oh, shit, this is not quite what I expected!'

"He's bringing it up there in the high 90s, maybe hitting 100 miles per hour on some fastballs, throwing strikes whenever and wherever he wants to, and he had that curve. What set Sandy's curve apart from most pitchers' is that you couldn't pick it up. It looked like a fastball all the way until it came to the plate chest high. You're ready to swing and boom! it drops out of sight. And it just didn't drop sharply into the dirt, it was strike three at the knees. Tom told you he went up there looking for a particular pitch because he was a good hitter. But guys like me, I just went up there looking for the ball. What else could you do?"

*Not much, not against Koufax or a Dodger pitching staff that doled out hits and runs to the Yankees as grudgingly as Dickens's Master ladled gruel to Oliver Twist. Over the next three games, Johnny Podres, Don Drysdale, and Koufax, making his second Series start, limited New York to two runs on a paltry 16 base hits. Los Angeles's starters encountered so little resistance from the opposition, Dodger manager Walter Alston used only one relief pitcher—left-hander Ron Perranoski—for a single inning's work in the entire Series. That bullpen call came in the ninth inning of the second game, a 4–1 loss that left the Yankees feeling like rubes flummoxed by a three-card-monte sharp:*

**Jim Bouton:** "Looking back, it was that second game that Johnny Podres beat us that drove the stake through our hearts. I don't really know why [Podres won]. If we had played three more games that series, Koufax and Drysdale may have done the same thing against us each time out; but we would have gotten to Podres, I'm sure of it. We certainly hit him hard enough, but nothing dropped in. . . ."

**Tom Tresh:** "I'll tell you how crafty Podres was, I don't even remember facing him in that Series. . . ."

**Bobby Richardson:** "I can't tell you how he got us out, don't recall the game he pitched at all. All I remember is Koufax and Drysdale. . . ."

**Ralph Houk:** "Oh, you better believe I remember him. What can you say, Podres was a pitcher's pitcher, a veteran. He didn't need a great fastball to get people out. He was throwing strikes, changing location and speeds beautifully. And he kept coming up with a little something extra when we got men on base. It was frustrating to watch from the dugout, because my memory is that we hit him hard, but the Dodgers kept catching the ball. I agree if we faced him again, we probably would have adjusted. . . ."

**Tommy Davis:** "Fine, but he would have adjusted, too. Johnny was smart and had a great change-up, the best ever, and the Yankees knew that. But I don't think they knew how great his curveball was, and he got a lot of key outs with it. Our pitching made us tough that whole Series, because, with all our speed on the bases, our team was built to do the little things that could win low-scoring games.

"Give you an example. In that second game with Podres pitching, Maury [Wills] led off the first inning with a single. Now he's moving off first, trying to get a good lead so he can steal second against Elston Howard, who everyone knew had a strong throwing arm.

"Junior Gilliam comes to the plate and having him in your starting lineup was like having a manager on the field. He was always thinking about how he could beat you. With Maury on, Junior set up so deep in the batter's box, the catcher would have to back off home plate just a bit. Now he has to make a longer throw to second. On close plays that can make a difference. Maury stole second, then moved to third on Junior's single. And Junior went to second when the Yankees tried to make a play on Maury at third. Willie Davis drove them both in. Right there, we had all the runs we needed to win that day. That's good, smart baseball."

**Phil Linz:** "Just starting Podres in Game Two, I think, was smart baseball. When you think of the Dodgers from that time, what do you think of? Koufax and Drysdale. You would have figured Alston to open the Series with his two main horses. Koufax starts Game One, so he can pitch three games if it goes seven, but if you start Drysdale in Game Two and you have a rainout, you might be able to bring him back for a third start if you have to, or use him a few innings in relief in a seventh game.

"Instead, Alston sandwiched Podres between Koufax and Drysdale. Give the manager some credit for this. If you wanted to beat the Yankees, you had to keep a fastball-hitting team like ours off balance. What I remember is how slow Johnny threw compared to Sandy and Don. It makes a big difference to face someone overpowering like Sandy, then, the very next day, face a guy whose ball you have to wait for. Some of those fastballs, you thought they'd never arrive at home plate. Podres just screwed up our timing. And then Drysdale, who threw everything hard, looked that much faster in Game Three. Don just shut us down. . . ."

*Los Angeles's hitters needed that kind of superlative effort, with the Yankees pitchers holding them to ten runs in four games and only three runs in the final two. But that was enough for the Dodgers to win the World Series four games to none as an offensive tide barely six inches deep swept away New York.*

**Jim Bouton:** "I drew Drysdale in Game Three and he was awesome that day, unhittable. In many ways as impressive as Koufax. Don's ball had tremendous movement, the way it would come not just up and in, but way in. He started a fastball on me that looked like it was coming down the middle of the plate. By the time I swung, it nearly hit me in the elbow, it had sailed in on me so much. He was a big guy, six-six, 230 pounds or so, a horse. So he maintained his velocity deep into the game.

"Before that game started, I was sitting on the bench in the dugout, trying to catch my breath, because it is all pretty overwhelming. Ralph Terry, a great guy, came over to me and said, 'You nervous, kid?' I admitted I was. He said, 'Well, when you go out there just remember this: No matter what happens, win or lose, 500 million Chinese Communists don't give a shit!' That was great, really gave me some perspective. I thought, 'Hey, I'm pitching in the World Series. What could be better than this.'

"The Dodgers scored one run in the first inning. With two men out, Tommy Davis singled off Bobby's [Richardson] shin to drive in Junior Gilliam. I've kidded Tommy that it took two bad hops, one off the mound, one at second base, for that to count as a base hit. It was probably the weakest single of his career, he was such a good line-drive hitter. That was the only run they scored, and it was enough. I don't want this to sound pompous, but I think that was the best-pitched game of the Series on both ends. You have to remember, we scored two runs off of Sandy even though he struck out fifteen.

"I sometimes wondered what would have happened had I opened against Koufax and pitched the same game I pitched against Drysdale. We would have won 2–1 and opened the Series one game up instead of a game down. It might have made a difference. Now let's take the fantasy further. I didn't pitch another World Series game until I faced the Cardinals in 1964 and won that game while giving up only a run. If I pitch that same game against Koufax in Game Four of the World Series, maybe we win again 2–1 instead of losing by that score. Now I'm facing Sandy in Game Seven. . . . If only there were an alternative universe."

*Fittingly, it was Koufax who ended the Yankees' season with a 2–1 Series-clinching win against Whitey Ford on October 6. While his pitches may have lacked the giddyap they demonstrated in Game One, Koufax earned even greater respect from at least one Yankee pitcher by proving himself to be resourceful as well as physically gifted:*

**Steve Hamilton (major-league pitcher, 1961–72; pitcher, New York Yankees, 1963–70):** "He had to be tired by that game. You know he pitched a lot of innings [311] during the season and was on three days' rest. So he couldn't have been throwing as hard, and at Dodger Stadium Sandy couldn't throw out of those white shirts in center field like he could in our ballpark, so our hitters got a better look at the ball.

"Koufax compensated for all that with control that was even better than the first game [Koufax had walked three batters in Game One; none in Game Four as he struck out eight]. I really admired the way he worked with what he had. He put our hitters behind in the count all day and mixed in a few more curveballs. It's not often you find a power pitcher who can improvise that way when his fastball might be a bit off. Mind you, he was still throwing harder than just about anyone else around. I couldn't throw that hard with a full season's rest. But you could see that day how Sandy was a pitcher, not just a thrower."

*After the sweep, Mickey Mantle said, "I don't care if the Dodgers beat us ten straight, I know we still have the better team." Most of Mantle's teammates did not share his bravado. New York's postgame clubhouse was a mortuary, and at least one Yankee who didn't play a single inning during the Series later explained how embarrassed the drubbing had left him:*

**Bud Daley:** "The way Koufax and the Dodgers beat us four straight, that's humiliating even when the games are close. I had a hand in losing that Series even though I didn't play. I was supposed to be the closer in 1963. Opening day Whitey gets in trouble in the ninth, I come in to get us out without surrendering a run. But I don't think I warmed up enough or maybe I strained something during the game. The next day I woke up with an elbow swollen so bad, I was through for the season.

"The Yankees sent me back home to Long Beach, California. When it looked like we'd be playing the Dodgers in the Series, Ralph Houk called, asking me to scout them. One report I sent said, 'Play Tommy Davis to pull, he never hits the ball to right field.' Third inning, first game, Davis singles to right. Two innings later, he gets an infield hit to second base. Then he singles to right again. Game Two, second time up, he hits the chalk line in right field for a triple. That pretty much took care of my career as a scout. . . ."

**Whitey Ford:** "Before we played the Dodgers, I asked Stan Williams—he had pitched with Los Angeles the year before—how to pitch Frank Howard. He was the biggest home-run threat the Dodgers had, and right-handed. Stan said, 'He has trouble with high fastballs.' So I threw him a high fastball in the second inning of the first game, and Frank hits a line drive over Tony Kubek [at shortstop] that kept rising until it hit a loudspeaker in center field, over 450 feet away. Home run. When we get to Game Four, we're down three games to none and I'm facing Sandy again, Williams tells me Howard can't handle a slow curve. I throw him one of those in the fifth inning, he hits it into the upper deck for another home run. So I guess we had a lot of bad scouting reports that Series; maybe that's why we lost. . . ."

**Tommy Davis:** "Did Bud tell them I couldn't hit to right field? Well, thank you very much, Mr. Daley. To be fair, a scout who just sees you for a series or two is at a disadvantage, because he might catch you when you're not at your best. Every hitter goes through a period where he gets away from the things that make him successful. Who knows, maybe Bud saw me in some games when I wasn't handling the outside pitch, trying to pull balls I should have taken the other way. But that was a pitch I usually hit well. The Yankee pitchers must have listened to Bud, because in those first couple of games they did pitch me away.

"I remember the triple in Game Two—in fact, I hit two of them that day. The second one, to left center in the eighth inning, drove in Willie Davis with our third run. But that triple Bud mentioned that went down the right-field line might have been the more important hit, a real turning point, although we didn't get a run out of it. You know why? Because Roger Maris raced over trying to make a diving catch on it. His momentum carried him into the right-field fence so hard, he injured his left arm and wrist. Put him out for the Series.

"We won the last two games 1–0 and 2–1 and I don't think the guys who took Roger's place did very much. That was a big bat to lose. I am never happy to see anyone get injured on the ballfield; you know what happened to my career after I hurt my ankle. But I have to admit, his injury helped our pitchers, because now they only had to face half of the Mantle-and-Maris combination.

"You know in that series, Sandy, Don, Junior, Johnny Podres, John Roseboro, and I had all been part of the Dodger organization when the Yankees would beat Brooklyn every year. So we were up for those games, and when we won we felt we had won for Brooklyn as well as Los Angeles. I had an uncle who was a tremendous Yankee fan, so crazy about them that when Brooklyn beat New York in 1955, he left town. I razzed him a bit after we won those four straight, and I think he became a bit of a Dodger fan after that."

*Perhaps Tommy Davis's uncle was willing to swap his pinstripes for Dodger Blue. But one Yankee loyalist refused to surrender his allegiance even though he happened to be wearing the uniform of the winning side:*

**Moose Skowron:** "Everybody in our clubhouse was happy about winning, but I had a different reaction, like something I never experienced in baseball before. The Yankees had traded me to the Dodgers for Stan Williams after the 1962 season. I'd had a bad year with Los Angeles, but with Whitey starting Game One in Yankee Stadium, Mr. Alston wanted to get another righty in there.

"He figured I knew Whitey pretty good, so he put me in the lineup. I get a couple of hits, couple of RBI, and we win. Mr. Alston puts me out there again. I get two more hits, including a homer. He leaves me at first for the rest of the Series. I hit .385, we win four straight, and I was miserable. Miserable! Later on the radio, I said, 'I'd wish I was playing on the loser.' Hey, I was being honest. Sure, I was lucky to be on another World Series winner with all that great pitching. But twelve years I was with New York, three in the minors, nine in the majors. I loved those guys and it killed me to beat them. My uniform might have said Los Angeles. But, in my heart, I was always a Yankee."

## ROCKING OUT IN CHICAGO

*T*hree straight losses to open the 1964 season should have told the Yankees that the pennant race wasn't going to be a cakewalk. Instead of rolling over the opposition as it had only the year before, New York stutter-stepped through its early schedule, losing nearly as often as winning. Ralph Houk was no longer in the dugout to rally his sluggish troops. Shortly after the 1963 World Series, Houk had moved into the Yankee front office as general manager. Yogi Berra was the new skipper, and he displayed admirable calm as both the Baltimore Orioles and Chicago White Sox edged past New York in the standings. He kept reminding reporters that the club was hurting—injuries were indeed hampering Mantle, Maris, and Kubek—and that everything would be righted once his stars regained their health.

But nagging ailments weren't the only contributors to the Yankee malaise. Even the halest members of New York's offense were compiling dreadful statistics. The 1962 American League Rookie of the Year, Tom Tresh, was experiencing the sophomore jinx a year late. He would spend most of the summer searching for his batting rhythm from both sides of the plate. First baseman Joe Pepitone was hitting timely home runs but little else. His slugging average among regular first basemen was nearly the lowest in baseball—and his on-base percentage was minuscule. Dead men walked more often than Pepitone.

Second baseman Bobby Richardson would hit .267 that season, acceptable for a middle infielder back then. But it was an empty average. Richardson had little power, and the second baseman's .296 on-base percentage was the worst mark of any major-league leadoff hitter with 300 or more at-bats. Clete Boyer, still a defensive marvel at third base, and the balky-backed Kubek, were even less productive.

*An unreliable bullpen also troubled Berra. He spent most of the season trying to find a reliable closer, a search that wouldn't end until the Yankees acquired right-hander Pedro Ramos from the Cleveland Indians in a September trade. New York remained a contender only by the dint of its impeccable defense, superb starting pitching, and Elston Howard's consistent excellence both at bat and behind the plate. Once Mantle and Maris regained their health, they combined with Howard to give the Yankees their only reliable run producers.*

*Despite the offensive shortcomings, New York managed to string together enough wins in late July to climb into first place. On August 6, the Bombers played the first of fifteen consecutive games against their primary rivals, the White Sox and Orioles. This was the time for New York to at last pull away from the other contenders. Instead, the Yankees lost ten of those fifteen games, including the final four straight to the White Sox in Chicago.*

*The Yankees left Comiskey Park after the final game in that series a glum and sour group. Berra's team was in third place, four and half games behind the leaders. Chicago's streets were sweating tar, the urban huggermugger mauled the pedestrians' ears, but inside the team bus, all was quiet as ice. There was none of the usual postgame banter or pranks that the players relied on to numb the sting of losing. These Yankees were as lively as zombies, a club ready to tank. Someone had to cut through the despair. It was the perfect time for a fledgling musician to haul out his ax:*

**Phil Linz:** "Yeah, my debut as a performer. Not exactly Carnegie Hall, was it? I'd only had that harmonica for a few days. . . ."

**Tom Tresh:** "Okay, if we're going to talk about the harmonica incident, I guess it's time for me to confess that I had a hand in Phil getting that thing. Music is a big part of my life. When I joined the Yankees I already played guitar, and one day in Baltimore I decided to buy a good harmonica. After I got it, Tony Kubek started playing it along with me, then he'd borrow it to practice. Tony liked it so much I hardly ever got a chance to play it again. Finally, I said, 'When we get to Chicago, we're going to Marshall Field's department store and get you a harmonica of your own so I can get mine back.'

"We get to Chicago, and just as Tony and I are leaving the hotel for Marshall Field's, who do we run into? Phil Linz coming through the lobby. He asked us where we were going. We told him, and he offered to join us. Now, up to that point I don't think Phil had any interest in harmonicas . . ."

**Phil Linz:** ". . . and Tom's right, I just liked department stores. Jim Bouton and I loved hanging out in them because, well, it was a great place to pick up girls. You'd talk to them, let them know you were a ballplayer, then saw where it went. So I didn't wake up that morning thinking, 'Gee, I think I'll go out and buy a musical instrument today.'. . ."

**Tom Tresh:** ". . . but after we bought Kubek's harmonica—a Hohner—Tony started playing it in the store. He does a rendition of 'Streets of Laredo'—about the only song he knew all the way through up to that point—as we walk out of the music department. And he plays it pretty well. Everybody's listening and applauding. Phil thinks this is pretty cool, so he says, 'I want one for me.' We turn around, go back to the music department. Phil buys a harmonica and he's having a ball with it right away. . . ."

**Phil Linz:** ". . . When we got to the ballpark, I was pretty upset because I found out I wouldn't be playing against Chicago. This was a big series for us. Our team had been sluggish all summer, but now it's late August, when we usually pull away, and we're only a game out of first place. The White Sox and Orioles are in front of us, but if we take three out of four in Chicago, we have a good chance of leaving in first place or tied for the lead. Any ballplayer who doesn't want to get into a series like that shouldn't be playing.

"My strength at that time was hitting left-handed pitching. Chicago's best pitchers were Gary Peters and Juan Pizarro, both left-handers I handled pretty well. Kubek was having trouble hitting all season, so I figured to get at least a couple of starts that series. In fact, any trouble I had with Yogi started when I was supposed to start a game. I'm trotting out to the shortstop position when Yogi—I have no idea why he made this last-minute change—sent Tony out there instead and pulled me back. You just don't embarrass a player like that in front of people. Yogi had been a player long enough that he should have known that.

"That series in Chicago was a disaster. The White Sox kicked our asses four straight and the club is really down. We don't have that old confidence like we always had in the past. I think a lot of us on the bus were thinking this just wasn't our year. Things looked bleak.

"It would be nice to say I started playing the harmonica to cheer everyone up, but that wasn't the case. I really don't know why I started playing. Subconsciously, I suppose it was a defiant act, showing my resentment at Yogi for not playing me. But as soon as I started playing 'Mary Had a Little Lamb'—that was a learner song that came on the harmonica's instruction sheet—Yogi yelled for me to knock it off. Now, the story is that I didn't hear Yogi and that when I asked Mickey what he had said, Mickey yelled, 'Yogi wants you to play it louder.' All that did happen—Mickey loved to get things going—but the truth is, I had heard what Yogi said; I just pretended not to hear him.

"So I kept it up and here comes Yogi, steaming. Told me to shove the harmonica up my ass and then he threw it at me like he was making a throw from home plate to second. Hard. He even raised his arm as if to hit me, but he didn't. Just stormed back to the front of the bus. I probably should have let it drop, but my ass was burning. I stood up on my seat and hollered, 'Why are you picking on me? I'm putting out a hundred percent every time I play. You should be talking to some of these other guys on this club who aren't hustling.' [Third-base coach] Frankie Crosetti told me to shut up. I told him, 'Fuck you, Cro.'

"What made this a big deal—a bad move on my part, really—was that the baseball writers traveled with us back then. So when we get to Boston to play the Red Sox the next day, I wake up and what do I find? War headlines in all the newspapers—bold black print, three inches thick on the front page—describing the incident. You know, 'TURMOIL ON THE YANKEES!' Then I find out it's getting coverage like this all over the country. People start sending me boxes of harmonicas, corncob harmonicas, baseball-bat harmonicas. Fans are singing 'Mary Had a Little Lamb' in the stands as soon as they see me. They're throwing harmonicas on the field. Pretty wild.

"That night, I apologized to Yogi. He shook my hand and hugged me. It was all forgotten, but then he said, 'Phil, with all the writers there, I have to fine you. How much do you think it should be?' He actually asked me, which, I think, tells you that Yogi still wasn't comfortable being a disciplinarian. I said, 'You're the manager.' He suggested $250 and I agreed, because I knew I was wrong.

"We were friends after that. In fact, he played me more than ever. The most ironic thing about all this is that Yogi and I always got along before and after the harmonica thing. On the Yankees that season, there were three schools of thought on Yogi. There were the veterans like Mickey and Whitey who came up when Yogi was a star. They got along with him fine.

"Then there were the younger veterans, many of them Ralph Houk guys, who complained that Yogi wasn't a strong enough leader. Tony Kubek was hurt early in the season, and after he got back he had a lot of little, nagging injuries, so he was out of the lineup a lot. Yogi put me at short. Then, when Tony got back into the lineup, he wasn't hitting. So Yogi played me a little more, not only against left-handers, but right-handers, too. Bobby Richardson and Tony spent a lot of time in Ralph's office complaining that Yogi was playing me too much instead of Tony. They didn't like that.

"Then you had the young players like me, Joe [Pepitone], Tom [Tresh], and Jim Bouton who really enjoyed playing for the guy. In my case, I loved him. He was still a player when I came up in 1962, and we'd go out for drinks. Of course, it helped that he liked me as a player and felt I could help the club with my speed. I didn't realize it at the time, but it makes a difference when a manager puts his confidence in you. It makes you play better.

"I paid his fine, but I came out ahead. A little later, Hohner Harmonica, whose sales had gone through the roof after the incident, asked me to endorse their product for $10,000. The next year, there was even an ad featuring me on the back of the *Yankee Yearbook*. It said, 'Play It Again, Phil.' And here's something hardly anyone ever writes about. That incident didn't end harmonica playing on the Yankees. We had this batting-practice pitcher named Spud Murray who was a great harmonica player. During that September stretch when we were winning game after game, he played for us every day, including on the bus, and by then we were having sing-alongs. We sang our way through the rest of the year. . . ."

*Sweet music, apparently. New York went 22–6 in September to cop the flag on the season's final day. So many people have written that Linz set the winning tone for that drive, you'd swear his Hohner was Mozart's Magic Flute. But this author found few Yankees who shared that view:*

**Jim Bouton:** "What fascinated me about the harmonica incident was the way the press portrayed it. The writers really played it up as something meaningful. Stuff like that happens during the course of any season, and I'm sure most of us on the team had started forgetting about it the next day. You had a few laughs over it and that was it. But the press wrote about it as if it was some extraordinary event—Yogi was losing control, the team was falling apart, et cetera.

"But then we won 18 out of 23 to climb from third and win the pennant, and the same writers were then saying the harmonica incident was the catalyst that got us going. It was the motivating factor that helped us win the pennant. I always got a kick out of that. Can you imagine a battle cry of 'Let's win this game for Phil's harmonica'? That doesn't happen except in sportswriters' stories where just because one event follows another, the two are somehow linked. According to the writers, no matter how we played, the harmonica was the cause. If we had lost it, it would have been the harmonica that finally broke us. But we won it, so it brought us together. Every club should carry a harmonica on the team bus."

**Phil Linz:** "I'm not going to tell you my harmonica turned us into winners. If anything, I think the incident had a positive effect on the team,

at least indirectly. It lightened us up and gave Yogi a chance to establish himself as a leader, someone who could put his foot down. There
had been too much horsing around all year, and that stopped after
Chicago. And I think my line about some guys not giving a hundred
percent made those players think about how they weren't hustling as
hard as they should. . . ."

**Tom Tresh:** "Phil is right about that one thing. I was upset before the
incident, because I didn't think some of the players were taking the
games seriously enough. It's like they either thought they could just
turn it on at any time and win the pennant, or they thought we were
through, so there was no sense in trying too hard. That bothered me.
Between the minors and majors, I had played on six straight champions—I'm one player who knows how Derek Jeter must feel—so I was
used to winning. Losing wasn't supposed to be fun, and too many guys
were fooling around while we fell further back in the race.

"I'm not saying we should have been walking around with our
heads hanging. Feeling really bad after a loss doesn't help you, just
puts more negative thoughts in your head. You have to turn the page,
get ready to win tomorrow. But we had some guys who, up to that
point, weren't ready to play all out. If what Phil said made them take a
look in the mirror, well, that was something we did need.

"But, when you get down to it, Bouton has the right slant on this.
Three things turned us around in 1964. First was Mel Stottlemyre
solidifying the pitching staff by coming out of the minors to win nine
games [while losing only three]. Here's a twenty-one-year-old kid
nobody knew coming out of nowhere with this great arm and super
control who has all the confidence—not a big head, mind you, but a
quiet self-assurance—of a Whitey Ford. . . ."

**Bobby Richardson:** "I want to second what Tom said. When Mel came
on board it was if he was on a par with Whitey, like we found another
ace. He threw the ball where he wanted to, kept the ball down. Mel
was not a strikeout pitcher, but he had the kind of hard sinker that

broke bats; I fielded a lot of weak pop-ups and softly hit grounders with him on the mound.

"I liked playing behind him, he was always ahead of the hitters. You get someone who throws hard but always runs the count 3–2, you're not as sharp because you can't get into a rhythm doubting the hitter will swing. When a pitcher is throwing a lot of strikes, you're up on your feet, ready all the time. Our infield was the best defensively, I thought, in the majors, so Mel was made for us. He gave us a huge boost. I think, too, that you should note Mickey got healthy. He had a great season, but he missed some games early, then he jammed his knee, so even when he played he was hurting. But by September, he was hitting as well as ever. Mickey was always a key for us. . . ."

**Tom Tresh:** ". . . Then Roger Maris gets red-hot. He was the best player in the league during the last six weeks of the season. With Roger, Mickey, and Ellie in the lineup together and hitting, the middle of our batting order was set and the rest of us followed. We all started hitting except for Tony, who was hurt. And, finally, Pedro Ramos came over from Cleveland in September to give us a bullpen closer. Yogi had tried four or five guys in that spot all season and none of them had been consistent. Pedro was unhittable for us."

**Phil Linz:** ". . . Pedro was the man for us, all right. You know, I roomed with him and he was a Cuban. He was getting so famous saving games for the Yankees, he was afraid Castro would have him kidnapped and brought back to play in Cuba. He slept with a loaded gun under his pillow. We didn't get him until after September first, so he couldn't pitch for us against the Cardinals in the World Series. If he had, we would have beaten St. Louis. . . ."

**Tom Tresh:** "Pedro, Mel, and Roger. You cross out any one of those three and we don't win in 1964 no matter how many songs Phil Linz plays. None of them had anything to do with the harmonica incident."

**Frank Crosetti:** "It was no turning point at all, near as I could tell. I'm almost sorry I got so upset over it. But what Phil did made it seem as if the losses didn't bother him. Back when I was a player, we didn't dare do things like that. You got beat in a ball game, you didn't fool around afterwards or Joe McCarthy would send you packing. And before he even said anything to you, Mr. Dickey or Mr. DiMaggio would let you know you were out of line. They didn't go in for any horsing around after a loss. But, looking back on it now, the thing with the harmonica wasn't really a big deal. I think what happened was ballplayers had changed and I just hadn't noticed it."

**Phil Linz:** "It's nice that, thirty-seven years after the fact, Cro says it wasn't a big deal. But back then, he was pissed and so was I. I resented the fact that he put an onus on me by saying this was the worst thing he'd ever witnessed on the Yankees. Yeah, Cro, worse than the time Ralph Houk beat the shit out of Ryne Duren on a train? Worse than all the stuff Babe Ruth pulled with his all-night parties when you were a player? Worse than Mickey Mantle coming in smashed before a game? But I probably should have apologized to Cro for cursing him out, and I never did. Don't let him tell you he didn't hold it against me. He ignored me after that, never hit another ball to me during practice.

"That hurt my career. During 1965, I knew Bobby Richardson would be retiring [after the 1966 season] and I thought second was my best position. I told Cro to watch me turn the ball over on the double play over there. This guy had been with New York for more than thirty years, and I knew he would have the manager's ear when they were figuring out the infield alignment. I wanted to show him I could be the regular second baseman when Bobby left. Second was my best spot. I could really get rid of the ball quickly, and my arm, which was average at short, was fine at second. Cro wouldn't even look at me. I got less playing time in 1965 even with Bobby and Tony having terrible years. By 1966, I was gone, traded to the Phillies for Ruben Amaro. I never got a shot to start again. So maybe, indirectly, I did pay a price for playing that harmonica."

## 1965: THE EMPIRE STRIKES OUT

*B*aseball had never witnessed a run like it. In 1964 the Yankees won their twenty-ninth American League pennant in forty-four years, although they would lose a closely contested seven-game World Series to the St. Louis Cardinals. Most managers who guide their teams that far into the postseason get a raise; New York skipper Yogi Berra got downsized.

The Yankees announced the firing only two days after the Series had ended. Journalists attend many press conferences expecting to hear a truth that's been massaged and manipulated until it's just a quarter-ounce shy of a lie. But George Orwell could have scripted the conference announcing Berra's removal. Yankee general manager Ralph Houk told the assembled writers that the World Series outcome had nothing to do with the decision to jettison Yogi. As if anyone in the cautious, corporate-minded Yankees front office would have found the sand to fire Berra had New York prevailed over St. Louis. No, Houk explained, the manager had to go because he couldn't overcome some vague "communication problems" Yogi had with his players.

Communication problems? How bad could they have been? Unless a plague of typos had visited every sports section in the country, New York did finish first in the American League standings. So why all the rumpus? Was Berra being released because he wasn't bilingual or couldn't speak in sign?

Houk didn't say. But he pointedly announced that the organization wasn't abandoning Yogi. Yankee management was too shrewd to sever its ties with such a fan favorite. Front-office flacks circulated a press release heralding how Berra had agreed to remain with the club as a "special field consultant" for an annual salary of $25,000. No office came with the position. That made sense as no position came with the position, either. You couldn't find a single Yankee executive who could identify what duties the now ex-manager would be assuming. As one reporter accurately observed, "It sounds as if Yogi isn't being kicked upstairs, he's sort of being kicked sideways."

Berra read the public relations ploy for what it was and decided he wasn't having any. Yankee pride. Yogi left the Bronx to become a player-

*coach under Casey Stengel with the New York Mets, and, boy, did the press ever revel in backhanding the Bombers over that defection.*

*Any good karma the Yankee team possessed accompanied Berra out the clubhouse door. Johnny Keane, himself only just resigned as manager of the Cardinals club that had bested New York in the Series, replaced Yogi in the dugout. Not an inspired choice there. Cain and Abel made for a more harmonious coupling than Keane and the Yankees would:*

**Clete Boyer:** "Johnny Keane was the absolutely wrong guy for our club. He was a hell of a good man, extremely religious, in many ways a beautiful guy. He would have made a hell of a college coach. But he didn't fit our clubhouse. Going outside the organization to replace Yogi, who we had all played with, was a dumb idea. Bringing in the guy who had just kicked our asses in the World Series was even dumber.

"Houk never wanted Yogi as manager in the first place. He was stuck behind Yogi at catcher for years, and I think he was jealous of him. That stuff about Yogi having communication problems with his players was pure bullshit. Maybe two or three players had complaints about Yogi, that happens on any club. But most of us got along with him and we all knew, even when we would kid around with him, that he was a smart baseball man. A winner. Yogi knew how to get the best out of a club. Hey, he took us to the World Series in 1964 and we weren't the best team in the league, and then he took the Mets to the World Series [in 1973] when they weren't even the best club in their division. You think that was a coincidence? Yogi let us play our game. He didn't overmanage, but when he did make a move it was always the right one. Doesn't mean it always worked, but it was a sound baseball choice. You understood the thinking that went behind his decisions.

"Keane, he had a funny way of managing. It was as if he still thought he was with the Cardinals with [Lou] Brock, [Curt] Flood, Bill White, my brother [Ken Boyer], and all those guys who could run. I mean, he would ask us to bunt in the first inning. Bunt! We were the fucking Yankees, we didn't bunt unless the game was close in the late innings.

"A ballplayer's job is to listen to his manager. But the manager has got to know his players, to utilize his personnel according to what they can do, what they are comfortable doing. We were a veteran ball club built for power, not the hit-and-run. Keane didn't understand that. . . ."

**Phil Linz:** "The third week of the season we were a couple of games below .500, not good but nothing to panic about, and John calls this meeting where he started bawling the hell out of us for not hustling. We all thought, 'What is with this guy? The season's not even a month old.' We often started slow, then caught a streak and pulled ahead when the race tightened, because we were money players. Johnny pushed the panic button way too early. Then he started questioning players on why they made a certain throw or play. It was demeaning. . . ."

**Clete Boyer:** ". . . There were times when we would be three or four runs down in a game, and Johnny would give the take sign to Mickey Mantle on 3 and 0. Mickey Fucking Mantle! This was a Hall of Famer, and Keane is flashing him the take sign. Mickey would just look at him like he couldn't believe it. You just didn't do something like that. Look at the way Billy Martin runs this club [At the time of the interview, Boyer was a coach with the 1982 Oakland A's]. When Rickey Henderson is on base, or Dwayne Murphy is at the plate, we don't have to give them too many signs. They know what they have to do. Cliff Johnson, on the other hand, needs a little more help, so he'll see more signs. Had Yogi stayed on as manager, there's no way we would have contended in 1965. But you can bet your ass we would have finished over .500, because Yogi would have used our roster better than John did. It's simply a matter of understanding your personnel. Keane didn't."

**Tom Tresh:** "More than once, Johnny sent someone like Ross Moschitto to the outfield to take Mickey's place with the glove while Mickey was already out there. Then Mickey would have to trot back to the dugout in front of the crowd. That was very embarrassing to Mickey, but he would never say anything about it. Mickey didn't deserve that. You know if you are going to substitute for anybody—but especially a Hall of Famer like Mickey Mantle—tell the player before he goes out there, don't do it in the middle of the inning as if you just realized he's incapable of playing out there. It was so unnecessary. Mickey was a pro, he knew where to play the hitters and he could still catch any fly ball he got under. He just couldn't move like he used to, and his arm was no longer strong.

"When a manager does that to his top star, he loses everybody's respect for no good reason. What are the odds that a ball is going to be hit to that particular fielder in a way that will affect that particular ball game? But what happens is, the move ends up having a negative effect on a lot of other ball games because you break down communication lines with your players. Every one of us idolized Mickey, and we knew darn well if Keane could do that to him, he could do that to us."

*On November 2, 1964, the Columbia Broadcasting System, the television conglomerate, announced that it had purchased 80 percent of the New York Yankees from Dan Topping and Del Webb for $11.2 million. Topping remained as club president. The network named one of its top honchos, Mike Burke, as executive vice president (Burke would succeed Topping as the Yankees' president and chairman of the board in 1966). CBS stock fell nearly two points on the day the sale became public knowledge. Someone on Wall Street must have worn out Gypsy's eyes analyzing that transaction, the sudden discount showed such prescience. New York finished sixth in 1965, strangers to the first division for the first time in forty years.*

*The Yankees granted Keane a contract extension for 1966 three weeks before the disappointing season concluded. Ralph Houk told the press, "We cannot blame our present position in the standings on the manager. We feel our present standing is the result of not having our club together for the entire season. While we do not like to use injuries as an alibi, it is true that we have not been able to play our club as a unit all season." Houk finished what amounted to his defense of Keane by assuring everyone listening that "Johnny and I are not concerned with this ball club. . . ."*

*They should have been. The Yankees opened the 1966 campaign with only four wins in their first twenty games. Houk, no press conferences left in him now, resigned as general manager to take Keane's place in the clubhouse. Yankee play improved with the managerial change, but not by much. New York finished last. Only two other Yankee teams had sunk that low in the twentieth century. Monumental stuff, but the CBS party line denied that New York's ailment was chronic, acting instead as if the club were merely going through a form of market correction.*

*Those network executives should have seen the plunge as more harbinger than aberration, should have treated the Yankees like a sitcom that needed canceling. Or a new cast. New York's injured, prematurely aging roster was desperate for an infusion of fresh talent. Unfortunately, the minor-league organization, so robust and fertile for decades, had turned fallow:*

**Clete Boyer:** "That new draft rule [first implemented in 1965] where you had to draft in reverse order of your finish really hurt us. Before that, the Yankees had their choice of the best ballplayers in the country, the best damned ballplayers in the world. Everybody wanted to play for us or for the Dodgers, so we signed a good share of them. We had so many good young players that if the team needed to pick up a spare part for the pennant race, you know, a Bob Cerv or a Bud Daley, we just bought them from some team for a bunch of prospects.

"But with the new draft rules you couldn't stockpile talent like that anymore. You could only sign one prospect per round the same as everybody else. [Yankee] management couldn't cope with that. Hell, we had a ton of guys like Norm Siebern and Deron Johnson, good ballplayers who could help your club. But they were all gone to other teams by 1965, and we had nothing left to replenish the pool.

"Anybody from our front office who tells you they had no idea we were about to slide down the chute is either a liar or blind. I wasn't shocked when we collapsed in '65, so why were they? Hell, I didn't think we were the best team in '64 when we won the pennant. Baltimore had a much better club, with Milt Pappas, Wally Bunker, and all that good young pitching, and they had a deep bullpen. Chicago was probably better than we were, too. We just sort of snuck by them. That's right. Those teams were young and they had never won anything. They let the race get tight in the end, and we knew how to win that kind of game while they didn't. But if you just studied our roster, you could see we didn't have the young stars like we used to."

**Mike Burke (New York Yankees president, 1966–73):** "That's true, but I have to disagree with Clete on one thing. The new draft rule didn't kill us, it only made it more difficult to rebuild. For example, in that first draft, a player like Rick Monday would have been perfect for us, with his power and speed, as the eventual successor to Mickey Mantle. But Oakland picked ahead of us in 1965 and signed him.

"Our problems started long before the draft was in place. Dan Topping and Del Webb had known for a number of years that they were going to divest themselves of the team. So they stopped spending money on talent, to make the Yankees' ledgers look as attractive as possible. Meanwhile, the other teams took advantage by giving bonuses to players who ordinarily would have signed with New York. And, let's be honest, the Yankees' reluctance to sign minority baseball players during the 1950s—a malodorous policy I'm happy to say we immediately reversed—also caught up with the team. The Frank Robinsons, Roberto Clementes, Willie Stargells, and Bob Gibsons, there were so many immensely talented athletes the club neglected to sign simply because of the color of their skin. We paid a price for that.

"By the time CBS took over the club, we discovered we had bought a pig in a poke. There was virtually no farm system left! Scouts— whom we had no opportunity to speak with before the sale—later told us there was only one position player of any quality who was coming up and that was Bobby Murcer. Among the pitchers, Fritz Peterson was the only one who inspired unanimous enthusiasm. Out of the two hundred or so players we had in the minors, that was it. The whole system had been left to go to seed. . . ."

**Steve Hamilton:** "When you saw what was coming into spring-training camp, especially compared to what we were used to, it was sad. Ross Moschitto was supposed to be one of our young superstars. He was very vain about his physique, used to strut around the locker room flexing his muscles and doing complex flexibility exercises. Very athletic. He never talked to anybody, and he used to comb his hair for six hours.

"His first base hit was in California after he had gone about 0 for 30. It was a solid line drive to left field. But when he got to first, he circled the bag and took some steps toward the dugout as if he had made an out. He had gotten so used to making outs, it had become a habit. The coach got his attention, and he had to slide into first base to avoid being thrown out on a single.

"Another time Ross made a diving catch and jazzed it up a little bit for the crowd. He did a double somersault and comes up throwing. Made one of the strongest throws I've ever seen. Unfortunately, it was right into the center-field bleachers! He had come up backwards and didn't know it. We screamed about that one for weeks. We had to laugh about something. Things were pretty bad by then.

"You know, it wasn't until I left the Yankees [in September 1970] that I realized how bare our farm system was. During my last few years with the club, the Yankees brought up Roy White, Bobby Murcer, Thurman Munson, and Stan Bahnsen and that was pretty much it. Four good players in four seasons. All the other homegrown prospects were busts.

"Then I go to my first spring training [in 1971] with the San Francisco Giants, and wow! They had George Foster, Gary Matthews, Dave Kingman, Gary Maddox, Chris Speier, and Steve Stone in camp for the first time. Six young kids like that just up from the minors, and all of them become All-Stars. Foster would eventually win an MVP Award, Stone a Cy Young, and both Foster and Kingman became home-run champions. Frank Duffy was there, one year later he was the starting shortstop [for the Cleveland Indians]. Fran Healy made our roster out of that camp. By 1973, Healy was a starting catcher for Kansas City.

"So we're talking about eight minor-leaguers who went on to significant major-league careers. And you have to remember the Giants already had Bobby Bonds, Ken Henderson, Ron Bryant, Tito Fuentes on their roster, established players already and all in their mid-twenties. The Giants didn't know what to do with all their young talent. Those players came up from the minors in a four-year period, nearly half the roster. Stack that up against the four guys, as good as they were, the Yankees had brought up during the same time, and you can see how far behind New York's minor-league organization was. . . ."

**Pete Mikkelsen (major-league pitcher, 1964–72; pitcher, New York Yankees, 1964–65):** "What does this tell you? In 1964 I came up and pretty much became the Yankee closer until Pedro Ramos arrived. I was just out of A ball. [In 1963] Al Downing also went from A ball to the majors. [In 1962] Jim Bouton, Joe Pepitone, Phil Linz, all three from Double-A to New York. Obviously the front office wasn't too thrilled with whatever talent they had at Triple-A. . . ."

**Jake Gibbs (catcher, New York Yankees, 1962–71):** ". . . but because they seemed to have a lot of talent scattered throughout the low minors, you didn't realize the organization was crumbling. I saw Bobby Murcer, Fritz Peterson, Roy White, Horace Clarke, Stan Bahnsen, and Jerry Kenney work their way up the system and onto the roster; they looked like fine ballplayers to me, so how was I to know New York wouldn't continue on top?

"But I can say the one thing I noticed about most of our hitting prospects—Murcer was the exception to this—was that they lacked real power. They were mostly fast players who might get an extra-base hit on something in the gap, but look, we'd play Minnesota and peck out a run, then another a few innings later, finally a third. Then Harmon Killebrew or Tony Oliva would get them all back with just one swing. Our pitchers were terrific, but from 1965 on, runs were scarce and we lost a lot of low-scoring ball games."

*At least two Yankees who were witnesses to the plummet understood how the front office could lull itself into believing that the good times weren't about to stop rolling, why there were few adequate replacements ready when the stars turned dim. They point out that it wasn't the years that had ganged up to break down the Bombers:*

**Whitey Ford:** "It's true, we didn't have any hot prospects in spring-training camp that I can remember, but I thought we'd win again in '65. There weren't many open positions, so where was a rookie going to fit in? People say that team got old all at once, but we really weren't that old. Going into spring training that year, I think Mickey and Ellie [Howard] were the only guys in the lineup over thirty, and Mickey was, what, thirty-two? I was thirty-seven, but I think Hamilton was the only other pitcher we had over thirty. . . ."

**Jim Bouton:** ". . . Mel [Stottlemyre], Al Downing, Bill Stafford, and I were all twenty-five or younger at the start of spring training in 1965. Right there, you had four kids with great arms who'd already proven they could win in the big leagues. I'm not sure you could find a young pitching staff today with our credentials. . . ."

*Counting the World Series, Bouton had won 41 games over the previous two seasons, Downing had already led the league in strikeouts, while Stafford had enjoyed two 14-win seasons before he was twenty-three.*

**Jim Bouton:** ". . . and Mel Stottlemyre looked like a Hall of Famer as soon as he joined us. With those kind of talented young arms, I figured we'd have two or three twenty-game winners every year for the next ten years. Sure, Whitey had that circulation problem in his left arm and that hampered him at times, curtailed his pitching against the Cardinals in the '64 World Series. But he'd been great during the regular season and he pitched well in 1965 . . ."

**Whitey Ford:** ". . . so what really happened wasn't that we got old, we got injured all at once, which made us seem older than we were. Ellie did slow down, then he got hurt. Then Mickey and Roger [Maris] went on the disabled list. Tony [Kubek] played hurt for the whole year, never really hit, then he retired, and he wasn't even thirty yet.

"Our depth wasn't what it used to be, so those injuries killed us. You know, in the past, if one of our outfielders got hurt, Bob Cerv would come off the bench and hit .300. When Phil Rizzuto left, Gil McDougald would take over at short and do a great job. In '65, I think Hector Lopez replaced Maris in the outfield. Hector was fine out there, but he didn't have Roger's power. And when Mickey and Ellie went down, we didn't have anyone else."

**Jim Bouton:** "With Mantle, Maris, Howard, Kubek, and Stafford all hurting, John reached a point where he did not want to hear about injuries. One morning after a start, fairly early in the season, I woke up with a toothache in my biceps. This wasn't the usual day-after-the-game soreness, but no one thought it was anything serious. Sports medicine wasn't as advanced back then as it is now. We didn't even call it sports medicine. The doctors told me that there was nothing wrong, the muscle was just tired. They also told me that pitching with the pain wouldn't worsen my condition. So I tried throwing through it. My arm just got worse, and so did my ERA.

"At first my arm only bothered me when I threw, which for a pitcher is like saying it only hurt me when I breathed. But by mid-season, I couldn't lift a half-gallon container of milk with it. Yet I still believed the doctors, still thought I could throw.

"John did nothing to discourage my thinking, just kept sending me out there. But pretty soon, as the losses mounted [Bouton would go 4–15 in 1965], John, Houk, and the front office started behaving as if my problems were in my head. Can you believe that? I was suddenly supposedly afraid to pitch against the Kansas City Athletics, but six months earlier, I had beaten the St. Louis Cardinals twice in the World Series. You would have thought John, of all people, would have remembered that, and realized my problem was in my arm and not my head. He just didn't want to know, as if by not acknowledging my injury, it would go away."

*With Mantle, Maris, and Howard ailing or absent from the batting order, no one stepped up to ignite the offense. The hitters remaining in the lineup struggled while the pitchers paid for their futility:*

**Steve Hamilton:** "Who did we have without our big three? Pepi [Joe Pepitone] had good power, but he was unstable. At the plate, he looked like a superstar one day, an easy out the next. And he wasn't the kind of hitter who could lead your offense. He drove in a lot of runs, but only when there were good people around him. When he had to take the responsibility, he was no good. Joe had a lot of blind spots at the plate. He was a .250 hitter who hardly ever walked. Obviously, you could pitch to him.

"Clete [Boyer] had more power than most people realized, but he was right-handed. Yankee Stadium swallowed most of his best shots. Roger Repoz came up from the minors with a reputation as a power hitter, but he wasn't ready. That put a lot of pressure on Tom Tresh. He was supposed to be the next big Yankee, the one who carried on the tradition of Mantle and DiMaggio.

"Don't get me wrong. Before he was hurt [in 1967], Tommy was an excellent hitter with power from both sides, but he was best as part of the mix, not the main guy. Tommy was purely a fastball hitter. When Mickey and Roger were out, pitchers could challenge him with breaking balls. You didn't care if you walked Tom Tresh then, because there was no one to drive him in. Our lineup didn't scare anyone anymore. . . ."

**Fritz Peterson (American League pitcher, 1966–76; pitcher, New York Yankees, 1966–74):** ". . . and it didn't give our pitchers much margin for error. We had to scratch for runs. If you fell behind by two or three you were in rough shape, because now you couldn't steal or hit and run, you had to go for the long ball and we weren't hitting many of them anymore.

"That fall was especially hard for a young player coming up from the minor-league system, because you were suddenly somewhat disillusioned. Here you signed with the Yankees thinking you're going to be in the World Series every year, that you will win a lot of ball games just pitching competently, because the Yanks score so many runs. Only you wind up on a club that has to scuffle to beat anybody. Before becoming a professional ballplayer, I had a chance to sign with one of two teams, the Kansas City Athletics or the Yankees. The scout from New York said, 'We'll top whatever Kansas City offers you.' He also pointed out that if a left-handed pitcher was going to make it, he might as well pitch for the Yankees, because the Stadium favored left-handers and you get that World Series bonus every year.

"This was 1963. My choice was between the perennial American League champions and the last-place A's. It was no contest. So in my eight-plus years with the Yankees, I never saw a World Series check, while the A's moved to Oakland and cashed three of them. I loved playing in New York—I had my only twenty-win season there—but it's kind of ironic, isn't it?

"The worst part of it was when Mickey called it quits [just before spring training started in 1969]. I could never understand why anyone would want to go across town to see the Mets when they could come to our park and see Mickey Mantle. Even if it was just to pinch-hit. You figured he was baseball history stepping out onto the field. With him gone, we had such a bad team, I felt fans had no reason at all to come and watch us."

**Steve Hamilton:** ". . . the thing that hurt me most wasn't our fans not coming, it was the fans on the road when we started losing. Not because they were booing us, but because they weren't. Once teams started beating the Yankees pretty regularly, their fans would cheer us whenever we rallied. It was as if they felt sorry for the club, for what we had been and no longer were. Oh, that got under my skin! I wanted so badly to make them boo us again. You knew you were good when people rooted against you. If we needed any evidence of how far we had fallen, those cheers on the road should have been enough."

*From 1965 to 1973, New York played also-ran baseball, posting sub-.500 records on five occasions and finishing within ten games of first place* *only once. In 1972 CBS finally vacated a business it never should have entered by selling the Yankees to George Steinbrenner, a shipbuilding magnate from Cleveland, Ohio, and fourteen limited partners for $10 million.*

## A NEW SHERIFF COMES TO TOWN:
## BILLY THE KID RETURNS TO NEW YORK

*A fter a decade of often middling play, New York finished a close second in the American League East in 1974. George Steinbrenner and his general manager, Gabe Paul, convinced the club was ready to take a division title if not a league championship, enhanced their roster by signing free-agent pitcher Catfish Hunter, a twenty-five-game winner and Cy Young Award recipient with the world champion Oakland A's, and trading Bobby Murcer to the San Francisco Giants for Bobby Bonds, a player considered by many managers to be baseball's finest all-around talent. Those two acquisitions to a team that had missed winning their division by only 1 $\frac{1}{2}$ games made the Yankees the consensus favorites to win their division.*

*Disappointment throttled the season. Early injuries deprived the Yankee lineup and starting rotation of vital performers. New York had to release Mel Stottlemyre, the team's ace for over a decade, during spring training after doctors uncovered a career-ending rotator-cuff tear in his right shoulder. Lou Piniella, a .305 hitter in 1974, sustained an inner-ear infection while bodysurfing in Puerto Rico, where the Yankees were playing an exhibition series against the Pittsburgh Pirates. "A real flukey injury, if you can call it that," Piniella recalled. "I wasn't really hurt, but the infection took away my balance at the plate all season." So much so, the left fielder slumped to .196. Ron Blomberg, the designated hitter the Yankees considered an integral part of their left-handed attack, tore his right shoulder muscles in late May and played only 34 games. Bobby Bonds missed two weeks after injuring his knee while misplaying a fly ball on June 7; he returned to the lineup a diminished player for the rest of the season.*

*Most devastating was an injury center fielder Elliott Maddox suffered on June 13. With Yankee Stadium still closed for renovations, the Yankees*

*were playing their second consecutive season at Shea Stadium, home park*
*for the New York Mets. Maddox was eager for the team to return to its*
*Bronx home. He thought the playing field in Flushing ill maintained, par-*
*ticularly the outfield, which even a moderate rainfall often reduced to a*
*marsh:*

**Elliott Maddox (major-league outfielder/third baseman, 1970–80; center
fielder, New York Yankees, 1974–76):** "It's not that it didn't drain well,
the outfield there didn't drain at all. If it rained on Monday, it would
still be wet the following Saturday. We had to put our feet in Baggies
before putting on our spikes, just to keep our feet dry. Every home
stand, the outfielders would go through one or two pairs of spikes.
The dampness would ruin them. On that evening I was injured the
surf, excuse me, turf, was so soggy, my spikes got tangled in it just as I
was coming in on a line drive to shallow center. My body lunged forward, but my foot was stuck in place and my knee collapsed under me.
I went down and couldn't get up."

*Neither could the Yankees. Maddox, in the midst of a second consecutive*
*.300 season, his on-base percentage an impressive .386, was playing Gold*
*Glove defense when his injury occurred. Recklessly galloping over wide*
*expanses of the outfield, Maddox had been changing the definition of his*
*position. Center field was no longer a patch of real estate situated between*
*left and right; it was wherever Elliott Maddox chose to roam. Manager Bill*
*Virdon counted on him to save the pitching staff runs and set the offense in*
*motion from the top of the lineup. It would be over a year before he could*
*play another inning for New York. With Piniella and Blomberg already*
*out and Bonds playing on a fragile knee of his own, the Yankees were no*
*longer deep enough to cover the loss of such a valuable player.*

*Virdon spent the rest of his tenure with the club cobbling together a*
*hodgepodge offense that never rose above mediocrity. New York's starting*
*rotation—led by Catfish Hunter's 23 wins—was first-rate, but it was often*
*undermined by closer Sparky Lyle, staggering through the worst season of*
*his career to that point, and an inconsistent bullpen. By August 1, 1975,*
*New York was in fourth place with a 53–51 record.*

*For George Steinbrenner, even more galling than the Yankees' lackluster performance on the field was the the shellacking his team was taking at the box office from its landlord, the New York Mets. Despite playing hardly any better than the Yankees, the Mets would outdraw the refugees from the Bronx by nearly 500,000 fans. Steinbrenner couldn't tolerate that. He sought the bold move, something that would ignite an M-80 under the behinds of his demoralized players and their yawning fans. So he replaced the bland Bill Virdon with the one skipper who set off pyrotechnics every time he entered a big-league clubhouse:*

**Marty Appel (former Yankees public relations director):** "There's a funny story connected to Billy Martin's hiring. Sometime around May during the 1975 season, word got to me that Billy was upset with me because I hadn't invited him to our 1975 Old Timers' game. It wasn't an oversight. Billy was managing the Texas Rangers and they were scheduled to play on the West Coast that day. It didn't seem practical to invite him. But, in hindsight, it's something I should have done as a courtesy. Billy always wore his Yankee heart on his sleeve, it didn't matter what team he was with. He was very offended by what he perceived to be a slight.

"When I discovered how upset he was, I made it a point to visit him the next time we played Texas. I poured it on a bit during my apology, telling Billy we couldn't possibly even think about holding an Old Timers' Day without him. He knew I was tossing a little BS, so he tossed it right back. He said, 'Fine, but what about Charlie Silvera here, he wasn't invited, either.' Charlie had been a backup catcher with the Yankees during the '50s and was one of Billy's coaches. So I said, 'Well, of course, we can't hold an Old Timers' Day without Charlie, either.' Billy laughed, and that was the end of it. But he got his invitation, and so did Charlie. A few days later, Texas fired him.

"Right after Billy got fired, Gabe Paul came in and told me he was taking a trip. If the press asked where he was, I was supposed to say he was on a scouting trip in Puerto Rico. Actually, he was heading to Denver, Colorado, where Billy was on a fishing expedition. On August 2, I was getting ready for that afternoon's Old Timers' Day,

when Gabe called me into his office. He said, 'Marty, I'd like to introduce you to our new manager.' It was Billy. I shook his hand, laughed,
and said, 'Well, I guess you *did* make it here for Old Timers' Day
after all.'"

*Billy Martin was a character so complex, so turbulent, Tennessee
Williams could have created him. Martin had earned a reputation for
being curt, even belligerent with anyone he distrusted. Yet friends often
found him loyal, generous, and solicitous, particularly in distressful times.
Impeccably mannered, even charming when he felt comfortable in your
society, Martin could regale crowds with Stengel stories until long after the
night had turned in. He was a Civil War buff so knowledgeable, he could
have taught a college course on the subject. A real sop, too, the kind
of guy who might go teary-eyed at the end of* It's a Wonderful Life.
*Sentimentalist, buddy forever, scholar, raconteur, dugout brainiac, Billy
was all of these.*

*But at heart, he was a baseball gangsta, a Berkeley street kid mad at his
father for leaving a little boy and his mother rejected and impoverished.
Mad at the world for failing to smother his pain in a consoling embrace.
Forget Grant and Lee. Billy was the one always at war. A brilliant baseball
mind, Martin succeeded despite his penchant for self-obliteration. He
accepted his first managing position in 1969 with the Minnesota Twins, a
sub-.500 team the previous year. Martin immediately transformed them
into division champions, only to be dismissed during the off-season after a
spat with the Minnesota front office.*

*After taking a year's hiatus to work as a broadcaster, Martin agreed to
manage the Detroit Tigers, a skillet-footed, elderly ball club that had
tumbled into a downward spiral—it had fallen to fourth in 1970 while
going 79–83—few thought it could reverse. Those few did not include the
ever-confident manager who tacked twelve wins onto Detroit's record, good
enough for a jump to second place in 1971. Martin then led the team to a
division championship the following year, only to be dismissed less than
twelve months later after a spat with the Detroit front office.*

*Billy replaced Whitey Herzog as manager of the Texas Rangers during
the last month of the 1973 season. Stumblebumbling their way to a 57–105*

*record, the Rangers had been one of the most inept clubs in baseball history. But in 1974 Martin pushed Texas to a strong second-place finish only to be dismissed in 1975 after a spat with . . . oh, you get the idea. In six years as a big-league manager, Billy had dramatically improved the fortunes of three moribund ball clubs—you will find few skippers in baseball history who could match that record—while establishing a pattern for alienating his bosses that seemed pathological.*

*Being Billy was always the problem. Martin too often behaved like someone who couldn't function beyond the cauldron, as if confrontation alone could stoke the embers of his passion and his dark genius. He sought out demons everywhere, spent most of his waking hours clawing for any advantage that would aid his ceaseless combat against them.*

*There was no such thing as a petty grievance to Billy. You rarely saw him strolling from any slight, real or imagined. His rage often alcohol-fueled, Martin had a long list of punch-outs to his credit. Numbered among them were his own players, at least one team executive, and the occasional mouthy barfly. You got the idea Martin would have roundhoused Gandhi had the Mahatma looked at him cross-eyed on the wrong day. But one suspected that every hook he threw, no matter whom the target, was chingraz-ing a phantom. That dad who walked. Billy could never beat back the haunting.*

*Martin's scuffling ways inevitably created conflict with his employers. That was a second battle he could not win. It made no difference how often the pink slip tapped Billy, he could always roust up some team eager to employ him. And why not? The men who run baseball prize talent, and Martin was one of those rare managers who could elevate a club just as if he were a superstar going yard in the middle of the lineup:*

**Ferguson Jenkins (major-league pitcher, 1965–83):** "Look at the record. As soon as Billy joined your team, you picked up ten wins. How many players can you say that about? And it's not like he only did that two or three times, which would have been remarkable enough. He eventually managed, what, four or five different teams [five], probably eight or nine if you count all the times he went back to the Yankees? And every place he went Billy made a difference with all sorts of teams.

Clubs built around speed and defense, clubs that featured power, whatever they had, Billy could work with it.

"That's no fluke. Yes, he couldn't win without the players, but a big part of a manager's job is identifying the players you can win with. In that area, Billy had two qualities that I don't think people fully appreciated. First, Billy had a great eye for talent, and second, he had the courage to stand behind difficult personnel decisions. Both of those came into play on the Rangers the first year I was with the club [1974]. During spring training Billy saw that Mike Hargrove was ready to hit major-league pitching and Jim Sundberg was ready to catch a major-league staff even though they were both Double-A players. You know the Rangers' front office thought he was rushing them, but Billy had the guts to give them starting jobs and challenge them to succeed.

"Now, with hindsight, it's easy to say those were two good players, but who else knew that back then? We had a team of veterans, rookies, and castoffs and Billy made it all work by trusting our ability to play and working with what he had. The Rangers had only two real power hitters in 1974, Jeff Burroughs and Toby Harrah. The rest of the lineup were line-drive hitters, mostly singles hitters, so we couldn't sit around waiting for the long ball. Billy had everybody running, stealing, taking the extra base, challenging the other team to throw us out.

"Outside of Steve Foucault, our closer, Billy didn't have much of a bullpen, so he went with his starters deep into the game. I had 29 complete games that season. I think Billy started to get a reputation back then as a manager who went long, maybe too long, with his starters, but that was a bad rap. He was simply going with a strength and covering up our weakness. That's what a winning manager does, he plays the hand he's been dealt for everything it's worth."

**Roy White (outfielder, New York Yankees, 1966–79):** "Oh, there was nobody like Billy! The moment he took over the club, you knew something was different. The dugout came alive. Don't get me wrong. [Martin predecessor] Bill Virdon was an excellent manager. He was especially good with outfielders. He taught me some things and he made Lou [Piniella] a much better fielder by teaching him how to position himself. Lou wasn't fast, but he could catch anything he got near. Virdon taught him to anticipate where the ball would be hit. He knew his baseball, and we won a lot of games because of our defense.

"But he was laid back. With Virdon, we didn't run very much and we hardly ever bunted or used the hit-and-run. We had a lineup that could do all of those things. [Yankee center fielder Elliott] Maddox, [second baseman Sandy] Alomar, [right fielder Bobby] Murcer, [catcher] Thurman Munson, and I could all run and bunt, but our speed wasn't utilized. Virdon ran a one-dimensional offense.

"When Billy came on board, everything was put on the table. There was nothing laid-back about him. He was on the attack all the time. You could just feel it. He was always probing, trying to find the other team's weakness, and he wanted us to do the same. And he was so unorthodox, you never knew what to expect. He wanted everyone to run, not just steal bases but challenge the other team's outfielders by taking the extra base. He put the opposing team on edge and kept them there.

"One game, I was on second and Piniella was hitting. Billy gave Lou the bunt sign, and Lou fouled the ball off as I broke for third. I went back to second and somehow missed the next sign. Now, in that situation, you would expect Lou to bunt again. Ninety-nine times out of a hundred that is the logical play, and I assumed Lou would put down another bunt. But this is Billy in the dugout, so forget what the book says. Billy calls for the hit-and-run. Nobody does that! Lou singled, but because I had missed the sign, I didn't score.

"After the inning, Billy asked if I had missed the sign and I admitted that I had. He told me to stay awake out there or it would cost me money next time. I knew from that day on that we had to keep on our toes because we had a manager who was capable of the unexpected. Having a manager like that drives a team. You don't want to miss a sign and embarrass yourself by messing up an inning. You also don't want to get fined. Billy was fiery and smart. He made us fiery and smart. . . ."

**Oscar Gamble (major-league outfielder/designated hitter, 1969–85; out-fielder/designated hitter, New York Yankees, 1976, 1979–84):** "From the first day of spring training in 1976 he kept each one of us focused on what we had to do to get the team to the World Series. That was the goal, and Billy kept it in front of us all year long. Each player knew his role, and mentally, it makes a great difference to a player when he knows what the manager expects of him. I was the left-handed hitter usually platooning with Lou Piniella. If a right-hander was scheduled to start the next day, I could start preparing for him the night before, prepare with more intensity than if I didn't know whether I'd be in the lineup. Left-hander on the mound, I would start thinking about what right-handed relievers might come into the game, because I knew Billy would get me up there against them.

"When you were on the bench, he used you like a coach, kept you in the game all the time. Billy used to flash the steal signs to players through me. Billy would also think many moves ahead of other managers. He would have us practice the play over and over again. Runners on first and third, man on first gets a big lead, then falls down so the pitcher fires over for a pickoff while the man on third scores. Who spends a lot of time practicing that? Billy, because he thought about how to win morning, noon, and night. You better believe his teams scored some runs with that play. If he was going to use me as a pinch hitter in the eighth, he might have me leave the bench to take my practice swings as early as the fourth, so I was warmed up and focused when I came to the plate. Billy just made it easier for everyone to do their job. He was, no question, the best manager I ever played for. The best manager I ever saw."

**Roy White:** "That first full season [1976] with him, we had Mickey [Rivers] batting leadoff and stealing bases. Mickey was the only guy I ever saw who could go out without any warm-up or stretching and run out a triple at full speed. When I batted second behind him, Billy let us do so many things, things I had always wanted to do but couldn't batting lower in the lineup: hit and run, pull running bunt plays, double-steal. It drove the opposition nuts. Mickey and I had signs between ourselves.

"Sometimes we would put the hit-and-run on, but the pitcher would throw a curveball. I'd take it because I knew there was no way any catcher was going to throw Mickey out on a breaking pitch. If it was a fastball where I wanted, I'd hit it to the opposite field, or, if I was batting left-handed, pull the ball. That would give us first and third with Thurman [Munson] coming up, and now we really had you in trouble. That was the most fun I ever had in baseball."

**Willie Randolph (major-league second baseman, 1975–92; second baseman, New York Yankees, 1976–88):** "Batting behind Mickey could be an adventure. When I batted behind him, we had signs between us, whether I was going to hit and run or take a couple of pitches to let him steal. But Mickey kept missing them. He'd come back to the dugout and say, 'Yeah, I got you.' And I'd say, 'What do you mean, you got me? Then why didn't you go!' He'd just shake his head like he understood, and I'd just laugh because I knew he missed the sign again. But it didn't matter, because he was such a great instinctive base stealer and so fast he could get away with mistakes. Billy understood Mickey and let him do his thing, and then Mickey would get all of us going.

"Billy's first year as manager of the Yankees was my rookie year with the club. People always talk about how fiery he was. He had a reputation for being a manager who favored working with veterans, a manager who couldn't tolerate rookie mistakes. For some reason Billy took to me. We were both second basemen, he liked the way I played the game, appreciated the speed and defense I brought to the table. I think he also believed I was as crazy as he was, so he didn't mess with me too much. We had a few light run-ins, but we got along pretty well. He knew I was hustling, so he never really jumped on me when I booted one or made a mistake. Instead he'd take me aside and tell me what I had done wrong, show me how to smooth out my game. It was constructive criticism. Billy was encouraging, which is exactly what a rookie needs. He had incredible motivational skills and he could get players on a team to rally around each other like it was us against the world. Billy was so aggressive, he made us feel as if we were all in a bunker together and that baseball was all about war. . . ."

**Bill Lee (major-league pitcher, 1969–82; pitcher, Boston Red Sox, 1969–78):** "I think it was the first series we [the Red Sox] played against them in '76. Some Yankee hit a routine ground ball and busted his ass all the way down to first. He was out, but after the play, some-one on our team, it might have been Yaz [Carl Yastrzemski] because he was playing first base, said, 'Hey, this is not the same club we beat up on last year.' And he was right. They looked like they were breath-ing fire every time they took the field. Just like storm troopers."

**George Medich (major-league pitcher, 1972–82; pitcher, New York Yankees, 1972–75):** "If you read Billy's book, *Number One,* you know Billy didn't care for me very much. Claimed he told the front office to trade me because whenever I lost I alibied that my team hadn't played well behind me. That was bullshit! I pitched six games for him when he joined the club near the end of the '75 season. I lost once. Anyone who knows me, just ask my teammates, will tell you I would never be stupid enough to say something like that.

"Even if it was true, if a bonehead play cost you a game, you don't say anything unless it is to the player alone, behind closed doors. You have to protect your teammates so they will play hard for you the next time. Just go back and read my postgame quotes in the newspaper. I never ripped anybody. But that was Billy. He didn't even have a nod-ding acquaintance with the truth, and stories like that help sell books.

"But despite that, I have to admit that the son of a bitch was the best manager I have ever seen. He would stalk up and down the dugout and ask the guys on the bench their opinions on what was happening at that moment. I'd never heard of any manager who did that. It was as if he was raising a team of managers. You never knew who he would ask next, it could even be the bat boy, and it kept you in the game at all times. Billy is known as a fighter, and he would get his teams fired up. But he was also a solid baseball man. There wasn't anything he didn't know about the game between the lines.

"He did have one weakness. He let personalities get in the way of his judgment. Billy used to say he would have put Mussolini in his lineup if he thought it would help him win. That may have been true as long as Benito didn't play tennis. We had a pitcher named Larry Gura who had thrown great for us in '74 and '75. Billy had him traded to Kansas City for practically nothing just because Gura played tennis. Billy called it a pussy game. I believe he figured anyone who played it wouldn't be tough enough to play for him, so he got rid of a good pitcher.

"He also cost the Yankees one of our better right-handed hitters just by showing up. Two odd things occurred after Billy was hired. First, Bill Virdon just vanished. Usually when a manager gets fired he gives a farewell address to the troops. Not Bill. We didn't see him until the following spring when he reappeared as the manager of the Houston Astros. I thought it was strange the way he disappeared. But what was much odder was the disappearance of Alex Johnson. You can understand a manager who was just fired wanting to clear out as quickly as possible. But Johnson was a player. It's not as if he had been released or traded. Alex had been with Martin in Texas, hit close to .300 for him. The day Billy joined the Yankees, Alex packed and walked out of the clubhouse. Never came back. After the season I ran into him and asked what had happened. Alex said that once he had heard that Billy Martin was the new manager, he was halfway across eastern Pennsylvania before the next pitch was thrown. He just knew that with Billy coming, he was gone."

**Sparky Anderson (major-league manager, 1970–95):** "I'll tell you what made Billy a great manager. He was absolutely fearless. You'll see a manager whose team is going bad, the press is getting on him, writing stories that he's about to be fired. The owner isn't supporting him. You go play his team, he's not willing to take any risks during the game. Doesn't want to do anything the press can point a finger at or he might get fired. Not Billy. He didn't care if his club was ten games in front or ten games behind with everybody saying he was gone the next time the team lost. He was going to manage the same way, call the same plays, and he didn't care what the consequences were."

## OCTOBER 15, 1976: CHAMBLISS ENDS THE DROUGHT

*After joining New York, Billy Martin spent the final 56 games of 1975 assessing his new team. He decided it needed an overhaul. Over the off-season Martin and Yankees general manager Gabe Paul refashioned the club, which had featured a largely one-base-at-a-time offense, with two brilliant trades that enhanced the Yankees' speed, defense, and pitching. On December 11, 1975, Paul sent Bobby Bonds, the team leader in home runs, to the California Angels for scatback center fielder and American League stolen-bases champion Mickey Rivers and Ed Figueroa, a right-handed pitcher who had won 16 games in 1975 while registering the fifth-lowest ERA in the league for baseball's worst-hitting team.*

*Immediately following the Bonds-Rivers exchange, the Yankee GM dispatched 16-game-winner George Medich to the Pittsburgh Pirates for the highly regarded second-base prospect Willie Randolph, a twenty-two-year-old who had established himself in the minor leagues as a patient contact hitter with an discerning batting eye, disarming speed, and unrestricted range at second base. New York also received two veteran pitchers in the deal, Dock Ellis, a right-hander who had reached double figures in wins during six of his eight seasons with the Pirates, and Ken Brett, once a hard-throwing left-hander, whose elbow woes had left his arm all con and curveballs. He still had more than enough to get by. Brett's deceptive, underpowering assortment of pitches had helped him compile a .603 winning percentage over the previous three seasons. Many, though, doubted that Billy would keep him around long. Martin preferred power pitchers, hard throwers with enough heat to make batters sweat blood; he had little patience for pitchers who nibbled at the strike zone.*

*Gabe Paul would trade Brett to the Chicago White Sox shortly after the 1976 season started. But the general manager's other four acquisitions played vital roles in helping Martin to transform the Yankees into a*

*multidimensional team. This was a run-and-gun club that, like its man-
ager, came to the ballpark ready to force the action at all times. Martin's
Yankees swiped bases with impunity. They played hit-and-run and bunted
when such plays were least expected. And with Rivers, usually backed by
Roy White or Willie Randolph, at the top of Martin's lineup, it seemed as if
New York started every game with runners on second and third.*

*Speed wasn't the offense's sole asset. When the Yankees weren't dashing
over opposing pitchers, they were bashing their best stuff off and over the
walls. Six New York regulars, including American League MVP Thurman
Munson and home-run champion Graig Nettles, reached double figures in
home runs. The Bomber defense was quick and smart, and it played behind
the deepest pitching staff in the league.*

*Martin and the Yankees pressured the opposition from the moment the
season opened. New York won 15 of its first 20 decisions and took the
American League East division title by $10\frac{1}{2}$ games. After eleven seasons
of disappointment, the Bombers were back in postseason play. But before
they could advance to the World Series, New York had to defeat the Kansas
City Royals, winners of the American League West, in a best-of-five League
Championship Series. The Yankees won the initial game of that set and
gained an additional edge when the Royals lost their best all-around player:*

**Amos Otis (major-league outfielder, 1967–84; center fielder, 1976 Kansas
City Royals):** "We opened that series in Kansas City. While I'm sure the
Yankees and their supporters were excited about getting back to the
postseason, it probably meant even more to us and our fans. The
Royals were an expansion team and had been around only since 1969,
so this was the first time they were playing any important games in
October. What happened to me that afternoon was kind of flukey,
since normally I wouldn't have been batting when I did.

"[Kansas City manager] Whitey Herzog decided to bat me leadoff
for that game. Freddie Patek was our regular leadoff man, and I usually
batted second, sometimes third, fourth, or even fifth. When Freddie
would get on, I'd take a pitch or two so he could steal second, then I'd
move him over to third or drive him in. You'd pay cash money to bat
behind guys like Freddie Patek, Mickey Rivers, or Willie Wilson. I

usually saw a lot of fastballs with Freddie on base, he was such an excellent base stealer.

"But the Yankees had a club that could do a lot of things to win even when their power was off. They could steal, hit and run, scratch out a run here and there. No matter who you play, you always want to score first. But you especially want to get a team like the Yankees down as soon as you can so you take away their ability to play for one run. So I think Whitey wanted me to lead us off with power to get us on the board real quick.

"I went up there thinking like a leadoff hitter in the first inning. Looking down at third, I could see that Nettles was playing me way back, which is where you would play a right-handed power hitter. A bunt seemed like a good idea to me. I got it down, but I didn't get it over quite far enough. Catfish Hunter was on the mound for the Yankees, and he was quick for a big man, an excellent fielder. He got to the ball so fast, I knew the play at first would be close. So I leaped into the air the final few feet down the baseline. Now, that's something you're absolutely not supposed to do as a base runner. You should run to the base, not leap to it. Leaping doesn't get you to the bag faster, it slows you down. But in the heat of a game, you're not thinking. Your instincts take over.

"My toes and the balls of my feet hit the edge of the bag in such a way that all my weight came down on my ankle. The pain was indescribable; Whitey had to take me out of the game. By the time I got to the dugout, my ankle was three times its usual size. One of the trainers had to cut off my shoe. About an hour later, X rays revealed that I had fractured the ankle. I missed the rest of the playoffs. You can't describe the frustration when something like that happens. You spend your whole career working towards one thing, getting to the World Series, and you never know how many chances you'll have. Then I get injured on only the second pitch I see."

*Even without the estimable Mr. Otis, Kansas City played the Yankees tough. The two teams split the first four games. Yankee Stadium was the scene for the tie-breaker. That game did not start off well for New York.*

*Royals first baseman John Mayberry—a prototype left-handed slugger built on the scale of a small condominium—hit an Ed Figueroa slider into the Stadium seats for a two-run Kansas City lead in the first inning. New York's leadoff hitter Mickey Rivers essayed a quick reply to the Mayberry blast—a high arcing triple against Kansas City's ace right-hander Dennis Leonard. Roy White's base hit scored Rivers, then White eventually scored the tying run on first baseman Chris Chambliss's sacrifice fly.*

*Kansas City took a one-run lead in the second, but when New York tallied twice in the third and sixth innings to go ahead 6–3, Yankee fans sent the Stadium all aquiver with chants of "Ed-die, Ed-die, Ed-die!" as Figueroa's mixture of fastballs, sliders, and breaking pitches stymied the Kansas City offense. He kept the Royals fishing for low strikes all night. However, in the seventh, a noticeably fatigued Figueroa started to get his pitches up, though no damage occurred that inning.*

*Martin closely watched Figueroa as the right-hander warmed up for the eighth. As soon as Royals right fielder Al Cowens led off with a base hit, the Yankee manager decided his pitcher could go no further. Left-hander Grant Jackson came on in relief. Jim Wohlford greeted him with a single. The Stadium suddenly went still. Up to the plate, representing the tying run, came Royals third baseman George Brett. More left-handed demolition crew than hitter, Brett had already tallied seven hits in seventeen at-bats during this series. This was the threat Martin had in mind when he had first summoned Jackson into the game.*

**George Brett (third baseman, Kansas City Royals, 1973–93):** "Jackson was a hard thrower. That situation, down by three, two men out, we're away in the eighth. I'm looking for something to pull, a pitch I can drive. How far away was that right-field fence back then, 310 feet? I knew I could hit a ball that far. . . ."

*Or farther. Brett hit Jackson's 0–1 fastball deep into the right-field seats to tie the score at 6–6. Mausoleums sound more raucous than the Stadium did as Brett circled the bases. Yankee fans sat mute, troubled, wondering if their evening was about to sour. Their team failed to score during its half of the eighth and the Royals couldn't push across a run in their next turns at bat. Here was one brute of a ball game. With the matchup well over three hours old, Kansas City's right-handed closer Mark Littell, who had been in there since the seventh inning, prepared to face leadoff hitter Chris Chambliss in the bottom of the ninth:*

**Chris Chambliss (major-league first baseman, 1971–88; first baseman, New York Yankees, 1974–79):** "In such a tense game, you want to get up to the plate and take your swings. But I had to wait before I hit against Littell, because some fans had thrown things on the field and the groundskeepers had to clear it all away. I was getting a little anxious during the delay. Which may be one of the reasons why, when I finally got up, I jumped on Littell's first pitch.

"Sometimes you'll see players drop their bats at home plate to admire the ball as it goes out of the park. They know they hit it so well, it's a home run from the moment it leaves their bats. This wasn't one of those. The ball I hit was more what you would call a towering drive with a lot of height, but I didn't know if it had enough distance to make it out. When I hit the ball, it looked as if the Royals right fielder had a bead on it. He moved back as if he was going to catch it. But at the very last second, he backed into the wall and the ball cleared it.

"Everybody went a little crazy as soon as they realized it was the game-winning home run. Fans came running out on the field. I definitely touched first and second as I rounded the bases, but someone tripped me between second and third. I'm trying to get up so I can finish, and fans are grabbing for my helmet. I had to tuck the helmet under my arm, just the way you would carry a football, before making my way to third base. Except when I get to where third was supposed to be, I couldn't find it! There was a mob of people over there, and I think someone stole the bag by then! All I could do was keep moving, but when I got towards home plate, the mob there was even bigger, so I just made for our dugout. I had to come out later on with a police escort to officially touch third and home."

*As far as everyone in Yankee Stadium was concerned, the game was over as soon as Chambliss's drive departed the field. It didn't make any difference that he was unable to step on third or home. Or did it?:*

**Bill Shannon (member of the Baseball Writers Association of America, and president of the New York Sports Museum and Hall of Fame):** "It would have made a difference if someone from the Royals had done some fast thinking. I had no way of telling whether Chris had touched third during that first trip around the bases, so I'm not surprised that he says he didn't. No one really made an issue of it at the time.

"But had Herzog and the Royals decided to challenge Chambliss's home run, you would have had one of the biggest baseball controversies of this century. Home runs, despite what a lot of fans probably think, are not automatic. Hitting the ball over the wall isn't what puts an official run up on the board. You must touch all the bases and home plate to do that.

"Just go back and find footage from the final game of the 1951 National League playoffs between the Brooklyn Dodgers and New York Giants. You'll see that Jackie Robinson and the umpires closely watched Bobby Thomson after he hit his Shot Heard Round the World, to make sure he touched every base and home plate. They understood the rules. He knew that if Thomson failed to touch a bag or the plate, the Dodgers could make an appeal to the umpires and possibly have Thomson ruled out.

"Since this is an uncommon play, let me explain how Kansas City could have nullified Chambliss's run. Let's start with what the Royals did not have to do. They did not have to scramble to retrieve the ball Chris hit over the wall before they could make any kind of play on him. As long as Kansas City remained on the field in fair territory after the ball was hit, they retained the right to appeal. You don't need the home-run ball to do that. All Whitey Herzog had to do was to tell the home-plate umpire or crew chief that he was making an appeal.

"Then he had to get his players in position and have Littell step on the pitching rubber with a new game ball. Littell could then throw over to George Brett at third base for the appeal play. Or he could have thrown to the catcher for an appeal at home plate. If the umpire didn't see Chambliss touch the bag or the plate—or at least see him touch the vicinity of third or home if the base or plate were no longer there—he could have called Chris out."

*We can assume that Chambliss would not have been a passive spectator to these proceedings. Couldn't the first baseman have raced over to tag third as well as home before anyone took Littell's throw?:*

**Bill Shannon:** "Once Littell puts that ball in play, it is considered live. In other words, say Chambliss had remained near home plate and started running as soon as he realized Herzog was calling for an appeal. He would have had to beat the throw to third or he's out. And if he only had enough time to reach third ahead of the play and then tried to go home, he would have been proceeding at his own peril. The Royals could have thrown him out at the plate.

"That would have been the scenario if Chambliss remained on the field throughout all this. However, and this is where it gets interesting, as I remember it, Chris ran into the Yankee dugout trying to escape that mob. That's important, because once he was in the dugout, Chris was ineligible to return to the playing field to tag the plate or the base! The Royals could have carried out their appeal play without having to worry about Chambliss running the bases again.

"Had the umpire called Chambliss out, the score still would have been tied, and play would have resumed at that point. Provided, of course, that Yankee fans hadn't murdered someone by then. I wonder if the Royals ever realized that they could have postponed the game's ending if they had just reacted quickly?"

**Amos Otis:** "We were too numb to react to anything. When Chambliss hit the homer, frustration set in right away. Especially for me, since I was hurt the whole series. You know over the years, a lot of people— not just Kansas City fans—have said we would have won those playoffs if I hadn't gotten hurt. You can't think that way. I could have gone 0 for 15 in the series, and maybe we lose in four games instead of five. No one can tell what would have happened.

"But at the time, it was agonizing for me and my teammates. We didn't think about any appeal plays as we left the field. Once we got back to the clubhouse, we saw the replay on television and that's when it dawned on a bunch of us that Chris never touched home plate. We weren't sure he touched third, either. The next day, we talked about it on the plane ride back, but there was nothing we could do.

"We'd have been right to call an appeal play. Unfortunately, no one thought about that at the time because of the way that Yankee Stadium crowd hit the field. All my teammates were thinking about was safety. I wasn't even on the field and I was a little scared. If someone—say, Whitey or one of the coaches—had realized we had an appeal at home or third and been able to keep the team on the field, no doubt we would have tried it.

"Part of the problem would have been finding an umpire who could restore some order so play could resume. It looked like there were 25,000 people hooting and hollering out there, and I think the umps left the field the same time Chambliss did. If we did find an umpire, it might have taken all night to clear everyone off. And if they did, and we won the appeal, I don't think we would have gotten out of the Stadium in one piece."

**Bill Shannon:** "Amos said something worth considering there. That crowd presented a further complication. Just imagine if the umpires and security had been unable to clear the field after the Royals insisted on an appeal play. The Yankees could have lost something more than just a home run. If the umpires tried, for what the crew chief thought was a reasonable amount of time, to clear the field and they failed, he could have ruled that play could not continue and forfeited the game and the American League pennant to the Royals. It was, after all, the home team's responsibility to clear the field, so they would have been penalized if their fans didn't disperse. What a mess that would have been! You can bet that every umpire there that night—as well as the league president and the baseball commissioner—were happy that Herzog and the Royals did not appeal. Because they would have had a good case."

*Any euphoria over Chambliss's home run would prove to be short-lived. The Yankees would lose the 1976 World Series to the Cincinnati Reds in four straight games.*

## THE GREENING OF REGGIE

*T*he off-season following the 1976 World Series was historic. During the previous spring an arbitrator had struck down the reserve clause that the owners had used to restrict the rise of their teams' payrolls. Suddenly, any player with at least six years of major-league service who had completed a season without signing a contract could peddle his skills to the highest bidder. Baltimore Orioles right fielder Reggie Jackson couldn't wait for the auction to begin. The thirty-year-old Jackson was a two-time home-run champion who had triggered the offense for three World Series–winning clubs while playing for the Oakland A's. Everyone in baseball agreed that the slugger would receive the largest contract of the initial free-agent crop. No one was quite certain, though, which team Reggie would choose to play for:*

**Ken Singleton (major-league outfielder/designated hitter, 1970–84; outfielder/designated hitter, Baltimore Orioles, 1974–84):** "I had been with the Montreal Expos before I was traded to Baltimore, and I know the Expos were hot to sign him. Reggie would have been Montreal's first marquee player since Rusty Staub. But free agency was such a new thing, no one knew what would happen. My salary, for instance, tripled in one season. Reggie showed up late when the Orioles got him [in a trade with the Oakland A's just before the start of the 1976 season], he was a salary holdout, missed the first month, and by the time he joined us we were already eight games behind the Yankees. We never recovered. But Reggie played great for us once he was in the lineup; in fact, he almost led the league in home runs.

"We've heard about all the trouble Reggie had in the clubhouse when he went to New York, but he wasn't a problem with Baltimore. Reggie had been the big man with Oakland, and he had those three World Series rings. Forget about the home runs, RBI, and those other numbers; there is nothing players look up to more than a guy who's proven he can deliver for a world champion. So it was easy for Reggie to take a leadership role with Baltimore, although it was one that may have gotten him in some trouble one day when we were playing Dock Ellis and the Yankees. . . ."

**Earl Weaver (manager, Baltimore Orioles, 1968–82, 1985–86):** ". . . Ellis threw one close to our shortstop Mark Belanger's head, really had Mark ducking up there. I have no idea if it was intentional. But Reggie thought it was. He stood up on the dugout steps and shouted, 'Hey, Ellis! If you want to throw at somebody, throw at me . . .'"

**Ken Singleton:** ". . . now I knew Ellis from when he was with Pittsburgh in the National League. This was not a guy to challenge. Dock would throw at anybody. He once hit the first five Cincinnati Reds he faced in a game just because he thought the Reds were intimidating the Pirates too much. So Dock's idea of teaching someone respect was to start the game with two runs in and the bases loaded. You could see he heard what Reggie was saying, and you knew he would answer him in his own way . . ."

**Earl Weaver:** ". . . the next time Reggie came up, Ellis hits him in the face. We had to take him out for X rays, his face was a mess, looked like the bones in it were broken. So we lost him for another week and a half . . ."

**Ken Singleton:** ". . . But when he came back he showed us all something. His very first game, we're watching to see if he's gun-shy, going to back off that plate a bit, or spin out on anything close. Uh-uh, he hung in on every pitch, and, first or second time up, hit a three-run homer. That's what you want to see when a teammate comes back from a beaning . . ."

**Earl Weaver:** ". . . oh, Reggie wasn't afraid of anything and he never gave me any trouble. Drove in a lot of big runs, even stole nearly 30 bases for us. I enjoyed having him on the team so much, I wanted the Orioles to sign him to a long-term deal. We tried. Reggie's agent, Gary Walker, had this fear of flying, so Hank Peters, our GM, had to fly back and forth to Walker's office in Arizona to negotiate. And Hank was getting frustrated. He told me, 'The figures they're talking about are mind-boggling!' Reggie was looking for something like $1.5 million for five years. Remember, no one knew where the free-agent market was going to go, not even Reggie and his agent.

"Hank finally got Reggie to agree to a one-year deal for $190,000, but we thought we still had a chance to sign him to something longer. Then the Kansas City Royals signed [first baseman] John Mayberry to a five-year deal for around $1 million. Oh boy, now Reggie and his agent were backing off their own numbers. Reggie figured if Mayberry, who'd only been in the league three or four years, could get that kind of contract, he was worth a lot more. And it turned out he was right."

*Perhaps Peters could have persuaded Reggie to ink a multiyear deal. But at least one Baltimore teammate believes that Jackson had another employer in mind all along:*

**Rudy May (major-league pitcher, 1965–83; pitcher, New York Yankees, 1974–76, 1980–83):** "I played with Reggie for half that season in Baltimore. I had spent the first part of the season pitching for the Yankees. The thing I remember most about him is, he hit a lot of home runs and won a lot of games for the Orioles. And he talked to me about leaving for big bucks the whole time he was there. There was a lot of speculation about where he would end up. I didn't think Baltimore could afford to keep him and there was a lot of talk about the Angels, the Expos, the Braves, and the Dodgers. Ted Turner of the

Braves wanted him badly because he [Turner] was just beginning to build his Superstation and Reggie was the kind of star just made for television.

"Despite all that speculation, I never had any doubts about where he was headed. Sometimes after hitting a big home run or driving in a couple of runs, he'd come back to the dugout and sit next to me. He'd quietly say, 'Hey man, how is it to play for the Yankees?' I said he would do best to stay where he was because he liked playing for Earl, the Orioles were always a contender, and there was no way he would ever get along with Billy [Martin] and George [Steinbrenner]. I knew both of them, and you could tell it wouldn't be a good mix. . . ."

**Irv Noren:** "I played with Billy and I was the third-base coach for all three of Oakland's World Series winners, so I knew Reggie. I could have told him that he and Billy would be at odds with each other. Not because of the way Reggie played, Billy would like that. Reggie busted his fanny on the field, not only at bat but running the bases and in the outfield, although he was prone to making errors. No, it was in the clubhouse where the trouble would come. Reggie was a good person, I liked him, but you could combine the egos of any five people you know and still not match Reggie's ego. He always wanted to be the center of attention and Billy was team-oriented, the kind of player and manager who believed that the welfare of the ball club was more important than any individual's performance. I didn't think Reggie would be able to easily blend in with Billy's system . . ."

**Rudy May:** ". . . but Reggie said, 'For the money they'll pay me I can get along with anybody.'"

*On November 29, 1976, Reggie Jackson signed a five-year, $2.96 million contract to play for the New York Yankees. It was the largest contract in baseball history to that time.*

**Ken Singleton:** "It turned out to be a bargain for New York, didn't it? If Reggie had stayed with us, the Yankees don't start that mini-dynasty they had. We could have been the club. And don't think Reggie doesn't know that. He's tweaked me several times about it. He asks, 'Ken, how many pennants did you win with Baltimore?' He knows the answer is two. Then he says, 'And how many seasons did you finish second?' And I tell him, 'Six.' Now comes the big smile as he says, 'Well, if you'd had me there all that time, you would have gone to the World Series in at least four of them.' And, you know what? He was probably right. Reggie could carry a club to the heights, make a good team a great one."

### REGGIE, REGGIE, REGGIE

*T*he heights were where Reggie and the Yankees were headed in *1977, although they needed a tightrope to cover the distance. Rudy May was right: Reggie and Billy Martin were a bad mix, two accelerants conspiring on a Molotov cocktail. They scrapped with each other all season and nearly came to blows in Fenway Park when Martin— who mistakenly believed Jackson was too much the prima donna to be a "team player"—removed Reggie from the field in mid-inning of a nationally televised game against the Red Sox. The right fielder had failed to chase down a Boston hit with enough gusto to satisfy his manager.*

**Billy Martin:** "Was I making an example of Reggie? You're damned right I was. Every spring I tell my teams one thing: I won't show them up as long as they don't embarrass me or the club on the field. Reggie strolled after that ball [Boston left fielder Jim] Rice hit, let a pop-up drop in for a base hit, then took his time chasing it down. I knew what I had to do. You don't hustle for your teammates, you don't deserve to play. So I told Paul Blair to go out there and tell Reggie he was through for the day. . . ."

**Rick Miller (major-league outfielder, 1971–85; reserve outfielder, 1977 Boston Red Sox):** "From our dugout, Reggie looked confused out there, so maybe he lost the ball at first. But he did take his time getting the ball and throwing it back towards the infield. I think Billy was justified in yanking him, although you knew the move was going to cause trouble. Of course, on the Red Sox, any friction the Yankees had was fine with us. . . ."

**Billy Martin:** ". . . soon as Reggie came into the dugout, I asked him what the hell he thought he was doing out there. He said he didn't know what I was talking about. Acted like I was picking on him. Then he said I had shown him up. I told him, 'You know my rules. If you show me up, I'm going to show you up.' He said something like, 'Who do you think you're talking to, old man?' and that's all I needed to hear. We went at each other. One of the players, I think it was Jimmy Wynn, grabbed Reggie. Then Yogi and Ellie grabbed me— they both have catcher's hands, very strong—or we'd have gone at it right there."

**Fran Healy (major-league catcher, 1969–78; reserve catcher, New York Yankees, 1976–78):** "Before Reggie came to New York, he was a good outfielder. Just ask Dick Williams, who even played him in center field with Oakland. But during the 1977 season, Reggie was having problems in the field and he had lost confidence in his defense. So when that ball got away from him, I think we were seeing his frustration. One thing you have to know about Reggie is that he always played hard. Very hard. You'd have to ask him whether he loafed on that particular ball, but I can understand why Billy thought Reggie wasn't hustling and why he reacted the way he did. I don't want to say that Billy had it in for Reggie. But after the Yankees signed Reggie, I was with Billy in the Yankee Stadium clubhouse. I remember him saying, 'I'll show him who's boss,' and wondering why on earth he would even be thinking that way when Reggie hadn't even played an inning for him yet. It was as if Billy was anticipating a problem."

**Willie Randolph:** "That was the Game of the Week on national TV, and I was surprised Billy would show Reggie up in front of millions of people, but I saw it coming. I was watching the bench right after the play, and I could see Paul Blair grabbing his glove. I was surprised, but

I wasn't totally surprised. These two men didn't like one another, and if Billy felt that he could get one up on you then he would do it. I don't think Reggie was coasting on that play. He didn't have the best hands in the world by then—I think Fran's right, his confidence in his defense was down—and he was just being overcautious. He was playing it safe, trying to get the ball back in, and so he didn't look aggressive out there. But I don't think he flubbed the play or loafed on purpose. Reggie did play hard, and he never wanted to embarrass himself in the field."

*Before that incident, Jackson and his manager had endured a spiky relationship. After it, they didn't have a relationship at all. Martin wasn't the only inhabitant of the Yankee clubhouse who found Jackson's behavior off-putting. Many players were alienated by Reggie's disparagement of team captain Thurman Munson in a* Sport Magazine *article ("I am the straw that stirs the drink . . . Munson thinks he can be the straw . . . but he can only stir it bad."), the way he snubbed their handshakes after hitting a game-tying home run against the Red Sox the very night the interview appeared in print, his nouveau riche habit of counting in front of them the hundred-dollar bills from his formidable roll, and his constantly referring to himself in the third person ("Having Reggie Jackson on your team is a show of force . . ."). Reggie behaved like a man who had joined the Yankees as a savior, as if they hadn't won the American League pennant without him the season before.*

*Around the major leagues, rival teams were waiting for the Yankee locker room—which writer Roger Angell later described as "the most joyless clubhouse I had ever been in"—to implode on controversy and strife, sending this pricey, talented group vaporizing into the ozone. They're still waiting. They must have forgotten how expert Martin was at using furor as a motivator or how Reggie had thrived playing for baseball's original dysfunctional family, Charlie Finley's Oakland A's. New York overcame all the celebrated intramural skirmishes to win their division and the American League pennant for the second consecutive season.*

*When the Yankees took the field against the Los Angeles Dodgers for the first game of the 1977 World Series, Reggie and his teammates finally had something in common. Both the club and the player were seeking redemption, the Yankees for that embarrassing Series sweep by the Cincinnati Reds the year before, and Jackson for an emotionally hellish regular season that had left his reputation sullied. They all got what they craved. New York beat Los Angeles four games to two in a Fall Classic made memorable by Reggie's "show of force" finale.*

*Jackson, who had already homered twice in the Series, opened the second inning of that sixth game by working out a walk against Los Angeles right-hander Burt Hooton. Chris Chambliss immediately followed with a two-run, game-tying homer into the right center-field bleachers. Two innings later, with the Dodgers ahead 3–2 and Thurman Munson on first, Jackson hit Hooton's first pitch into the right-field stands to give New York a lead it would not relinquish.*

*In the fifth, Reggie again blackjacked the first pitch he saw, sending Dodger reliever Elias Sosa's fastball into the right-field seats. Two pitches, two home runs. The game was nearly superfluous by the time Jackson's next at-bat spun around. When Reggie bounded from that on-deck circle, the Stadium crowd rose to its feet, a mob roaring not for victory but for history. Above the din, you could hear the cosmic tumblers clicking, as if some celestial Jimmy Valentine was jigging the dials and handle. Only this was no safe Jackson was breaking into. He was going to crack open the whole season, declare it his own in letters writ so large they would crowd the moon from the Bronx night. All that with just one more swing:*

**Reggie Jackson (major-league outfielder/designated hitter, 1967–87; right fielder, New York Yankees, 1977–81):** "The Dodgers were trying to bust me inside that series, so I backed off the plate some six inches. Look at the photo from that night and you'll see how far I am off the plate. It was a small adjustment, but the second time up, Hooton threw his first pitch inside, and I got around on it. I hit it on a line into the right-field seats. The pitch Sosa threw me, again inside, was the one I wasn't sure of when I hit it. I hooked it a little and couldn't tell if it was going out until it did. But that pitch the knuckleballer [Charlie Hough] threw me for the first pitch in the eighth . . ."

**Charlie Hough (major-league pitcher, 1970–94; pitcher, 1977 Los Angeles Dodgers):** ". . . was a pitch I could live with. Reggie's adjustment at the plate didn't make any difference to me. When you throw a knuckler, you don't throw hard enough to bust anyone inside and you really have no idea where the pitch is going to end up. You can let the knuckleball go from the same release point time after time, and each pitch will react differently. It's the erratic nature of the pitch, that butterfly movement, that makes it so hard to hit, not speed or location. The one thing you don't want is for the knuckler to spin, because then it loses that erratic movement and it's nothing more than a batting-practice pitch. The knuckler I threw Reggie did not spin at all, it moved well and broke down over the plate around his knees, a good first pitch in a good spot . . ."

**Reggie Jackson:** ". . . that looked like a beach ball coming up to the plate. There was no doubt about that one . . ."

*Beach ball? Hough's knuckler must have resembled a beached whale, Reggie got so much of it. He hit an arcing drive that ended its flight deep in the right-center-field seats, some 425 feet from home plate. Three consecutive homers on only three swings. No one had ever done that in a World Series game. Jackson finished the evening with five RBI, all the runs starter Mike Torrez would need to record an 8–4 complete-game victory:*

**Mike Torrez (major-league pitcher, 1967–84; pitcher, 1977 New York Yankees):** "I wasn't even supposed to start that game. I'd pitched and won Game Three three days earlier. It was Eddie Figueroa's turn. Billy was going to start me in the seventh game if there was one. But the [index] finger on Eddie's right hand was tender. He told [Yankee trainer] Gene Monahan about it. Soon as Billy found out, he called me into his office, asked how I felt, and when I told him I felt good, he asked if I wanted to pitch Game Six. Well, who wouldn't want that start? Pitching on three days' rest was nothing for me to think about. I loved to work. I told him, 'Hell, yes, Billy, you know I'm always ready to go.'

"One of the reasons Billy gave me the ball, I think, was that he liked my confidence. When I pitched Game Three, Dusty Baker hit that [third-inning] three-run homer to tie it. Boy, was I pissed. If he hit a good pitch, that would have been bad enough. But I was really mad at myself for hanging a slider when I was throwing so good. As soon as I got back to our bench, I told Billy, 'Don't worry about it. They're not scoring another run.' And that's what happened. They didn't score another run and we won.

"So Billy was comfortable with me. Unfortunately, before he could tell Figueroa about the switch, Eddie had heard a rumor that he was being passed over. He came to me and said, 'Mike, are you pitching the sixth game?' Now I'm on the spot. Billy had told me not to say anything, that he would tell Eddie. But I couldn't lie, so I admitted it. Eddie was pissed. His finger was sore, but he didn't want to miss that start. In fact, he threatened to quit the team. But that got smoothed over. A team can straighten out almost anything when it wins. Our club was a prime example of that all season. I got along with Reggie pretty well, but he sure pissed a lot of people off in our clubhouse. They were happy to have him after that sixth game, though, you can believe that."

**Willie Randolph:** "I'll tell you a little story about that final game of the '77 World Series. Just before the start of the ninth inning, I told myself in the dugout not to get too excited when we won. I knew the game was ours, there was no way this club was going to blow a five-run lead. I reminded myself to grab my hat and get off the field as fast as possible. I remembered how crazy the fans went when Chris [Chambliss] hit the home run that won the pennant for us the year before. I wanted to hold on to my hat, because if some fan went to grab it, you could get your eye poked out.

"So I go out to second base very cool and composed, got everything planned. [Yankee pitcher] Mike Torrez gives up a run but gets two outs. Lee Lacy comes up as a pinch hitter. The Dodgers are down by four runs, so he's just trying to do anything he can to get on base. Mike is throwing strikes, so you can't go up there looking for a walk. I think Lacy figured the last thing we'd be looking for in that situation was a bunt. So that's what he did. Mike made a good pitch up in the strike zone, hard pitch to bunt. The ball goes up and Torrez is right there, underneath the pop-up, calling for it. It seemed to take a long time to come down, but Mike catches it. We win! We're world champions! And I go nuts. I forget everything I told myself. I start shouting like a crazy man, leaping in the air. All of a sudden some kid creeps up behind me and whap! He's got my hat and some of my hair. And yes, he nearly did poke me in the eye. I had to tackle him to get my hat back.

"When I got up I looked into our dugout. It was a mob scene. Half of Yankee Stadium was in there. When I got to the dugout, I saw two cops have got some fan by the neck and they're choking him. It was my father! He had gotten as excited as I did and had run out onto the field. I ran over and explained who he was and they let him go. We went into the clubhouse and he got soaked with champagne just like he was part of the team. Well, he was part of my team. That celebration was great, especially after that mismatch with the Reds. Now we were on top. We had shown everybody.

"Watching Reggie that night was something I will never forget. I can't even say I was surprised by the three home runs. Surprise is something you experience when the unexpected happens. This was beyond the unexpected. I couldn't believe that the man was coming out of his face the way he was in such a huge game. Bang! Bang! Bang! You could just see the confidence beaming from the man every time he walked to the plate; you almost felt sorry for their pitchers. And that typified what this team was all about. We had such a feeling that we could get the job done when we had to. Reggie brought that with him. When he played with the Oakland A's and they were winning all those titles, they didn't take a backseat to anyone. We all learned a lot from him about how to win, the power of believing that no one is better than you, and how the game is supposed to be played. He made all of us a little bit better."

**Charlie Hough:** "Check his record, Reggie made every team he joined better. What impressed me the most about that night was that he homered on the first pitch off three different pitchers with completely contrasting pitching styles. For a hitter to be able to successfully make that many instant adjustments from one at-bat to another in that kind of pressure situation is amazing. What you saw that night was a Hall of Fame slugger demonstrating why he was a Hall of Famer."

## COMEBACK

*Whatever made Billy Martin run in ceaseless overdrive, his World Series success did not stall his pace. Or mellow him. Martin arrived in Florida for the opening of his team's 1978 spring training camp cordial as a hangman, the chip on his shoulder no weightier than a Yankee Stadium monument. Before the start of New York's first official workout one reporter innocently inquired whether Martin believed his club could win a second consecutive World Series. Flashing dagger eyes at the journalist, the manager replied in tones clipped and disdainful, "I didn't come down here to get a suntan."*

*Martin ran an uneventful camp and left Florida confident he was once again entering a season with the finest team in the major leagues. But from Opening Day on, injuries decimated his lineup and pitching staff. By July 17, the Yankees were foundering in fourth place, 14 games behind the Red Sox. That was the evening Martin suspended Reggie Jackson for disregarding one of his signs during a loss to the Kansas City Royals. The hostilities between right fielder and manager had resumed. Six days later Martin himself was fired for making intemperate remarks about Jackson and Yankee owner George Steinbrenner to the press. The Bombers looked about done:*

**Bill Lee:** "You know the baseball adage It's never over until it's over. Players say that to the media when the team is down because they don't want to give up hope. And if they're up, they say it because they don't want to appear too cocky. But when the Yankees dropped 14 games behind us and Martin was fired, we didn't care that it was only mid-July, we figured the race was over, at least as far as New York was concerned. There was no way they were going to catch us."

*Bob Lemon, dismissed as manager by the Chicago White Sox only three weeks earlier, succeeded Martin in the Yankee dugout. Even-tempered and accessible, Lemon immediately restored serenity and order to the combat-fatigued Yankee clubhouse. Martin had been fiddling with his lineup all season. By the time Lemon arrived, Thurman Munson was playing right field, Reggie Jackson was a part-time designated hitter, and Roy White was platooning in left with Lou Piniella. Lemon returned Jackson to right, put Munson back behind the plate, and penciled both White and Piniella into his everyday lineup. The offense, sputtering since Opening Day, immediately revived:*

**Bob Lemon (major-league pitcher, 1946–58; major-league manager, 1970–72, 1977–82):** "It didn't take a genius to make those moves. That was the lineup they won the World Series with the season before, so why not go with something that worked? We weren't going to win without Reggie out there every day providing power in the cleanup spot, and I had other hitters who could DH. Every manager would tell you they never wanted to see Lou or Roy coming to the plate with the game on the line. As for Thurman, I've always been a great believer that pitching wins pennants and every great pitching staff needs a catcher to lead it. When I was with Cleveland [in 1954] and we won all those [111] games, Jim Hegan was behind the plate making our jobs easier by calling a great game day in, day out. Thurman's arm was bothering him, but he was a smart catcher. He knew the weaknesses of every hitter in the league. I needed that experience behind the plate so our pitchers could do their jobs."

*As injured players regained their health, New York resumed winning. Boston, meanwhile, began to wilt, a circumstance that did not surprise many residents of that clubhouse in the Bronx:*

**Bucky Dent (major-league shortstop, 1973–84; shortstop, New York Yankees, 1977–82):** "I don't think anyone on our team ever gave up. We'd had a lot of injuries—Don Gullett, Catfish [Hunter], Mickey Rivers, and Willie were on the DL and a lot of guys had nagging injuries that they played through. I missed some time. Thurman Munson's knees ached him all summer, so he couldn't drive off his legs to hit. But we figured if we got most of the team back, we'd be all right. And that's what happened. As we got healthy, we started to win. Boston slipped and then they got hit by injuries.

"As soon as we started knocking some games off their lead, we figured we could catch them. No one talked about winning every game or taking ten in a row to get back into it. Instead, we figured we just had to win every series, take two out of three, or three out of four from every team we played. If we could just pick up a game a week until September, we knew we had a shot, because we had seven games against them that month. That's what we were shooting for. . . ."

**Mike Heath (major-league catcher, 1978–91; reserve catcher, 1978 New York Yankees):** "I was a rookie that year and I couldn't help thinking there was no way to catch the Sox. I figured we were playing for second place because Baltimore and Milwaukee were only a few games in front of us. But how do you make up fourteen games in ten weeks? At least that's what I thought at first. But all the veterans thought we would still pass them. . . ."

**Lou Piniella (major-league outfielder/designated hitter, 1964, 1968–1984; outfielder/designated hitter, New York Yankees, 1974–84):** ". . . I remember telling Mike that Boston wouldn't stay there. I didn't like their depth and I thought their bullpen was thin. They hadn't had a slump all season and every team goes through their share, even the best clubs. We had a veteran team that had a history of playing better as the season got later. I knew we could still catch them . . ."

**Mike Heath:** ". . . after I heard that enough times from everyone on our team, I started to believe it."

**Lou Piniella:** ". . . we all believed it. As Boston started to slide just like we figured, that became the most exciting thing I've ever been involved with. I'd come to the park every day knowing we had to win, and later leave the park having won. And it seemed like each win cut another game off Boston's lead. . . ."

*New York finished August with eight consecutive victories as they moved into second place, 6½ lengths behind Boston. While the Red Sox lost five of their first seven games in September, the Yankees won four out of six. By the time New York arrived in Fenway Park on September 7 for a four-game series, Boston's lead had shrunk to four games:*

**Bill Lee:** "The Yankees came in so hot, one of our coaches later said, 'They'll never play that well for that many games as long as they have assholes.' Meanwhile, we got injured and tired. [Right fielder] Dwight Evans got beaned so bad, he was suffering from vertigo for months. He'd get dizzy circling under fly balls and he was seeing double at the plate. Butch Hobson's right elbow was so messed up from crashing into walls trying to catch foul pops, he had to run halfway to first base before getting off a throw. [Second baseman Jerry] Remy fractured his wrist, and that hurt us immensely because he was one of the few guys on the team who could ignite a rally with his speed. Yaz stopped hitting with a bad back.

"When our regulars folded at the knees, we didn't have the bench to replace them. And you can blame [Boston manager Don] Zimmer and the front office for that. They wanted a God Bless America kind of team. So they got rid of all the free spirits like Bernie Carbo, the best fourth outfielder in baseball. In 1977 he had 15 home runs [in only 228 at-bats], three of them as a pinch hitter. And they let Rick Miller, who gave us speed and defense off the bench, get away."

**Rick Miller:** "During the off-season [in 1977], I had joined the California Angels, where I got more playing time. From my perspective, Zimmer single-handedly cost the Red Sox the pennant in 1978. Zim played his same nine guys every day that year, no matter what. Take a look at their roster and see how many bench players got 100 or more at-bats. . . ."

*Only two Boston subs, utility infielders Jack Brohamer (244) and Frank Duffy (104), had as many as 100 at-bats. By contrast, five Yankee irregulars batted 100 or more times.*

**Rick Miller:** ". . . if a guy was ill or injured, Zim would say, 'Hey, you can play today, right?' and stick him in the lineup. By the end of August those guys were so tired they would have lost a twenty-five-game lead. Smart managers use their bench so that the subs don't go stale and the regulars stay fresh through the pennant stretch. You know Cal Ripken set that record for consecutive games played, all well and good, but was it really good for his team? Ballplayers need rest. Zimmer didn't seem to understand that and it cost him and the Red Sox."

**Bill Lee:** ". . . Garry Hancock was the backup outfielder. Good glove, but a .220 hitter with no power. Not exactly Bernie Carbo. Jack Brohamer filled in for Remy and Hobson. A professional fielder, but again, he could not hit. Bob Bailey was a hell of a hitter, but Zimmer used him so little, he never got into a groove.

"Compare that to when the Yankees were hurting early in the season. Mickey Rivers goes down, Gary Thomasson hits .300 while he's out. Dent is on the DL, Fred Stanley catches everything at shortstop and scratches his way on base in key situations. Their bench was good enough to keep them above .500 or they would have been too far behind to launch their comeback. We couldn't play .500 after our guys started dropping. That made the difference.

"When we played the Yankees early in the season, they were pathetic. Half their lineup was missing, they looked like zombies on the field. But when they came to our park for those four games in September, they were the most intense team I've ever seen. It was like stepping into a bathtub with Jaws. Evey time we turned around they chomped off another limb. By the fourth inning of the first game, we were huddled in our dugout shaking our heads in disbelief. It was like we were Butch Cassidy and the Sundance Kid wondering, 'Who are those guys?' They definitely weren't the same club we'd played in June.

"We had the wrong attitude going into that series. We kept saying, 'All we need to do is split and we're fine.' The Yankees, you could see it in their body language, they weren't interested in splitting anything. They came in to sweep, and that's just what they did—15–3, 13–2, 7–0, and 7–4. We weren't in a single game. The Boston Massacre. By the time the Yankees left, we looked like we had just spent a month wandering through some demilitarized zone in Cambodia."

**Bucky Dent:** ". . . Once we took those four games and left Boston tied for first, we knew we were going to take it. Our hitters were all healthy and whaling on the ball. But the big thing was our pitching. Goose [Gossage] was blowing people away out of the bullpen. Catfish—man, he looked like he was through in June—was back on a [six-game] winning streak, pitching as good as ever, [Ron] Guidry was unbeatable, and Eddie [Figueroa] went on a roll. Don't forget Jim Beattie, because he was a key. He looked very tentative, like he was afraid to throw strikes through the first part of the season . . ."

**Bill Lee:** ". . . that motherfucker had that deer-in-the-headlights look when he pitched against us in June. We hit so many long balls off his weak shit, we drove him back to the minors right after the game. But when he faced us in Fenway [September 7], it was like he'd undergone a complete personality change. He was throwing hand grenades to home plate with an attitude that said, 'Hit this, asshole!' We didn't score off him until the ninth, and the Yankees were ahead by two touchdowns by then."

**Bucky Dent:** ". . . from that game on, Beattie trusted his stuff more. He challenged hitters and got them out. With him, Cat, Gator [Ron Guidry], and Figueroa in the rotation, you knew we had a chance to win every series. We were going to be tough to catch."

*The following weekend the Yankees won two out of three from the Red Sox in Yankee Stadium to establish their own two-and-a-half-game lead. The Bombers continued winning, yet they couldn't pull any further ahead.*

*During the final two weeks of the 1978 season, New York and Boston were two bumper cars jawlocked in a slender alleyway. Boston juked and jostled until New York's lead fell to a single game. For several days, it looked as if the Red Sox would trim it no further. On the final Sunday of the season, it was the Yankees who finally buckled, losing to Cleveland. A Boston win left the two teams tied for first place in the American League East. The two teams would meet in a single-game playoff to decide the division championship.*

*A coin toss had already designated Fenway Park as the site of the October 2 tie-breaker. Mike Torrez, who had signed with Boston as a free agent during the 1977 off-season, started for the Red Sox. The right-hander had been a valuable acquisition for Boston. His 16 wins were the second-highest total on the Red Sox pitching staff and his fifteen complete games had granted much-needed relief to his team's sparse, overworked bullpen. New York answered him with Ron Guidry, the nearly unhittable left-hander whose 24 wins had kept the Yankees in the pennant race throughout the summer.*

*Boston took a one-run lead in the first inning when Red Sox left fielder Carl Yastrzemski sent a Guidry fastball into the right-field stands. The Sox scored again in the sixth on a Jim Rice single. Few two-run leads ever appeared larger. The slightly built Guidry, pitching on three days' rest rather than his customary four, struggled with each batter. Conversely, the often-erratic Torrez—even when pitching his best, the right-hander was prone to surrendering an alarming number of base runners—seemed at his peak. During his first six innings on the mound, only two Yankees had managed hits.*

*The New York seventh began uneventfully. Graig Nettles led off with a harmless fly ball to right. But Roy White and Chris Chambliss followed with sharply hit singles. Boston fans—by now inured to losing big games to the Yankees—prepared themselves for the deluge. However, when Jim Spencer hit a fly ball for the second out of the inning, you could feel tension release its hammerlock on the ancient ballpark. Bucky Dent was New York's next scheduled batter. As Boston fans reminded themselves, this shortstop was the tamest hitter in the Yankee lineup. And Torrez still looked indomitable despite the two New York hits:*

**Mike Torrez:** "Those singles by Roy [White] and Chris [Chambliss] didn't bother me a bit. I felt comfortable on the mound, locked in. I don't think I've ever had sharper concentration. Even after Spencer hit that fly ball for the second out of the inning, I didn't let up when Bucky came up. I had played with him the year before and I knew how tough he could be. He didn't strike out much, and he was strong for his size.

"He took my first pitch, a slider, for a strike. Then he banged another slider off his foot. Strike two . . ."

**Bucky Dent:** "I had gone to the plate that inning carrying a cracked bat. I was using Mickey Rivers's bat that day—felt very comfortable with it—but I had broken it during batting practice. It was a crack, under the tape, so small you could barely see it. When I went up to the plate for that at-bat against Torrez, I pulled the broken bat out of the rack without realizing it. While [Yankee trainer] Gene Monahan worked on my ankle, Mickey noticed my mistake. He said, 'You've got the wrong bat, man. That one's the cracked one.' So he gave me his other bat and I went back to the batter's box . . ."

**Mike Torrez:** "Bucky had limped around for a few minutes before Gene worked on him. That seemed like an eternity for me and—I don't mean to use this as an excuse—it robbed me of that extra bit of concentration. Suddenly, I wasn't as finely tuned as I had been. . . . When he finally got back up, [Boston catcher Carlton] Fisk called for a fastball inside. You see, we were going to jam him. Now, I could have thrown him another slider, he's down no balls, two strikes. Instead, I wanted to back him off the plate with a fastball, a waste pitch, then come back with the slider away. But instead of just throwing the ball like I had all afternoon, I tried to guide the pitch a bit and I didn't get the ball in deep enough and . . ."

**Don Zimmer (major-league manager, 1972–91; manager, Boston Red Sox, 1976–80):** ". . . Dent lofted the ball to left field. To be honest, I didn't think it was hit that well. The moment it left his bat I thought, 'Good, the inning's over.' It looked like an out from where I was sitting. Then I saw Carl [Yastrzemski] start to back up and I thought, 'Wait a minute. That damned thing's off the wall!' I start thinking tie ball game and I'm waiting for Yaz to play the carom, but he never stops looking up! I remember standing there sort of stunned. I think the whole ballpark went quiet, and I'm standing there saying, 'Oh my, it's in the net.'"

**Bucky Dent:** ". . . funny thing, I had no idea where the ball was. I was no home-run hitter by any means, but I had gone up to the plate looking to drive the ball for extra bases. In that situation you want to score the runners and get yourself in scoring position for the next batter. The moment I hit the pitch I ran my tail off. I knew it was on the line, but I had no idea how high the ball was. I figured it was off the wall and I was hoping to hustle to second with the lead run. I didn't find out I had hit a home run until I passed first base and saw the umpire's signal. I didn't actually see the home run until I caught it on videotape later. One thing I did pick up on right away was the reaction of the Fenway fans after they realized what had happened. That park was like a morgue. You couldn't hear anything except for the guys in our dugout and a few brave Yankee fans clapping.

"Later on, people asked me if I was excited after hitting the homer. To tell the truth, I didn't realize the magnitude of what I had done until long after it was over. In a moment like that, all you're focused on is winning. You're more concerned with the game's outcome than with being a hero. Remember, it was only the seventh inning and the home run gave us just a one-run lead. The whole thing didn't hit me until after the World Series."

*A dramatic moment, to be sure, but there were still two innings of baseball left to play. Torrez followed Dent's homer by walking Mickey Rivers. Zimmer brought Bob Stanley, an all-purpose right-hander who could start, close, or pitch long relief, into the game. Rivers stole second base, then scored the Yankees' fourth run when Thurman Munson doubled. Reggie Jackson,*

*no doubt noting that the clubhouse calendar had turned to October, led off
the eighth with a home run, making the score 5–2, New York.*

**Bob Stanley (pitcher, Boston Red Sox, 1977–89):** ". . . just two days
before, I had pitched [seven scoreless innings in a start] against
Toronto. I'd been pitching well [15–2, 10 saves, 2.60 ERA], and
Zimmer liked to play the hot hand. But I probably shouldn't have
been out there after pitching so much on Saturday. Fans blame
Mike for the Dent home run, but if I could have held the Yankees, it's
a different ball game. That home run by Reggie in the eighth hurt
us. . . ."

*Boston rallied for two runs in the bottom of that inning. When the Red
Sox came to the plate in the ninth, New York led 5–4. Yankee closer Goose
Gossage was on the mound to pitch his third inning in relief of Guidry.
During the off-season, New York had chosen to invest in the free agent
Gossage rather than sign Mike Torrez to a lucrative long-term contract. It
was a sound decision. Gossage's record with the Pittsburgh Pirates in 1977
had established him as one of baseball's dominant closers. He had entered
the game against the Red Sox as the American League leader in saves. But
when he first joined New York for the 1978 season, the pressures of playing
in a demanding city after signing a rich, highly publicized contract had
weighed on his performance:*

**Goose Gossage (major-league pitcher, 1972–94; pitcher, New York
Yankees, 1978–83):** "I did not get off to a good start when I joined the
Yankees in 1978. Even after I had that rough start, my teammates
didn't get down on me. They knew what I could do. They kept me
loose by getting on my case. One game, the car was bringing me in
from the bullpen. Mickey Rivers, who was in center field, throws himself in front of the car and he starts screaming, 'No, not him! Anybody
but him!' I told him to get off the car and get ready to catch the shit I
was going to throw up there. We got to the mound, I got out of the car
and threw one pitch. The batter whacks it to deep center. Mickey had
to race about sixty miles at full speed to get it. When we got to the

dugout he gave me this pop-eyed look and said, 'Hey, man, you weren't kidding, were you?'

"Another time, Thurman [Munson] came to the mound during a game. I had just been brought in, and the winning run was up at the plate. Thurman said, 'Well, Goose, you've given up home runs to lose games and thrown wild pitches. You've lost on base hits and you've got beaten on errors. You've done it all. What have you got planned for us today?'

"Right after that, different game, Thurman came out as I took the mound and said, 'Well, someone sure has confidence in you.' I said, 'What do you mean?' He laughed and said, 'Look at your center fielder.' I turned and saw Mickey Rivers already facing the center-field wall in a sprinting position. All I could see was the number on his back.

"The fans weren't laughing, though. We lost four of our first five games in '78, and I was charged with two of those losses. When we got back to New York for the home opener and [Yankee p.a. announcer] Bob Sheppard introduced me during the pregame ceremonies, the crowd let me have it. There was more than 60,000 people there that day, and I swear it sounded like every one of them was booing me. [Yankee left-hander] Kenny Holtzman, he'd been called out just before me, turned to me with a big smile and said, 'That's not "Goose!" they're yelling, buddy.' I just nodded at the crowd like it didn't bother me, but inside I was thinking, 'All right, you mother-fuckers. Boo all you want. By the time this season is over, I'll have all of you cheering.'"

*This was his opportunity to win their cheers for a lifetime. Dwight Evans hit an unimposing fly ball to left field for the first out. Rick Burleson, the Boston shortstop, worked Gossage for a walk. Red Sox second baseman Jerry Remy entered the batter's box. Picking on a low fastball, the left-hand-hitting Remy pulled a line drive to Lou Piniella in right. A certain double. However, Piniella made what became the crucial play of the game by pretending to draw a bead on a ball he had lost in the sun. The "catch that wasn't" kept the speedy Burleson and Remy at first and second.*

*Piniella's was the kind of heady play the Yankees seemed to routinely make during their dramatic stretch run:*

**Lou Piniella:** "As I went out to right field in the ninth, I kept thinking, I hope they don't hit the ball to me, because it was almost impossible to see out there. It was really bad. The sun was right in my eyes, especially down the line. I had even mentioned it to some of the guys. I was playing shallow for Jerry Remy, he didn't have much power. When he hit the ball, I never saw it, couldn't tell you where it was, so I had to play on instinct.

"I had noticed the trajectory of his swing and figured the ball had to be hit on the line. I took a few steps over without letting the base runner know I had lost sight of the ball. If you let the base runner know you're having problems out there, he'll take off on you. So I stayed as calm as I could and decoyed that I was going to make the catch. All of a sudden, the ball drops out of the sun and hits in front of me. It bounced to my left, and I grabbed it quickly to get off a good throw to third. That's what kept Burleson from advancing."

*Had Burleson been able to advance to third on Remy's single, he might have subsequently scored the tying run when Jim Rice hit a deep fly to Piniella for the second out. That run would have radically altered the complexion of the game, with Boston having all the momentum. Instead, the next Boston hitter faced Gossage with runners on first and third and two men out.*

*In medieval battles, opposing generals leading equally strong forces were loath to risk the heavy casualties that an all-out conflict was bound to incur. So the two commanders would often agree to a round of champions, a duel or joust between the most formidable warriors from each side. The army whose knight prevailed took the day.*

*That is what the 1978 baseball season came down to that afternoon in Boston. For months these two powerful clubs had mauled each other until they were separated by only a single run in the final frame of a sudden-death playoff. Now the division championship would be decided by a duel between Goose Gossage, the most intimidating closer in baseball, and Carl*

*Yastrzemski, a Boston legend, the much-storied hero of Boston's Impossible Dream pennant-winning season in 1967. Gossage knew his opponent's reputation:*

**Goose Gossage:** "The night before that game, I had a feeling that I would end up facing Yaz for the last out, and that's exactly what happened. We were up 5–4, two men out, two men on, bottom of the ninth, and here he comes. My legs were shaking. Never had a feeling like that before. I told someone it was like being led in front of a firing squad. Yaz was a strong, veteran fastball hitter who had come through in the clutch so many times to win big games for the Red Sox. He had a great eye, and I knew he wouldn't be overswinging out of nervousness. Rice, [Fred] Lynn, Fisk, Evans, they were all great, but Yaz was the last guy I wanted to face in that spot.

"I had to calm down, so I started talking to myself. I thought, 'All right, what's the worst thing that can happen here?' And my answer was, 'I'll be home in Colorado tomorrow looking at the mountains.' Suddenly I'm very calm. I put my foot on the rubber and just went right at him. Yaz was still a great fastball hitter, but that was my best pitch, so that's what I was going with. I did not want to go home losing the game on some half-assed breaking ball. . . ."

**Carl Yastrzemski (outfielder, Boston Red Sox, 1961–83):** "You knew Gossage wasn't going to try to fool you. He threw everything hard, so you went up to the plate looking for a fastball. But that pitch he threw me that afternoon came in even faster than I thought. . . ."

**Goose Gossage:** ". . . I can't tell you how hard I threw that pitch, but it might have been one of the hardest pitches I've ever thrown. Afterwards Thurman commented that it had something extra on it . . ."

**Carl Yastrzemski:** ". . . I had a good look at it as it came up to the plate just around my knees. That's usually a good pitch for me. But just as I got the head of the bat out, the ball exploded. I tried turning on it, but I just got underneath the ball . . ."

**Goose Gossage:** ". . . that pitch rode in on his hands, and he popped it up to Nettles. Later Graig told me that during Yaz's at-bat, he was saying to himself, 'Pop him up, pop him up, pop him up,' and when I did, he says he thought, 'But not to me!'"

*Nettles's fevered imagination may have been entertaining doubts, but his hands were confident and sure. Yaz's pop-up hung for an interminable moment, suspended for so long it seemed to taunt the crowd below before settling into the third baseman's glove. Gossage received credit for the save as Ron Guidry recorded his major-league-leading 25th win. New York sprinted to Kansas City for the start of the American League playoffs while Boston and its fans trudged off into another forlorn winter of what-iffing, victimized once again by those damned Yankees.*

## LIGHTNING STRIKES

*I*t was appropriate that Ron Guidry notched the win in that division-clinching game. The player journalists had dubbed Louisiana Lightning had kept his team in the pennant race all season. No other Yankee pitcher, not even Whitey Ford, had ever looked so incapable of losing. A lean bundle of nerveless energy, Guidry called upon reserves of strength that belied his unimposing physique. Everything he threw was hard. Unlike most starters, who needed at least three pitches to baffle and subdue major-league hitters, the Cajun lefty took to the mound with only two weapons of choice. The way he made them dance, two were enough.

The Guidry slider—a vicious, biting scythe imparted to him by Yankee closer Sparky Lyle—was a conjurer's pitch that flashed toward the hitter near eye level before vanishing under his bat. Guidry's fastball was among those rarest of heaters that appeared to gain velocity while it leaped at the plate. Add his unerring control and a cavalryman's mental toughness to his spare but potent arsenal, and you understood why batters found this lefty one hard piece of work. Like a Dizzy Dean or a Sandy Koufax, Guidry's stud strut to the mound at the start of a game would immediately lift his entire team. Everyone on the Yankees was convinced that he was invincible. During the 1978 season they weren't alone in that conviction:

**Ron Guidry (pitcher, New York Yankees, 1975–88):** "People don't remember this because I finished 25 and 3, but the 1978 season started kind of slow for me, at least as far as wins went. I had a couple of no-decisions in my first few games. But I had pitched well and didn't get charged with any losses. Then I went on a roll and it seemed like every time I went out there I knew I wasn't just going to win, I was going to blow people away. And I did. When I lost my first game, I figured, 'This is just a temporary setback, because I'm not going to lose again.' I won thirteen in a row, lost, won two in a row, lost again, then won eight in a row before I lost one more. Then I didn't lose again for the rest of the year.

"In Milwaukee, Mike Caldwell beat me. In Baltimore, it was Mike Flanagan, and in Toronto, Mike Willis. Willis won only three games that whole year, so I guess if your name was Mike, and you were pitching against me, you had a chance to win. But not much of one. You had to be great to beat me, had to pitch your best game. I don't want that to come out wrong, but that was how I felt. No matter who the other guy was, if he didn't pitch the best game of his life he was going to lose . . ."

**Ken Singleton:** ". . . and a lot of his opponents felt the same way. Let me tell you about one of those 'Mike' losses, because even though Guidry got an L that night, it demonstrates how much respect hitters had for him. We were playing the Yankees that season, Mike Flanagan is on the mound for us, and we are losing 1–0. Dent makes a throwing error, a ball Chambliss couldn't dig out of the dirt, and we have a man on first.

"The next batter, Doug DeCinces, comes to the plate and hits a line drive, one of the hardest-hit balls I've ever seen. It just clears the left-center-field fence, which was much deeper than it is now, for a two-run homer. Normally, that happens, a guy might come into the dugout saying, 'Okay, let's get some more now,' you know, exhorting his teammates to put some more runs on the board? Doug comes into the dugout, looks at Mike Flanagan, and says, 'We're not getting any more runs, so you better make that stand up.' And he was right. Mike beat him 2–1, a loss that dropped Gator's record all the way down to 15–2. We upset him so much, he went out and won his next seven or eight in a row."

**Ron Guidry:** "That was the year everyone started clapping when I had two strikes on the batter. You see that all the time now, but I don't think that had ever been done before, at least not start after start. The night I struck out eighteen Angels [June 17], I could hear the clapping and that was unusual. Usually I would hear something in the distance, like it's at the end of a tunnel, but you're concentrating so hard you can't describe quite what it is.

"But that night against California there were 35,000 fans in the Stadium and they were rocking the place. Everything went my way, and the Angels helped me a little. They were swinging—and missing—at everything I threw up there, fastballs in their eyes, sliders in the dirt. After a while, the Angels hitters were so determined not to strike out, they came up to the plate swinging defensively. It was almost funny after a while. They were even chanting out the number of strikeouts from the California dugout. . . ."

**Rick Miller:** ". . . One of the reasons he struck out so many that night is because our lineup was stacked with right-handed hitters and Guidry was tougher on righties than lefties. That hard, hard slider of his looked like a low strike until the last minute, when it would break down and in on right-handers. He could make them look ridiculous with that pitch. They'd be swinging and missing at pitches that would bounce in the dirt or be off their ankles. And he had an up-and-away fastball. You're looking for that slider down, you had no chance against that high fastball.

"Lefties had a better shot, because the slider didn't look like a strike to us like it did to righties. We couldn't hit it anyway, so we'd just take it. Then he'd end up throwing us more fastballs or switch the slider to the inside of the plate. Like most left-handers, I was a low-ball hitter so I didn't mind facing him, but I still couldn't do much with him that season. Nobody could."

**Bucky Dent:** "I was on the bench with an injury, so I didn't play the night Guidry struck out all those Angels, but I had a ringside seat in the dugout. Overpowering? He had so much stuff that night, I watched an entire lineup of big-league hitters just try to make contact, anything to put the ball in play. After a while, it looked like guys who just fouled off the ball were happy to do that. He was just throwing the ball right by them."

**Amos Otis:** "Every hitter in baseball should've taken out a contract on Sparky Lyle for teaching Guidry that slider. Ron actually improved on the pitch. Guidry threw his slider much harder than Sparky, as hard as anyone could throw it. It looked like a fastball until it got to home plate, then it broke straight down, more like a hard, fast, nasty curveball. If you went up looking for it, you still couldn't hit it, and if you did look for it, Guidry could smoke you with a fastball. The best slider I ever saw belonged to Steve Carlton, but, for at least two or three seasons, Guidry's slider was just as tough."

**Bill Lee:** "From a pitcher's standpoint, Guidry had four things going that year that put him on another planet from everyone else. First, velocity and control. There have been very few pitchers who could throw that hard while staying around the plate. It seemed like every hitter who faced him entered the batter's box behind in the count. You expected control like that from a guy like me who never threw all that hard, but it's exceptional in a pitcher with Guidry's velocity. Second was his endurance. Most power pitchers could go hard at you for six or seven innings, but then they went to other pitches more—provided they had them—as their velocity dropped. Guidry threw just as hard on pitch 121 as pitch one. Great stuff all the way through. You watched him pitch—and he was a little guy—and thought, 'When's his arm going to fall off?' but it never did. A lot of that was mechanics. Guidry had textbook mechanics, there was no wasted energy in his motion.

"Third was the action on his slider. Some sliders bite, this slider cut like a buzz saw, just sawed your bat in two. It had such great late movement, it was hard to make good contact with it, and even if you did hit it squarely, it was a bitch to elevate, so you couldn't hit him for distance.

"Finally, Guidry had quick feet. Most people don't realize this, but the great power pitchers—someone like Pedro Martinez today—usually have quick feet. A pitcher cannot throw a baseball until his landing foot is down. . . ."

*The pitcher who finished second to Guidry in the voting for the 1978 American League Cy Young Award agreed with Lee's assessment:*

**Mike Caldwell (major-league pitcher, 1971–84; pitcher, 1978 Milwaukee Brewers):** "That's a good point. Pitchers throw against their front side a little bit. Watch Pedro Martinez and some of these hard throwers today, you see how firmly that front foot is planted after their release. Having quick feet is an indication that you're an exceptionally coordinated athlete, and we know Guidry had great reflexes, could field his position so well, he won a few Gold Gloves. A pitcher with a great arm like Guidry or Martinez, who can get that landing foot down quicker, gets through his release point quicker . . ."

**Bill Lee:** ". . . and the ball gets to the batter before he's ready for it. Give me two pitchers who both throw 90 miles per hour, one who hits that landing foot in a flash, and one who's more deliberate in his windup. To the batter, the pitcher with the quicker feet is going to seem to have the better fastball. It doesn't matter what the Juggs gun reads. It will be as if the ball is right on top of you before you're even set to swing, and then it explodes.

"That was how most of Guidry's pitches looked that season. I know Jim Rice won the MVP Award that year, and I'm not going to dispute that choice. But without Guidry, the Yankees don't come near us in '78. He'd get two quick strikes on you and then you were meat. Guidry lost only three games that year, and it seemed as if the teams that beat him should have apologized for it."

**Ron Guidry:** "In the playoffs against Kansas City that year, we had the Royals down two games to one. I was scheduled to pitch the fourth game, and a lot of the reporters were asking the Royals how they felt about having to beat me to have any chance at all of winning the pennant. George Brett got so sick of hearing the question he said, 'Ron Guidry isn't God.' Just before the game that night I sent George a note. It read, 'George, maybe I'm not God, but right now, I'm the closest thing to it.'

"Of course, George hit a triple off me in the first inning of that game and scored the first run of the night, so he got some revenge. Great hitter. But that was the only run the Royals scored that evening. Graig [Nettles] hit a home run to tie it in the second, and Roy [White] hit one out in the sixth. Two runs. That year, that was about all I needed. We rode those right into the Series."

*The media billed the 1978 World Series as a grudge fight, a Texas-style death match between the Los Angeles Dodgers and their tormentors from the previous October. New York arrived in L.A. for the first game confident, but disadvantaged. Willie Randolph, their All-Star second baseman, had pulled a hamstring just as the season ended. He would miss the entire Fall Classic. A pulled leg muscle was hampering the speed of center fielder Mickey Rivers. First baseman Chris Chambliss, the Yankees' most reliable hitter throughout much of the season, was also troubled by leg problems that made it difficult for him to drive the ball with any power.*

*After the Dodgers won the first two Series games on their home field, it appeared as if these Yankees had finally run out of miracles. But Los Angeles made two grave errors. The first occurred when Dodger second baseman Davey Lopes, after hitting the second of two first-game home runs, flashed the "We're Number One" sign as he rounded the bases. His action piqued a Yankee team that was best left unperturbed.*

*The second error proved more serious than the first. The Dodgers failed to beat Guidry in the Series' third game, on a rare night when New York's Top Gun was eminently beatable:*

**Ron Guidry:** "The way Lopes behaved and the things the Dodgers said after those first two games, acting like they had the Series sewn up, really pissed us off. I always believed we were a team with a lot of class. Even when we were beating Los Angeles the year before, we didn't say anything about it, we just did it. Same thing against Boston and Kansas City. We respected our opponents and figured, 'Hey, if you want to talk, let's do it out there between the lines.'

"There were a bunch of us in the clubhouse early on the day I was scheduled to pitch [October 13, 1978]. Thurman [Munson] came in steaming. He had just read some more Dodger quotes saying this was going to be their year, and he said, 'If this was any other team but Los Angeles, I might say just forget it. But the way these guys have been carrying on, mouthing off, I would like nothing better than to kick their asses four straight.' So he turned to me and said, 'If you got enough to win this game, let's take the next three and go home.'

"As it turned out, I didn't have my best stuff that night. I'd pitched a lot of innings in the last month of the season and had started against Boston in that playoff game on short rest. I was still feeling it. But [Yankee third baseman] Graig Nettles was incredible that night. He made four plays that have to be among the best ever made and saved me at least six runs. Caught balls from out of nowhere.

"We won that game and won again the next day. Now we had the edge, because we had one more game here [at Yankee Stadium] and the Dodgers were looking kind of stiff. All of a sudden they had developed laryngitis or something, because the chattering stopped.

"They collapsed completely in that fifth game. We kept getting hit after hit, and then the Dodgers started to make errors and mental mistakes. You know, good players always want the ball hit to them, they want all the tough plays. Like Graig in my game. But the Dodgers looked like they were thinking, 'Please don't hit the ball to me!'

"We beat them 12–2 and that really ticked us off, because as soon as it was over we realized the team now had to fly cross-country to Los Angeles for only one game and then come all the way back home. We knew, though we kept it to ourselves, there was no way they were going to force us to play a seventh game.

"Catfish [Hunter] was even more confident than any of us. He was scheduled to start the sixth game and he had already reserved a flight back to his home in North Carolina for that same evening. He knew he was going to close the deal. I think we would have beaten Los Angeles no matter what, but Lopes and the Dodgers with all that talk made it a lot easier for us to turn our motivation up a notch or two. That 1978 club, it really wasn't a good idea to get us angry."

*Catfish Hunter made his flight. He received credit for the win as New York defeated Los Angeles 7–2. Gossage pitched two scoreless innings to close the victory. Fenway scourge Bucky Dent hit .417 with seven RBI to win the Series MVP Award. Brian Doyle, Willie Randolph's replacement at second base, further supported Bill Lee's contention that New York possessed a superior bench by batting .438 in six games. The victory gave the Yankees their twenty-second World Series Championship. No other club could claim as many as ten.*

## GEORGE BRETT: THE SILENCE OF THE FANS

*T he Kansas City Royals had reached the American League playoffs in 1976, '77, and '78, only to lose on all three occasions to the New York Yankees. In 1980 the two teams met once again for the league championship. To a man the Royals believed that these Yankees were vulnerable. Key Bombers who had frustrated Kansas City in the past were no longer on New York's roster. The Royals also entered this fray with a plan, one as uncomplicated as the "wait and fire" strategy employed so successfully by Wellington at Waterloo. "The idea," said Kansas City right fielder Clint Hurdle, "is to do anything we can to get an early lead and keep [Goose] Gossage in the Yankee bullpen. No one wants to see him come in with the game on the line. He is the master of disaster."*

**Amos Otis:** "Ballplayers aren't going to admit to fear. Go up to the plate intimidated and you might as well sit down without taking your cuts. But we all have a healthy respect for what can happen if you get hit by a baseball that's being thrown 90-plus miles an hour. You have to have that respect so you don't fall asleep up there and get caught.

"Gossage increased that respect level. Here you have this guy on the mound, six-three, 230 pounds, coming into the game looking like he has an attitude. His hat is pulled down so far over his eyes, you're not even sure he can see you, and while Goose actually had pretty good control for such a hard thrower, he's just wild enough to keep you loose up there. He threw, what? 97 miles an hour, sometimes hit 100, and his ball moved. Plus he had this deceptive pitching motion—like he needed that—all arms and legs coming at you at once with the ball, making it that much more difficult to pick up the pitch. On top of that, he had by then developed a real nasty bat-breaking slider, something he threw a lot in 1980. Not fair. Baseball should have outlawed him from using any kind of breaking pitch.

"There were a lot of great relievers in the league when I played. We had Quis [Dan Quisenberry] on our team, a super reliever, and he had just as many saves as Goose that year. But with a runner on third and no one out, there was a chance you could score off Quis, because he didn't throw hard. A runner might score on a ground ball or a long fly. But Goose could come in and just stop your offense right there; you know, strike out the first two hitters, then get the third out on a weak pop-up. Goose could shut you down like no other reliever around at that time. Hurdle was right; he was the master of disaster."

*These Royals had a master of disaster of their own, only he wasn't a pitcher. Third baseman George Brett had spent the summer trying to become the first major-leaguer since Ted Williams to bat .400. He missed by only ten points, settling for a major-league-leading .390. In 117 games Brett, who played his home games in a park notoriously unkind to sluggers, hit 24 home runs while gathering 118 RBI. He won what many consider the real triple crown by leading his league in slugging and on-base percentage as well as batting average. Brett had played in all three of the League Championship Series the Royals had lost to New York. An unrelenting competitor, he had no intention of being on the short side in a fourth.*

*Opening the series in Kansas City on October 7, Brett and his teammates kept Gossage in the bullpen while winning the first two games, 7–2 and*

*3–2. Yankee Stadium was the site of Game Three on October 10. With one more victory, the Royals would finally reach the Promised Land. Kansas City took a 1–0 lead in the fifth inning off Yankee starter Tommy John, but New York recaptured the lead with two runs in the sixth.*

*Kansas City responded promptly. In the top of the seventh, Royals left fielder Willie Wilson's elbows-flailing scamper turned a dunking slap shot into a two-out double, chasing John and summoning the Goose into the game. The moment Kansas City had dreaded was at hand.*

*Gossage came rumbling onto the diamond his usual self—raging, hot, smoking, looking like you could fry eggs on the bill of his cap. Just glancing his way you knew this was no average flamethrower. He would be dealing napalm from the mound, engulfing home plate in roaring sheets of the stuff. And to the Yankees young captain, that usually smelled like victory.*

*UL Washington knew what was coming. As you watched the Royals shortstop walk toward the batter's box, you got the impression he was tiptoeing so as not to rile the prickly reliever any further. He didn't appear scared; he just didn't look as if he was approaching his task with a whole lot of incentive. But kneeling behind UL in the on-deck circle was the Kansas City equalizer, concentrated and cool, ready—no, eager—to meet the Gossage inferno with a little heat of his own:*

**George Brett:** "Going into that third game, we'd heard from a lot of people about how the Yankees always found a way to beat us in the past. They were wondering how we were going to blow this one even with a two-games-to-none lead. Those people didn't realize something and we did. These were not the same Yankees who had beaten us in the past. Thurman [Munson] had died in that plane crash [during the 1979 season]. Chambliss, White, and Rivers weren't there anymore, and those guys used to kill us. Rivers and White must have hit .400 against us. This was a different group, and we were very confident for that third game.

"UL was the first batter to face Goose. He hit a high chopper over the mound, and Willie Randolph made a great play just to get it and make a throw. But with UL's speed, he beat it out. I came up, first and third, two men out and we're down by a run. This is the Goose out there. I had faced him enough times to know Gossage wasn't going to start me with any change-ups. In that situation he was going to go with his best. I wasn't sure if it would be his fastball or the slider, so I just looked for something hard.

"That first pitch he threw to me was right down the middle. I doubt Goose wanted to make it that good. Remember, he could have walked me without giving up a run, there were only two men on. I had come up planning to pull the ball. With Yankee Stadium's close right-field seats, I figured anything hit in the air was a bonus. Well, I did get it into the air for a three-run homer, and we ended up beating the Yankees, 4–2. That's how it stayed.

"I've got to tell you, that was sweet. I was there in '76, '77, and '78 as a member of those losing teams. There's nothing more frustrating to a ballplayer than getting that close to the World Series, and missing out. I remembered how the Yankee fans went crazy when Chris Chambliss hit that home run to beat us in 1976. Yankee fans were always noisy when their teams were winning; they were noisy when New York had the lead that night. So I guess the biggest thrill of all, in that moment as I circled the bases, was getting to hear just how quiet 56,000-plus people could get in this stadium. That was the most fun I'd had in a long time. We lost the World Series to the Phillies that year, but 1980 is still a great memory for me."

### OUT AT HOME

*B*rett's heroics might not have eliminated the Yankees if not for a controversial play that occurred during the second game of those playoffs. Playing in Kansas City, New York was behind, 3–2, in the eighth inning. Second baseman Willie Randolph led off that frame with a base hit. Two outs later, Bob Watson hit what looked to be a game-tying double. Then the ball caromed perfectly to Royals left fielder Willie Wilson:

**Amos Otis:** As the center fielder and senior player, I was the captain of the outfield, so I worked with Willie on his throwing. Willie didn't have a strong arm; it was his only weakness as an outfielder, because he could cover more ground than anyone in baseball and catch anything he got to. We worked for hours on his release so he could get rid of the ball quickly, with no wasted motion after it was caught.

"What made that play against Bob, though, wasn't the throw itself, it was the positioning. Willie was in the right spot to get that ball and make the play, and that, no matter what Yankee fans might have thought, was not luck. We had a system in our outfield. As the captain, everyone keyed off me. The other two outfielders and I would set up the same distance from each other on every play. How far that distance was depended on how much range whoever was playing that day had.

"When Al Cowens was our regular right fielder, I gave him more room to cover because he could fly. But when Clint Hurdle took over, I had to cheat a few steps towards him, because he wasn't as fast as Al. Throughout the game, the other outfielders would watch me; if I moved two steps to my right on a batter, so did they. Exactly the same two steps. We did this for each hitter.

"When Watson came to the plate—a right-handed pull hitter, basically, who I knew we would pitch inside—I moved two steps to my left. So did Willie. That's why he didn't have to move very far to get to Watson's carom, and he got rid of that ball lickety-split. . . ."

*Wilson's release was quick but his throw was weak, a rainbow lob toward home that could not have reached the plate in time to intercept Randolph. Fortunately for Kansas City fans, George Brett was perfectly positioned for the cutoff. Wheeling around and making a pinpoint throw of his own, the third baseman nailed Randolph before he could score. The play killed any hopes the Yankees had for a rally.*

*Yankee owner George Steinbrenner, claiming third-base coach Mike Ferraro had erred by sending Randolph in, blamed his coach for the eventual loss of that game. He wondered why Ferraro had failed to notice that Randolph had stumbled while rounding second base. He also intimated that Ferraro had shown a similar lack of alertness throughout the season. Within a week of the Royals' playoff sweep of New York, Steinbrenner tried to hire Boston Red Sox manager Don Zimmer to replace Ferraro at third base.*

*When Yankee manager Dick Howser firmly opposed the firing of his coach, both men were dismissed. All this because Ferraro had allegedly made a crucial mistake in sending his runner home. However, had anyone bothered to ask Willie Randolph, he would have discovered that the third-base coach had nothing to do with the second baseman's decision to score:*

**Willie Randolph:** "Mike wasn't involved in that play at all. I was going regardless of the third-base coach. No one talks about the fact that I was trying to steal third right before Bob got the hit, but my back foot slipped from under me and I stopped. That's what's meant when we call this a game of inches. That split second killed me, because I got thrown out on a bang-bang play.

"When Watson hit that ball, I figured there was still no way I couldn't score. The way the ball bounced back to Willie [Wilson] was so unusual. Most of the time, you expect a ball hit out there to roll around for days. So when I rounded third, I wasn't even looking for Mike. I was going in all the way, because I knew it would tie the game up. Bob would have gone to second, maybe even third depending on how the Royals played the throw, cut it off or let it go through. Then we would have had the momentum. I was even laughing as I rounded third, because I knew we had them.

"But then, as I approached the plate, I felt the mood of the [Kansas City] crowd change; you can't always sense that, but I did that night. Willie grabbed that carom, threw to his cutoff man, and Brett was there. George made a perfect throw, and I was out. I don't slip on that first step, I'm safe. Brett's throw is off by an inch, I'm safe. I was as shocked as anybody, but you couldn't blame anybody, especially Mike. That's baseball."

**Amos Otis:** "Willie and I see this the same way. Randolph was right all the way in going for home plate, and if Ferraro was sending him, he made the correct call. It took two perfect throws to get him. Willie

Wilson's throw to Brett wasn't a classic; it might not have had much on it. But it couldn't have been more accurate. George didn't have to lunge for the ball, and it left him beautifully positioned to nail Randolph. No one can be blamed for that. If Wilson bobbles the ball for an instant, or his throw comes in a fraction too late or it's off by two inches, Randolph scores. The Yankees have a shot at tying the Series, and Ferraro probably gets a raise."

*New York would recapture the American League championship in 1981, only to lose the World Series to the Los Angeles Dodgers. The franchise would not appear in another Fall Classic until 1996.*

## TORRE'S TEAM SWIPES THE SUBWAY

*When Joe Torre assumed the role of Yankee manager for the 1996 season, he inherited a roster that included such All-Stars as David Cone, Wade Boggs, John Wetteland, Paul O'Neill, Mike Stanley, Jimmy Key, and Ruben Sierra. It was a team long on talent but short on balance. Buck Showalter, Torre's predecessor as Yankee skipper, had rarely employed baseball's subtler weapons such as the hit-and-run play, and he had little regard for base stealing. With the exception of center fielder Bernie Williams, his Yankees were slow, their offense heavily dependent on the long ball to score runs. It was exactly the kind of team a smart opposing manager could exploit:*

**Sparky Anderson:** "I loved playing against those teams that go station-to-station, taking one base at a time while they wait for someone to hit a home run. Give me good pitching and we can stop that kind of team cold. Just keep their hitters out of the air or make them drive the ball to the deepest part of the park where your outfielders can catch them, and they have no other way to beat you. And most home-run hitters take long, hard swings, so they're easier to strike out. Did you see what Pedro Martinez did to McGwire, Sosa, and those National League sluggers in the [1998] All-Star Game? He just threw the ball by them. When a batter strikes out, your offense is stuck.

"But a team that can run makes things happen. Stolen bases are only a small part of what I mean. You give me players who can go from first to third, fake steals, do something that injects movement into the game, and we'll drive the other team crazy. Their defense will have a hard time getting set and we'll have holes opening up to hit through. And fast players will cover more ground for you on defense. You give me those players who can run, back them up with a good pitching staff, and we'll chase that team of sluggers right out of the ballpark."

*Torre had his own version of the Anderson credo. He reconfigured his club by teaching it to play what Joe Morgan, the ESPN analyst and Hall of Fame second baseman, later characterized as "National League–style ball in American League ballparks." The manager installed the speedy rookie Derek Jeter at shortstop. Mike Stanley, a slugging catcher of below-average defensive skills, was allowed to leave as a free agent. Torre and his bench coach Don Zimmer then lobbied Yankee general manager Bob Watson to trade prospects to the Colorado Rockies for Joe Girardi, a quick, nimble catcher with a reputation as a first-rate handler of pitchers. Tim Raines, a former National League stolen-base champion, arrived to platoon in left field and as the designated hitter. With a few other additions and Torre's constant prodding, the Bronx Bombers became a band on the run, a street gang of crafty sprinters who bunted, executed the hit-and-run, stole bases, and moved runners along with productive outs while still hitting its share of long balls. It was a thinking team that played edgy, wide-open, opportunistic baseball.*

*The results of Torre's makeover were dazzling. From 1996 to 1999, the Yankees captured three pennants and three World Series championships, the last two on four-game sweeps of the San Diego Padres and the Atlanta Braves. The 1998 team set an American League regular-season record [which the Seattle Mariners surpassed in 2001] by amassing 114 wins. Only a narrow loss to the Cleveland Indians in the 1997 American League Divisional Series prevented New York from making four consecutive World Series appearances.*

*However, by 2000 Torre appeared to be leading a club in decline. New York won only 87 times during that season to finish first in the American League East by a scant two games over a mediocre Boston Red Sox team.*

*They were especially listless in September as they recorded seven consecutive losses to close out the month. Despite all that, as soon as the playoffs began, the Yankees revived themselves. New York eliminated Oakland and Seattle to take the American League pennant. Torre's Bombers had positioned themselves to become the first team to win three consecutive World Series since the 1972–74 Oakland A's. To match the A's record, the Yankees would have to defeat the National League champion New York Mets. It would be the first time the two franchises had ever met each other in post-season play.*

*Game One took place in Yankee Stadium on October 21. New York City hadn't hosted a Subway Series game in 44 years, but the Yankees and Mets made up for that by playing one of the more memorable contests in Fall Classic history. No one would know the identity of the winner until 4 hours and 51 minutes after the opening pitch had been thrown. Andy Pettitte started for the Bombers; Al Leiter, who began his career in the Yankees farm system, was on the mound for the Mets. It looked like a pitchers' duel from the start. Although Pettitte's fastball seemed to lack its customary whoosh in the early innings, he spotted his pitches brilliantly and kept the Mets hitters off balance and guessing wrong. Leiter's stuff appeared stronger, his control even sharper as his cutter gnawed at the Yankees' bats. Both left-handers maintained shutouts through five.*

*In the sixth inning the Mets verged on scoring, but a base-running blunder cost them at least a run. With rookie right fielder Timo Perez on first, Mets first baseman Todd Zeile pulled a Pettitte fastball deep down the left-field line. Perez, a swift yet unschooled base runner, slowed perceptibly as he rounded second. He had presumed Zeile's long fly would clear the fence fair and that he could trot into home plate on the front end of a two-run homer. Unfortunately for the rookie, the Yankees left fielder and shortstop weren't presuming anything:*

**David Justice (major-league outfielder, 1989–present; left fielder, New York Yankees, 2000–2001):** "Zeile had a good swing on that ball. As soon as he hit it, I knew there was no way I could catch it on the fly. So I set up to play the carom off the wall to prevent the man on first from scoring. I understand why Timo reacted the way he did, because for a few moments it looked like that drive might go out. But you can't take anything for granted in this game. When that ball hit off the top of the wall and came back, I was in good position to get the bounce and get off the throw quickly. I did my job, but as far as I am concerned, it was Derek [Jeter] who made this play work . . ."

**Derek Jeter (shortstop, New York Yankees, 1996–present):** "When the ball was hit, I really couldn't tell whether it was a home run or not, but until I'm absolutely sure it cleared the fence, I have to assume the ball will be in play. So I ran out to take the cutoff. As I did, I took a glance to my left and could see that Timo hadn't gotten to third yet. The throw was a little to my left, so I basically had to catch it and throw it as quickly as possible even if I didn't have much time to set . . ."

**David Justice:** ". . . Actually, Derek was running towards me when he caught the ball and he had to spin around immediately, which means he couldn't get everything behind his throw. But we all know the kind of arm he has. He still got a bullet off. Timo is very fast, but he didn't run full out the whole way. I'm sure he thought the ball was out, and by the time he speeded up, the throw was already coming in. Which is what allowed us to get him at home plate. That was a huge break, because in a Series where the first team to get to four [wins] is the champion, you have to minimize mistakes. . . ."

*Pettitte finished the sixth without allowing a run. Leiter encountered a jam of his own during the bottom of the inning. With Chuck Knoblauch on second and Derek Jeter on third, he faced David Justice, the Yankees' leading power threat. Justice is an analytical hitter who can adapt to a pitcher from one plate appearance to the next. After five-plus innings of watching Leiter work the Yankee hitters, he had seen enough to know exactly how he wanted to approach this crucial at-bat:*

**David Justice:** "Leiter is a very tough lefty. He throws in the nineties, his fastball was running in on me, backing me from the plate. I had already resigned myself to the fact that if he misses any further in, he's going to hit me. No one likes to get hit, but for a left-handed hitter to be successful against lefties you have to accept that you're going to get plunked occasionally. I didn't want to start opening my front shoulder up, because if I do that I can't hit the ball away and that's what I was looking for, a ball from the middle of the plate out that I could drive to the opposite field. The way he was pitching me, I figured he was trying to get me to look inside, so he must be ready to go outside. On 2 and 1, he threw me a breaking ball away. My mechanics were sound, I kept that shoulder in, and I made solid contact. The ball found the left-center-field gap for a double. . . ."

*Knoblauch and Jeter crossed home plate. The Mets responded by tallying three runs of their own in the seventh to establish a 3–2 lead. That's where the score stood when Mets closer Armando Benitez entered the game in the bottom of the ninth. Benitez, all 6´4˝ and 250 pounds of him, roamed onto the field resembling a character out of celluloid. The reliever as Godzilla, except the Japanese icon never threw this hard. After Benitez retired the first batter he faced, the Yankees countered the monster with Paul O'Neill, the team's right fielder and resident gladiator, a thoughtful, soft-spoken gentleman off the field who played baseball with the delicacy of Mad Max storming the Thunderdome.*

*O'Neill was known the league over for his intensity. Your average professional baseball player might vent his frustration over a prolonged slump, a hitless game, or a particularly unproductive at-bat. O'Neill? He could get pissed off over bad swings. There weren't many of those. As Derek Jeter once observed, "O'Neill can flat out hit." At thirty-seven, the right fielder no longer had quite the bat speed that had won him a batting title in 1994. All the same, he was a master of working pitchers into advantageous hitting counts and he still possessed one of the best pair of eyes in the major leagues. Fighting to keep pace against Benitez's ultra fastball, O'Neil fouled off one close offering after another while taking any ball that strayed from the strike zone. It was a ten-pitch Armageddon in a single plate appearance. When it was over, O'Neill stood on first, the recipient of a hard-won base on balls:*

**Derek Jeter:** "That at-bat right there shows you what Paul O'Neill means to this club. Not just that he got on base in that situation, but the way he reminds everyone how to play the game, not by words but by example. Look at how he battled Benitez on every pitch. Paul's intense, everybody knows he thinks he should get a hit every time up. But that's a great approach, and he's taught me from the time I got here not to give away any at-bats. . . ."

**Paul O'Neill (major-league outfielder, 1985–2001; right fielder, New York Yankees, 1993–2001):** "I approach every at-bat the same, you continue to battle. The big thing with two strikes is not to panic. You still have to try to get a good pitch to hit. Against a guy like Benitez, you're in a little more trouble because he throws so hard. The key for me is to try to stick with what I do and not try to get into the pitcher's head. I'm the type of hitter who focuses on what I do at the plate mechanically, rather than try to guess along with the pitcher to try to figure out what he's going to do. That's my theory. Other people will look for a particular location. At times I will do that, but once Benitez had two strikes on me, I'm looking at the whole strike zone. Anything near it, I've got to make contact. When that at-bat was over and he walked me, I had a sense of relief. I hadn't given away the at-bat by swinging at a bad pitch. That's a World Series game, the opener, we're down by a run, so the thought there is to get on base any way you can. The great thing about this team is, you never feel as if you have to do it by yourself, you don't have to be the guy who hits the home run that ties the game. Once I got on, my walk meant nothing until the hitters behind me did their job."

*When things go against him, Benitez often steps from the mound, puts his hands on his hips, and tilts his nose skyward. It is the pose of a potentate raising his nostrils above a noxious aroma, a bit of body language that reveals when Benitez is wrestling with his confidence as well as his stuff. It is the pose Benitez struck as O'Neill jogged to first base. Scott Brosius was due up next, but Joe Torre instead inserted left-handed Luis Polonia into the lineup. Benitez served up a hitter's pitch, a fastball that caught too much of the plate, and Polonia singled O'Neill to second. The next batter, second baseman Jose Vizcaino, slapped another single over shortstop to load the bases. Chuck Knoblauch followed with a towering fly ball to Mets left fielder Joe McEwing. O'Neill tagged up. Tie ball game.*

*After that, the Yankees had several chances to win, but the Mets repulsed each assault. Mets reliever Dennis Cook opened the tenth by walking his first two batters. Manager Bobby Valentine removed him in favor of Glendon Rusch, who promptly delivered a wild pitch to Yankee first baseman Tino Martinez:*

**Glendon Rusch (major-league pitcher, 1997–present; pitcher, New York Mets, 2000–present):** "Before I threw it, any kind of out would have been good in that situation, because the worst that can happen, unless there is an error on a throw, is that the Yankees move up to second and third with two men out. And if I can get a ground ball with Tino up, there's a chance for a double play. But the wild pitch changes your approach a little, because now the Yankees can score without a hit. And if they score, the game's over. So I needed a pop-up, a strikeout, something short that would keep the base runners where they were . . ."

*Runners on second and third and nobody out. Bobby Valentine moved in his infielders and outfielders to cut off the run at the plate.*

**Glendon Rusch:** ". . . my best shot, I thought, was to come in on Tino with a fastball. I'd faced Martinez when I pitched in the American League, and we all know he has excellent power, so if you come inside you have to jam him good. If your pitch doesn't get in on him enough, he's going to do some damage. I threw him a fastball and jammed him enough that he didn't get much distance on it even though he had a good swing."

*Martinez looped Rusch's pitch into shallow left field, and McEwing skedaddled in to catch the pop fly some twenty feet from the lip of the infield for the first out of the inning. Valentine ordered Rusch to intention-*

*ally walk Yankee catcher Jorge Posada, filling the bases while creating the potential for a force play at every base. The strategy worked. O'Neill chopped an innocuous grounder up the middle that second baseman Edgardo Alfonzo turned into an inning-ending double play.*

*The Yankees threatened again in the eleventh, putting runners at second and third with two outs. Though they failed to score, they continued to pressure the Mets pitchers. After one out in the twelfth, Tino Martinez singled off reliever Turk Wendell. Posada lined a double, Martinez stopping at third. Wendell intentionally walked O'Neill to load the bases as Valentine once again ordered his fielders to play in. Pinch hitter Luis Sojo hit a weak foul ball for the second out. Yankee second baseman Jose Vizcaino, a former teammate of Wendell's when both were with the Chicago Cubs, came to the batter's box reminding himself to keep things simple:*

**Jose Vizcaino (major-league infielder, 1989–present; reserve infielder, 2000 New York Yankees):** "Coming up with the bases loaded in a big game like that, where if you score one run the ball game is over, I'm not really looking for a particular pitch. I'm just looking for the first pitch to be a strike. I know Turk has to get the ball over. So I'm looking for a pitch I could hit up the middle. Turk gave me what I was looking for and I hit it into left field. It was the most exciting moment in my career, to be the hero in a game like that. When I first came to the Yankees, I was excited, because you know they have a chance to go into the postseason and win. But I never pictured that I would be in that situation and come through."

*Yankee Stadium reverberated with cheers as Martinez scampered to home plate carrying the winning run. At first base Vizcaino leaped into the air and pumped his fist toward the night sky. His teammates, led by shortstop Derek Jeter, mobbed him in celebration. It was a game that had showcased the nuances that had brought Torre's team so much recent triumph. The Yankees' patience at the plate, their textbook defense, stubborn pitching, and superb base running were all on display, as well as an intangible factor:*

**Paul O'Neill:** "We've lost before, and you use that as an inspiration to continue winning because you don't want to go through that again. We had won the World Series in 1996, so we were coming off that and wanted to return. But [in 1997] we lost a close series to the Indians that ended our season. That was the worst defeat of my career, because that series was in our hands. We had almost won it the night before and we were ahead in the final game. It takes a while for it to sink in that you're not going to the park tomorrow, that you're going home. You always want to be the last team that has to go home. So it was something that was hard to take, and no one has forgotten that. . . ."

**Bernie Williams (center fielder, New York Yankees, 1991–present):** ". . . The key here is, we are persistent. No one in our clubhouse ever gives up. Every team makes mistakes. The club that minimizes its mistakes and takes advantage of the opposition's mistakes is going to go a long way, especially in the short series of the postseason. That's something we've been able to do ever since Joe got here. . . ."

*If the Bombers' opening victory was about patience and persistence, fury was the dominant theme for Game Two. It was Yankee starter Roger Clemens who introduced that element as he commandeered center stage in this muscular, urban passion play. Nothing unusual there. Clemens often works the diamond incensed, his every pitch a rant. He is an athlete who plumbs his feelings, many of them as dark as they are deep, to keep himself honed and engaged:*

**Roger Clemens (major-league pitcher, 1984–present; pitcher, New York Yankees, 1999–present):** "The way I prepare, the physical work I do, my mental approach is pretty good. But if I'm scuffling with my location, seeing things I shouldn't see, or hearing sounds I shouldn't hear, I know my focus needs to be sharper and I can regroup. It's all a game within a game. You're sixty feet six inches from home plate. The game is between you and your catcher and somewhat the hitter. But you are focused on everything that enables you to get the job done.

"One way you can heighten your game is with emotions. I've played on emotion quite a bit and I ask myself to do things emotionally if I have to. It can be a combination of things, whether I have to think about family members before I go out there, like my mother being ill, for instance, or my grandmother . . . I have children at home who are growing up, and I'm missing part of that. They've made tremendous sacrifices for me to continue pitching. I take all that to the mound. I always feel as if I'm pitching for a lot of people who did a lot of work behind the scenes just so I could get here, as well as for my teammates.

"Like here at home with our fans. There might be a family of four or five that has come out to see you, I get letters all the time that they are coming to a certain game just to watch me pitch, so I want to perform well for them. That's just having respect for the game. Maybe that's why I still feel I have the same intensity as I did when I was twenty-two years old. I take pitching very seriously. I enjoy kidding with these guys here, they're great teammates, but they know when it's time for me to take the mound, I'm very serious about what I do."

*When Mets right fielder Timo Perez faked a bunt on the very first pitch of the game, Clemens spouted an expletive, then struck the hitter out on fastballs so rapid they reduced Perez's swing to a mere grope. The right-hander threw three straight pitches past second baseman Edgardo Alfonzo for out number two, then waited for Mets catcher Mike Piazza to take his turn at bat.*

*For weeks the media had ballyhooed this confrontation. Clemens had hit Piazza in the head with a pitch during an interleague game on July 8, inflicting a concussion on the Mets All-Star catcher. Many journalists suggested the beaning had been intentional—before that at-bat Piazza had gone 7 for 12 against Clemens with three home runs. This would be the first time the two players had faced each other since the incident.*

*Clemens threw two fastballs by Piazza for strikes. After wasting a pitch out of the strike zone, he came back inside sporting a 99-mph missile that shattered Piazza's bat into three pieces. The ball skipped foul as the bat barrel bounced up to Clemens. Gloving the broken lumber as if it were a ground ball, the pitcher fired it sidearm toward Piazza, who was jogging up the first-base line. The jagged barrel missed scything Piazza's legs by inches. Chaos ensued. The Mets coaches and players immediately rushed the field, where a horde of Yankees met them for the usual baseball shoving match. Joe Torre had to physically restrain Mets coach John Stearns from attacking Clemens. An obviously stunned Piazza pursued the pitcher while demanding to know why Clemens had tossed the object in his path. He couldn't get an answer.*

**Mike Piazza (major-league catcher, 1992–present; catcher, New York Mets, 1998–present):** "I was more confused and shocked by the whole thing. First, I was disoriented because after the bat shattered I had no idea where the ball was. No clue. Then I wondered if he would tell me that it was an accident, but he didn't say anything. I kept asking him, 'What is your problem?' He didn't say anything to me, he just talked to the umpire. You know, I didn't really see what happened. My head was down, I couldn't see the ball, and I was moving towards first, so I had no idea he caught the bat. I was trying to pick up the ball, so I took my eyes off him. I didn't know if it was grounder or a pop-up.

"So when I started jogging down the line, I asked him what his problem was and he didn't respond. I have no idea what his intentions were, or even if he had any. By the time I was asking him, other parties were intervening, so I didn't find out anything. It was bizarre."

*Clemens later admitted to being equally perplexed by Piazza's actions:*

**Roger Clemens:** "I was extremely emotional that first inning. All day long the guys were concerned that all the talk that week about that game in July [when he beaned Piazza] had gotten me down, and they wanted to keep my confidence up. Before I let go of the bat, I had no idea Mike had run up the line. It was a foul ball, so I assumed he wouldn't be running. That's what I was telling the umpire, that there was absolutely no intent. Yes, I was fired up, but all I tried to do was sling the bat towards the on-deck circle. I had no idea he was running."

*The umpires quickly cleared the field—no punches were thrown, so no one was ejected—and play resumed. Clemens retired Piazza to end the inning. Then the pitcher retreated to a sanctuary where he could tame his emotions:*

**Roger Clemens:** "For that World Series, my intensity was exactly where I wanted it to be going in. But now I got to a point where I had to sit in the sauna to be by myself to focus on the game and nothing else. I wasn't having any part of the nonsense that was going on. I wasn't going to allow this to become a grudge match, to affect my teammates and what we were trying to accomplish. If the media wanted to talk it up, well, that was disappointing, because they made this issue bigger than the game itself. I felt once that at-bat was over, we had to go back to playing baseball, play the game like it was supposed to be."

*In the Mets dugout, Bobby Valentine asked his players what had happened. The manager hadn't seen Clemens throw the bat because he, like Piazza, had been looking for the ball. There was no consensus. "Some guys thought Roger just swung the bat in that direction," Valentine later explained, "some thought he threw it at Mike." Valentine added that he would have said something to the umpires about possibly ejecting Clemens had anyone convinced him that the pitcher had acted deliberately.*

*Banishing Clemens from the field certainly would have improved the Mets' chances of winning the ball game. To counter Rocket Roger in peak form, the National Leaguers needed an equally dominating performance from their own starter. They didn't get it. Mike Hampton struggled against the Yankees almost from the outset. Even while the left-hander retired the first two batters he faced, his stuff seemed cranky and rebellious. He tried to right himself by speeding up his delivery, a modification that only made him more erratic. Hampton walked the Yankees number-three hitter, David Justice, on four pitches before throwing four more consecutive balls to Bernie Williams.*

*Despite his wildness, he still had a chance to emerge from the inning unscathed if he could retire Tino Martinez. The Mets figured to have the edge in that duel. Martinez had just endured his worst season as a regular and had been particularly vulnerable against the outside breaking ball, a Hampton specialty. But as the postseason neared, the first baseman had made an adjustment:*

**Tino Martinez (major-league first baseman, 1990–present; first baseman, New York Yankees, 1996–2001):** "I had struggled most of 2000 and it was frustrating, but I started to swing the bat really well in September. By then, I felt we were going to make the playoffs and I wanted to get my swing down for the postseason. Somewhere along the line, I had started trying to hit home runs to make up for my low batting average and I ended up burying myself completely.

"But from September through the postseason, I started hitting the ball the other way, really going back to being the hitter I was in the past. I told myself to let the home runs take care of themselves instead of trying to force them. Use the whole field. Hampton was struggling that first inning, walked a few guys and he struggled to get the two outs he had. My thought was that he didn't have his good stuff, and we had him on the ropes. So this was our chance to jump out to a big early lead, maybe even knock him out of the game. We had to go for it, because eventually he'd find his stuff and then cruise along. But you also have to know how to go for it. Against a tough pitcher like Hampton, you don't try to hit the ball out of the park. Anytime a left-handed hitter goes up trying to pull Hampton, he's done. I told myself to stay back and go to the opposite field."

*Martinez lined a single to left field, sending Justice sprinting around third with the first run of the game. Hampton promptly fell behind Posada, who singled past second base to plate Bernie Williams. That was all the scoring the Yankees could muster in that inning; Hampton struck out Paul O'Neill to finally retire the side, but Scott Brosius led off the second inning with a home run, pushing the score to 3–0. Hampton would allow one more run before leaving the game after six innings.*

*Meanwhile, his teammates were helpless against Clemens. One Juggs gun clocked the Rocket's fastball as high as 99 mph, his splitter at 94, a mind-boggling speed for a pitch that swerves and dives so precipitously. Clemens's splitter accounted for several strikeouts, but for most of the game, the right-hander subdued the Mets with raw heat:*

**Roger Clemens:** "I'm still essentially a power pitcher, but I'll feature the split when I need to. I've had it since 1988, 1989. Early in my career I could pitch up in the zone, and I continued to do that into the late '80s because the umpires called that a strike, something they're trying to do again. I use the splitter a little more now, but I don't use it as much as some people may think. You'll see it on the highlights because it might have been an out pitch in a particular situation, so fans think it's a dominant part of your repertoire. But I don't feature it that much, because it is difficult on your arm and if you fall in love with it, I think it detracts from your fastball. You'll see how guys who throw it a lot will lose velocity, pitchers like Mike Scott and Jack Morris. If I feature it fifteen times in a 130-pitch game, it's not too much."

*Everything Clemens threw that night was too much for his opponents. The pitcher turned the batter's box into a hothouse for those Met hitters, and all but Todd Zeile wilted. Clemens left the game leading 6–0 after pitching eight innings. He had struck out nine while yielding only two base hits—both to Zeile—and nary a base on balls. Piazza finally put the Mets on the scoreboard with a two-run homer off Yankee reliever Jeff Nelson in the ninth, and center fielder Jay Payton brought his team within one by hitting a three-run shot off Mariano Rivera. The Mets would get no closer. Rivera struck out shortstop Kurt Abbott to save the win for Clemens.*

*Two nights later the Mets hushed any talk of a Yankee sweep by prevailing 4–2 in Game Three at Shea Stadium. Reliever John Franco received credit for the victory in relief of starter Rick Reed. Yankees right-hander Orlando Hernández had brought an 8–0 postseason record into that game, and he performed admirably. Changing speeds and varying his arm angle on each hip-hop pitch, El Duque baffled the Mets for seven innngs. But with the score tied 2–2 in the eighth, Mets left fielder Benny Agbayani solved the puzzle:*

**Benny Agbayani (outfielder, New York Mets, 1998–present):** "After he escaped with the bases loaded in the sixth, we were shaking our heads wondering what you had to do to beat this guy. I mean, he was tough. My first two at-bats, I wasn't following my plan. I wanted Hernández to elevate the ball a little more so I could make good contact. But I was swinging at bad pitches, which is what he makes you do. He comes at you with different angles and he changes that leg kick; sometimes it's higher than others. He brings the ball from right by his ear on one pitch, then the next, I swear, it seems he's bringing it from his shoe . . ."

**Jay Payton (center fielder, New York Mets, 1998–present):** ". . . and he has that jerky movement to go with that leg kick, so you have all that to block out plus he keeps the ball hidden longer than most pitchers. You don't pick up the pitch out of his hand immediately, which makes his curveball more effective, because you have less time to read it."

**Robin Ventura (major-league third baseman, 1989–present; third baseman, New York Mets, 1999–2001):** ". . . I knew from playing in the American League that he will try to jump ahead of you. Orlando throws strikes. And once he's ahead of you, it's like he makes up pitches out there. But early in the count, when he is trying to get it over, that's when you have your best chance. Don't let him play with your head . . ."

**Jay Payton:** ". . . and don't underrate his fastball. He's not overpowering, but he gets it up there in the low 90s. That's excellent, because when a hitter can't pick up the pitch right away, it seems to be on top of you quicker, and you have less time to react. When he throws that breaking ball from the side, it's going to be more three to nine, over the top it's more twelve to six. When he drops down, the ball runs in on you more. He's unique with his quirks, no one like him I've ever seen . . ."

**Benny Agbayani:** ". . . He never seems to throw the same pitch at the same speed twice in a row. His slider breaks late, so it looks hittable right until the moment you swing. Then it breaks out of the zone. And when you don't expect it, he can throw the ball right by you. He's a pitcher. When I went up in the eighth, [Mets pitching coach] Tom Robson reminded me to be patient, to let Hernández come in with a ball a little bit up, because he got me out twice when I was swinging at balls out of the zone. So I went up there looking for a pitch up, something I could drive into the outfield. The ball went all the way to the wall in left center, far enough that Todd [Zeile] was able to score from first with the go-ahead run. What was great about that game was that John [Franco] got the victory. He's been in this game a long time and this was his first World Series, so it was nice to help him win one in front of the hometown fans."

*That defeat not only sullied Hernández's impeccable postseason record, it also ended the Yankees' fourteen-game World Series winning streak, the longest unbeaten streak in major-league championship play. The following evening Mets right-hander Bobby Jones started against Yankee left-hander Denny Neagle. Whatever momentum the Mets had gained with their victory against Hernández stalled on Jones's first pitch of the game. With Jose Vizcaino and Chuck Knoblauch slumping, Torre had elected to use Derek Jeter as his leadoff hitter. Jones later admitted he had expected Jeter to take a pitch or two during his first trip to the plate. A mistake:*

**Derek Jeter:** "I was looking for a fastball. I'm an aggressive hitter. I've batted leadoff before, but I'm not a typical leadoff hitter who takes a lot of pitches trying to draw a walk. I stay aggressive, especially against someone like Bobby who has good control and throws strikes. If Bobby left a pitch over the plate, I was going to be swinging. Yes, I heard later that he didn't expect me to swing at the first pitch. That was a good thing. . . ."

*Jones's pitch was a change-up, phat and inviting. Jeter attacked it with brio, hammering a home run deep into the left-field stands to give the Yankees an immediate lead. One inning later Paul O'Neill pulled Jones's limping fastball into the right-field corner. The drive skipped past Timo*

*Perez and caromed sideways off the wall. O'Neill dashed to third for his second triple in two games. Bobby Valentine elected to walk the next batter, the switch-hitting Jorge Posada, in favor of pitching to Scott Brosius. The Yankee third baseman hit a sacrifice fly to put his team two runs in front.*

*The Mets couldn't score against Neagle over the first two innings. Jeter opened the third with a line drive that short-hopped the right-center-field wall for a triple. Valentine decided to play his infield back, a dicey strategy since it effectively conceded a run on any ground ball, and the next batter, Luis Sojo, tended to hit grounders. When Sojo slapped a bouncer to second, Jeter scored. Yankees 3, Mets 0. Jones squiggled out of the inning without allowing another run.*

*Timo Perez opened the bottom of the third for the Mets with a line-drive single up the middle, a ball hit so hard it sent Neagle diving to the ground. With one out, Mike Piazza took a Neagle change-up low and away for ball one. Neagle's next pitch was another change-up, this time closer to the plate:*

**Mike Piazza:** "The key here was, I was able to get the barrel of the bat on the ball because I recognized the pitch early. The tough part of it was that the pitch kept going away. It was not a bad pitch by any means, down and away, just on the plate. I had to reach out for it. But I had committed, so I just followed through and hit it out of the ballpark."

*Piazza's home run cut the Yankee lead to 3–2. That was still the score when Piazza faced Neagle again with nobody on and two men out in the fifth inning. Neagle had retired the first two batters on easy fly balls and he needed only one more out to qualify for the victory, provided his club maintained the lead. That didn't persuade Joe Torre to let his soft-tossing left-hander test Piazza again. He stepped out of the Yankees dugout to dismiss Neagle and summon David Cone from his bullpen. It was a move the normally patient Torre might not have made if the calendar hadn't read October:*

**Joe Torre:** "When you're managing during the season, you're doing things to help you in the long run. When you get into a short series, you're doing things for today. When you have, I can't say a plan, but as it develops, as it goes along, you have to do what you think is right to get an out, to get an inning, to get a hit. Don Zimmer taught me that my first year here, in '96, especially when dealing with pitchers. And, you know, Denny was obviously disappointed. When I went out there and looked in his eye, he was shocked. It was just something that if I hadn't done it and had thought about doing it, and something had happened, I never would have been able to forgive myself for it.

"Mike [Piazza] is one of those players who is in scoring position when he gets in the batter's box. Obviously, Neagle didn't know that that was going to happen, but David Cone knew in the top of that inning that he was going to pitch to Mike. He [Piazza] had a couple of good swings off Neagle, hit the home run even though I didn't think it was a bad pitch. And I just made up my mind that he [Cone] was going to pitch to Piazza at that point. . . ."

*Cone, a twenty-game winner in 1998 and the former leader of the Yankee pitching staff, had suffered through a horrendous 2000 season. His ERA had rarely dropped below 6.50 and his once dominating fastball never topped 90 miles an hour. The Cone slider, the right-hander's signature pitch, arrived flat at home plate in start after start. His pitching was so consistently dreadful, Cone doubted Torre would include him on the postseason roster. On this night, however, for at least one batter, Cone was an ace reborn. He threw sharp, vintage sliders to Piazza to retire the catcher on a pop-up to second base. It would be his only appearance of the Series; he had made it a memorable one:*

**David Cone (major-league pitcher, 1986–present; pitcher, New York Yankees, 1995–2000):** "This one surely meant something. You get a big out, you contribute to the win, everybody's happy, it means a lot. It's gratifying to be able to do anything at this point. I thought this was a huge game—first, because it's the middle game of the three on the road. But second, the rotation turns over, we see their top two pitchers again—and Leiter and Hampton are tough. So this was huge. . . . I don't recall what Joe said to me, it was brief, you know, something about Here it is, you've got two outs, you need one more."

*A deadly triad of Yankees firemen—Nelson to Stanton to Rivera—kept the Mets off the scoreboard for the rest of the night. The Mets knew all about Rivera, of course. Mariano was the closest thing to an automatic save in baseball. Yet it was the middleman of the Bombers' relief trio who was making an indelible impression on the National League champs. Mike Stanton was fanning the Mets' batters in clusters, swinging strikeouts that told us the left-hander wasn't merely overpowering hitters, he was confusing them as well:*

**Jay Payton:** "He was something of a surprise only because Mariano is the guy everyone focuses on. But Mike is just a terrific pitcher and a lot more than just a left-handed setup man, because he's effective against righties as well as lefties. He does a great job mixing up his pitches and he throws very hard. He threw everything at us, his split, the slider, the curve, his fastball. We couldn't be sure what to look for. And he's smart. When you're looking for something else, he would throw three straight fastballs. He didn't seem to have any pattern . . ."

*Which, for Stanton, is a pitching pattern:*

**Mike Stanton (major-league pitcher, 1989–present; pitcher, New York Yankees, 1997–present):** ". . . I was getting ahead of the hitters, and once you do that you open up your options as a pitcher. When you fall behind, it narrows down your options. Once I get ahead, I expand the strike zone. Make my other pitches look like fastballs, then surprise the hitter with a fastball, throw a pitch that looks like a strike until it breaks outside of the strike zone.

"Jay is right, I'm not just a left-handed setup man, though I've heard myself described that way. I probably face twice as many right-handed hitters as left-handed; to be successful I have to get those right-handed batters out. So I throw four pitches—fastball, curve, slider, and my split for a change. Mix them up, change speeds. I picked up the split in '97 and it's given me something off-speed that moves away from right-handers. The key with the split is arm speed and using the same arm slot as your fastball, because deception is such a big part of that pitch. It's a down-breaking fastball without the speed. In the Subway Series, [Todd] Pratt and Alfonzo saw splits, but I'll go in some situations and never use it. Or I might not use my curveball. My pattern changes from day to day. I can't predict what I will throw until I'm in the situation, and I think that unpredictability helps me. If I don't know, how can the hitter?

"In fact, when I'm throwing the ball well, usually the only time I see the hitter is when he first steps into the batter's box. You recognize who it is, and from there you go over whatever the scouting reports say or what you know about the hitter to decide how you want to go about facing him. Then I just try to make quality pitches with a positive frame of mind.

"Even if you make your pitches, sometimes you won't get the result you're looking for, but that's basically what I'm going to do. I pitch to my strengths, and if it happens to be the batter's strength, so be it. I am not one to go by the adage never get beat by your second- or third-best pitch. If I'm trying to get the hitter out with my splitter, then that's my best pitch, because that's the pitch I think will get the hitter out. You have to make a commitment.

"For me everything comes down to your mental approach. To succeed in the postseason, you have to be able to turn it up a notch but still stay within yourself. You have to discover that happy medium between getting too up or too far down. As a reliever, I find, you don't have to put just the bad behind you, but the good as well. Take each game as a new event. Concentration is usually my problem. You play 162 games, plus spring training, that's a long season and no one can have peak concentration every day. The grind is grueling. Usually when someone struggles in this game, it's because of their concentration. Your concentration and confidence can go up and down every day. The two go hand in hand.

"But when you're in the pennant run and postseason, concentration isn't a problem, the games are too important. Then I actually have to calm down, to keep from trying to do too much. When I get too revved up, I'm not thinking out there. So I step back and remind myself to actually pitch rather than just try to throw everything as hard as I can. Move the ball around, review how I want to attack each hitter. I also use mental imaging to prepare, been using it for quite a few years. I don't picture a particular hitter, or visualize whether or not he swings. Instead I see myself making a particular quality pitch, then I step up and perform."

*Stanton and his teammates, as focused a group as any that has ever played hardball, had stepped up and performed so well, the Yankees needed only one more win for their threepeat. Game Five at Shea Stadium would become the Subway Series in microcosm. In a reprise of the Series opener, Andy Pettitte started against Al Leiter. The Yankees took a one-run lead in the top of the second inning when Bernie Williams snapped a twenty-two-at-bat hitless streak with a home run on a Leiter cutter lacking its usual fangs:*

**Bernie Williams:** "He was throwing a lot of cutters, so I was looking inside a bit more than usual. He threw me low and in, low and in, and I kept fouling them off. He just happened to throw one that didn't break in low and hard enough. I was able to connect with it. It's kind of hard to hit a cutter and pull it fair. He is one of the toughest lefties in baseball, so I was very fortunate."

*The Mets responded against Andy Pettitte in their half of the inning. With one man out, right fielder Bubba Trammell walked. Jay Payton followed with a single to right center field. A Kurt Abbott groundout advanced the runners to second and third. Leiter came up, not much of a hitter during his career, but a good bunter, something he proved to the Yankees by dragging a maneuver out of the Ty Cobb playbook:*

**Andy Pettitte (pitcher, New York Yankees, 1995–present):** "That was a great job by Leiter. I threw a four-seamer away, so I'm kind of falling off the mound that way [toward the third-base side] and I was very surprised. He laid down a perfect bunt. He got it right by me, with me falling off the mound, and T. [Tino Martinez] bobbled it a bit and that bobble was enough just to jar me a little bit there . . ."

**Tino Martinez:** "I'll tell you how good a play that was. Leiter did the job even though the bunt didn't surprise me. Al kept looking at me as if he wanted to see how I was positioned, so I thought he might bunt, but it was a perfect drag bunt right past the pitcher towards the second-base side. I tried to force-throw to Andy, and he dropped it. We may have gotten Leiter had everything gone right, but that bunt couldn't have been better placed. It was a real work of art."

**Andy Pettitte:** "That second inning, it rattled me a little bit and I had to regain my focus there. You get a couple of pitches where you feel like you make good pitches and things don't work out the way you want them to. So your concentration gets broken a little bit there, but you try as hard as you can to stay focused and locked in."

*Pettitte remained locked in; he wouldn't allow the Mets another run. Leiter matched his intensity as well as his results. He worked aggressively, brushing several Yankees off the plate with hard stuff inside, an approach that made his late-breaking cutters on the outer portion of home plate that much more effective. But in the sixth inning, he tried to get fancy with Derek Jeter and the Yankee shortstop made him pay:*

**Derek Jeter:** "Leiter is probably tougher on right-handers than left-handers, because he throws that cutter so hard, it moves in on right-handed hitters quickly. You think you have a good pitch to hit, but before you know it, the ball is in on your hands. He's real tough. He doubled up on change-ups. That first pitch was a ball, a tight inside cutter, I believe. The second pitch was a change-up for a ball, so I was looking fastball, but he threw another change-up. Only this time he left it up over the middle of the plate and I was lucky enough to hit it out."

*The game was tied 2–2. Pettitte and Leiter held it there through seven. Leiter opened the eighth by striking out Tino Martinez and Paul O'Neill, a performance that convinced Bobby Valentine that his ace still had enough velocity and command to continue pitching. Jorge Posada was the next batter. The Yankee catcher was a hitting anomaly. Posada was that rare switch-hitter with home-run power from both sides of the plate. Despite his propensity for fanning on breaking balls out of the strike zone, Posada had developed such an acute batting eye, he had finished among the league leaders in walks. A stubborn out, as Leiter soon discovered.*

*With two strikes against him, Posada fouled off three funky, dancing cutters before coaxing a walk. Brosius followed with a single to left on Leiter's 141st offering; the Met lefty hadn't been stretched that far in any start during the 2000 season. Posada stopped at second. In the Mets bullpen, John Franco was warmed and standing with his arms crossed, waiting to see if his manager would summon him into the game. Valentine never budged. He was sticking with his left-hander, paying tribute to an athlete's fortitude. Leiter's pitching had been so inspired, so ballsy, he had unsettled the city's very geography. For at least one evening, the heart of New York was on that mound in Queens. Valentine wasn't about to abandon him.*

*Luis Sojo, an eighth-inning replacement for Vizcaino at second base, came to the plate. The utility infielder had played on all three of Torre's World Series–winning Yankee teams. He had repeatedly demonstrated a knack for getting key hits in critical situations. Yet in Game Four of the series, Sojo had taken several uncharacteristically wild swings and, he felt, gotten himself out. He was determined to revert to form against Leiter:*

**Luis Sojo (major-league infielder, 1990–2001; reserve infielder, New York Yankees, 1996–2001):** "I didn't play until Game Four of the World Series, and in my first at-bats I was trying to pull everything. That's what happens when you don't play, because when you get in, you don't want to get beat by the fastball. Leiter is tough, I had two hits off of him in a game when I was with the Pirates and those were all the hits I ever had off him. When I came to the plate that inning, [first-base coach] Lee Mazzilli reminded me to stay up the middle, to hit the ball towards right field. Kurt Abbott was at shortstop for the Mets and I could see he was playing me to pull, leaving this wide hole in the middle of the infield. So when I pinch-hit, I kept all that in my mind. Leiter has that great cutter, but I figured he would want to get ahead of me with his first pitch, so it probably wouldn't be that nasty. He knew I rarely swing at the first pitch. He threw me a fastball that went from the middle [of the plate] in on me, and I was able to inside-out the ball and it worked. A ground ball up the middle . . ."

*Sojo's grounder bounded past Mets shortstop Kurt Abbott into center field. Posada, one of the slower Yankees, chugged around third base as Mets center fielder Jay Payton came up with the ball:*

**Jay Payton:** "I doubt anyone in the world thought I had a chance to make a play on Posada. I had to run in full out on that ball, it wasn't hit very hard. That's one of those plays where the ball was placed perfectly and hit just well enough. Had Luis hit that ball harder, say, a line drive past the infield, we might have gotten Posada or maybe Jorge doesn't even try to score because the ball might have gotten to me that much quicker. I charged the ball hard, reached the ball in good throwing position, and almost made a good play. But it wasn't good enough. . . ."

**Mike Piazza:** "It was a good throw, but I had only two choices on that play, come out to take the throw or stay back to block the plate. I felt that I had to let the ball come to me. If I had gotten out in front of the plate, I would have given the plate to Posada to slide by . . ."

**Bobby Valentine:** "If that ball is a fraction of a second sooner, or an inch away from the runner's leg, Mike would have caught it and tagged him out . . ."

*Piazza planted himself on the baseline as Posada lunged toward the mound side of home plate. Payton's throw struck the Yankee catcher in the leg and skipped into the Mets dugout. Brosius came around to score while Sojo hurried to third. Leiter's evening was over. He left the ball game to a standing ovation with two men out in the eighth. At the postgame press conference, a reporter asked Valentine why he allowed his pitcher to throw so many pitches, 142 in all. The manager defended his choice:*

**Bobby Valentine:** "I talked to Al yesterday and he was determined to win this game. He said, 'You don't have to worry about intentional walks; you don't have to worry about pitch counts. I can throw 150 pitches, I'm going to give it everything I have. I'm going to be the guy to get the victory tomorrow.' And he walked his talk every step of the way, I thought, today. He battled them and he gave it everything he had. . . . I wasn't going to bring in a righty to face Polonia. Or for Sojo, it was either Al or Johnny [Franco], and Johnny had thrown three days in a row. I decided to go with Al. I thought that striking out the first two guys, and the pitches he threw to Posada, made me think he had plenty. . . . In the dugout, I said, Congratulations on a super season and a great job. I asked him if he still thought he had enough and he said he had plenty. He thought he had Posada on strikes—he just missed—and he was confident he was going to get Sojo. . . ."

*Valentine's decision to stay with Leiter, to honor a commitment to his left-hander's will and moxie, was understood by everyone in the Yankee dugout:*

**Joe Torre:** "Bobby made the right choice. I think that that's an emotional choice that nobody should second-guess, because he [Leiter] put his blood and guts into that one. . . ."

**Scott Brosius (major-league third baseman, 1991–2001; third baseman, New York Yankees, 1998–2001):** "You wouldn't second-guess Bobby for leaving Al in the game if you were hitting against him. I thought he was still pitching well. It looked to me like his cutter had the same bite. I went up there looking for it and was lucky enough to get the hit, but it's not as if we were hitting him hard that inning. Our hits just found holes. . . ."

**Bernie Williams:** "The thing about that game was that Al rose to another level as the innings went along. Not necessarily faster, but his location, command, and choice of pitches kept getting better. He threw a lot of pitches to spots that were unhittable. My last at-bat he struck me out on a slider that I just didn't think he would throw in that situation. He looked like he was getting stronger, so why take him out? It was inspiring to watch. Here his team was facing possible elimination and he just let it rip. He threw his whole self into that game. In all the postseason games we've played, that was probably the best I've ever seen a pitcher throw against us. Even though he lost—I mean, once you throw 142 pitches, come on, you're good but you're not made of steel—he gave it all he had. I certainly tip my cap to him."

*John Franco relieved Leiter and retired Yankee pinch hitter Glenallen Hill to end the eighth. Mike Stanton pitched scoreless ball for his team in the bottom of that inning. With the Yankees leading 4–2 in the ninth, Joe Torre brought in right-handed closer Mariano Rivera to terminate the Mets' October ride. Bobby Valentine's squad had proven as resilient a foe as any the Bombers had faced in six consecutive years of postseason play. This club knew no quit. Still, as Rivera warmed up on the Shea Stadium mound, everyone in the Mets dugout realized what a formidable obstacle he represented:*

**Joe McEwing (major-league infielder/outfielder, 1998–present; utility player, New York Mets, 2000–present):** "You sit there on the bench thinking, 'What's the problem? This guy's a one-pitch pitcher. We all know what's coming. Why aren't we hitting him?' Then guys come back to the bench shaking their head . . ."

**Jay Payton:** ". . . I actually feel comfortable against Rivera, I had that home run off of him in Game Two. I can see why others don't, though. They say he's a one-pitch pitcher, but that's not so. He has a straight fastball that tails a little that he throws in the mid 90s, then he has that awesome cutter that bites in on a right-handed hitter's hands. And now he has that hard sinker. A great part of it, too, is his confidence. He looks like he believes he can get anybody out in any situation, and that's a big part of winning. Also, he has the stuff to back it up. He has great location, puts the ball where he wants it. At this level, it's all about location. If you throw a hundred miles per hour down the middle, we will hit you. But throw 87 and paint the black with it all the time, and you're tough to hit. He throws that cutter close at 97, 98, 99, and puts it where he wants, too, with movement. That's almost unfair. . . ."

**Robin Ventura:** ". . . Left-handed hitters usually have an edge against right-handed pitchers, but he's no ordinary right-hander. He has that cutter that comes into a lefty and every now and again he sinks something. Mariano doesn't really throw anything straight. He throws so awfully hard, but you can adjust to speed. The movement on that cutter keeps you off guard. I told myself I would not get beat by that pitch. But he just did a great job. He threw a 93-mph fastball on the outside part of the plate and I was just not prepared for it.' . . ."

**Benny Agbayani:** ". . . We all knew that he was a closer on top of his game. You can't say he's a one-pitch pitcher. That cut fastball comes in right on your hands, or he can cut it away. He makes it move in or out, and both pitches usually go to tough spots. Then he can blow a high fastball by you. He throws the kind of fastball that you think you get a good look at when it leaves his hand, it looks firm, but then it just explodes past you. No one I've seen throws a ball that moves like that. . . ."

**Tino Martinez:** ". . . He's so good, and his pitches move so much, you have to stay on your toes when you play defense behind him. The problem with Mariano when he's at the top of his game is, he can lull you. He comes in and just overpowers the first two hitters, you think no one is going to touch him. You have to stop yourself. Because with a one- or two-run lead you don't want anyone to get on. But you end up watching him like you're a spectator, he makes it look so easy, and you have to say, 'Hey, I might get the next ball hit to me, stay awake! . . ."

**Mariano Rivera (pitcher, New York Yankees, 1995–present):** "... To tell you the truth, I can't tell exactly why the cutter does what it does. When I first came up I threw the ball hard but it didn't move a lot. I knew I had to get the ball to move or batters would hit it no matter how hard I threw. So I just practiced with a lot of different grips until I found one that got the best movement. ..."

*Rivera opened the ninth by striking out reserve outfielder Darryl Hamilton. Agbayani, one of the better batting eyes in the Mets lineup, worked the Yankee closer for a walk, then stole second unopposed. Second baseman Edgardo Alfonzo's long fly ball out moved Agbayani to third base. Two down. Mike Piazza, the most productive hitting catcher in major-league baseball history, entered the batter's box as the potential game-tying run with his team one out away from elimination. He knew what to look for:*

**Mike Piazza:** "... the cutter, naturally. You have to look for it and you have to be quick. One of the things that fools you about Mariano is his incredibly smooth mechanics. The ball gets on you so fast, he is difficult to time. The cutter is in your zone for a split moment, then it's off your barrel. He is very talented. You know what's coming most of the time, you still can't hit it. That at-bat in the last inning of Game Five, that was one of my best swings I've had against the guy, I hit the ball well ..."

*With the count 0 and 1, Piazza unleashed a slugger's hack, the impact of bat against ball producing a sound that screamed home run. In the Yankee dugout, the manager was certain that Piazza had resuscitated his team's season:*

**Joe Torre:** "... That was probably the most scared I've been, when Mike hit that ball, because anytime he hits a ball in the air it's a home run in my mind. I saw Bernie all of a sudden sort of trotting over for it ..."

**Bernie Williams:** "... I've seen Mike hit balls just like that and they just fly out of the ballpark. The way he hit that ball, I started running back. The first few moments, you have a good idea if it is going to stay in the park or not, and I wasn't sure this would. But that ball just started to die, which was unusual for the way he hit it . . ."

**Mariano Rivera:** ". . . When Mike swung it looked like he was going to hit it in front of the plate, which I'm sure is what he thought. But at the last moment, that ball bit in on him, not that much. Just enough. So he hit it right below the barrel. You know he is a great hitter, because he still hit that pitch pretty good. I watched Bernie chase it . . ."

**Bernie Williams:** ". . . I remember thinking, 'I've got a bead on this . . .'"

**Joe Torre:** ". . . and I said, 'Wow, I must have misread that one . . .'"

**Bernie Williams:** ". . . I realized that it wasn't going to make the wall so I better get back fast and make sure I catch it. With both hands. I still have that ball in my home, I had everybody sign it. Mariano wanted it, but there was no way I was going to give it to him."

*Williams's catch sealed the Yankees' twenty-sixth World Series victory. Afterward, the sportswriters elected Jeter the Series' Most Valuable Player, an appropriate pick given his consistent play throughout the Fall Classic and his home-run heroics in the final two games. He graciously accepted the award in the Bombers' champagne-soaked clubhouse. But when it came time for the Yankees to ride down the Valley of Champions during the ticker-tape parade New York City threw in their honor, the shortstop demurred when organizers invited him to ride in a float apart from his teammates. His gesture underscored the Torre philosophy, with its emphasis on team accomplishment rather than individual performance, that had made the New York Yankees the most successful franchise in baseball during the manager's tenure.*

**Derek Jeter:** "They had the infielders on the infield float and then they had my name with MVP on this little thing in the front they wanted me to stand on. I really couldn't do that. The way I see it, you could have picked a name out of a hat and named the MVP. . . ."

**Bernie Williams:** "It's always questionable whether we have the best talent, player for player, from season to season. Who can say that? But, as a club, we've been able to incorporate all the aspects of our game and put it together for a team effort. You know we have meetings and review teams and we go through different players. Every team has one, two, three, however many hitters you especially have to be aware of, superstars who are always dangerous or good hitters who are hot, the guys swinging the bat well. We go over how to play each one of them. And I have to wonder what the other teams say about us as a club, how they choose which guys they have to be aware of, because I don't think there's a definite answer to that. Anyone on our team can beat you . . ."

**Roger Clemens:** ". . . and that all starts with Joe Torre. He knows how to deal with every personality on this club. We don't emphasize stats in here. I've often said I can go 10 and 10 during the regular season as long as we win most of my starts—I don't care who gets credit for the win—and Skip gives me the ball in the postseason. When we do add new guys, they get in line real quick with the program, because they see how it works.

"It's like a slow-moving train where everybody has a chance to jump on board and we all work for a common goal. Joe and Mr. Steinbrenner want rugged individuals who are ready to battle to the end. These days you have to look a little deeper than just whether a guy can throw 95 or hit the ball 425 feet. You have to look into their character and judge their insides. And when you have depth like we do, players with the determination you see here, you can't focus on everybody.

"Like, Scotty Brosius is down there batting eighth or ninth, a pitcher might forget about him. You think you can sneak a fastball by him, and he gets you. I can tell you as a pitcher that when you have to concentrate so hard on everybody we send to the plate, it's wearing. . . ."

**Al Leiter:** "... The Yankees lineup, it just seems that they constantly pound you. Even the so-called reprieve of six, seven, eight, nine. Normally you get an out down there ..."

**Roger Clemens:** "... and when a team gives us an extra out, we jump on them. It's like chum in the water and our guys can smell it. Then they get after it. You can feel that sense of purpose. We go into our attack mode...."

**Derek Jeter:** "... Our manager has taught us what we have to do to win. Everyone on this team plays hard and is ready to perform when he calls on them. Let's look at the first game of the Series. Vizcaino is the man. He doesn't get that hit, we'd still be playing Game One. The last game, Luis [Sojo] comes up as the hero ..."

**Luis Sojo:** "... Vizcaino and I really got to know each other last season. We're both utility infielders doing the same job, and we would share information. He said to me one day, 'We are the secret weapons on this team.' Well, in the World Series, he drove in the winning run in Game One, I drove in the winning run in Game Five. When he and I celebrated in the locker room afterwards, I reminded him of that. The secret weapons came through...."

**Derek Jeter:** "... You don't win without contributions like that, especially when the two teams are so evenly matched and you know you're going to call on your bench for pinch hitters and pinch runners in the late innings. It takes special individuals to play those roles. For instance, I don't know how Luis does what he does. It's tough for any player to take a day, two days, three days off and get back into the swing. Here is a guy who sometimes only plays once every two weeks, but he's productive. Almost every time he plays he does something in the field or at the plate to help us win. There is no way I could do his job as well as he does it. He's a very valuable commodity.

"Then you look at the rest of the team. Remember what Paul O'Neill did game after game? He had his little slump in September, but we knew he'd be there for us. He put it all together in the biggest games of the season, and not one of us were surprised. Stanton and Rivera, the way they shut everyone down. Think of how tough Andy Pettitte was in this Series, in every big game he's ever pitched for us. The second game of a series like this is so important, and Roger [Clemens] just took over in that one. Tino, David Justice, and Brosius came up with big hits. Bernie was stuck in a slump, but he comes up huge in Game Five. And Knoblauch drove in the game-tying run with a sacrifice fly in the first game after O'Neill has that tremendous at-bat. No one talks about that very much, but we don't take the first game without it, and Game One in a Series can set a tone.

"That's how we win, not relying on any one guy but getting contributions from every single person on this roster. That's what I'd like people to remember about this team. From the manager to the coaches to every player in here, we have a clubhouse filled with MVPs."

## ABOUT THE INTERVIEWS

Portions of quotes by Steve Hamilton, Roy White, Lou Piniella, Mike Burke, Ron Guidry, Willie Randolph, Mike Torrez, Goose Gossage, George Medich, George Brett, Don Zimmer (speaking about the Dent home run), and Bucky Dent have appeared in an earlier book I wrote on the Yankees in 1983. Back then space constraints compelled an editor to cleave many of the quotes. They are presented here in a fuller context. Whenever possible I gave the subjects who were interviewed during the early '80s an opportunity to review what they had said and provide additional information or retell their story. The following list includes those subjects whom I spoke to or corresponded with between 1980 and 1985, but not since:

Mickey Mantle, Billy Martin, Mike Burke, Elliott Maddox, Marty Appel, George Medich, Chris Chambliss, Lefty Gomez, Phil Rizzuto, Woody English, Steve Hamilton, George Brett, Rudy May, Reggie Jackson, Mike Torrez, Roy White, Bob Lemon, Mike Heath, Lou Piniella, Ron Guidry, Goose Gossage, Bucky Dent, Bob Stanley, and Carl Yastrzemski.

Jim Bouton was gracious enough to take the time to review what he had told me in 1982, then retell the anecdote in greater detail without altering the facts and with the fresh perspective of hindsight.

# INDEX